Selling Guantánamo

UNIVERSITY PRESS OF FLORIDA

Florida A&M University, Tallahassee
Florida Atlantic University, Boca Raton
Florida Gulf Coast University, Ft. Myers
Florida International University, Miami
Florida State University, Tallahassee
New College of Florida, Sarasota
University of Central Florida, Orlando
University of Florida, Gainesville
University of North Florida, Jacksonville
University of South Florida, Tampa
University of West Florida, Pensacola

John Hickman

University Press of Florida
Gainesville · Tallahassee · Tampa · Boca Raton
Pensacola · Orlando · Miami · Jacksonville · Ft. Myers · Sarasota

SELLING GUANTÁNAMO

**Exploding the Propaganda Surrounding
America's Most Notorious Military Prison**

This book may be available in an electronic edition.

18 17 16 15 14 13   6 5 4 3 2 1

A record of cataloging-in-publication data is available from
the Library of Congress.
ISBN 978-0-8130-4455-2

University Press of Florida
15 Northwest 15th Street
Gainesville, FL 32611-2079
http://www.upf.com

To John M. Hickman, Fred L. Long, Marvin L. Sissel, Chong Lim Kim, and Alice Fleetwood Bartee.

Contents

Introduction

In January 2002, twenty men were selected from a much larger population of prisoners because they seemed unusual to their American captors. They were transported to the far side of the planet and delivered to a tropical island that would seem, if not for the electrified fences and the heavily armed military personnel, like paradise. The prisoners were exhibited to junketing politicians, diplomats, and other elites. Even the press was given a glimpse of the shackled men in orange jumpsuits. Over the course of months and years, the military base in the southeastern corner of the island transformed into a prison camp housing approximately seven hundred captives. The men, some just boys, were subjected to a range of sophisticated physical and psychological tortures, held incommunicado and indefinitely. Today they are still threatened with prosecution, yet denied minimal due-process rights.

That much of the story is familiar.

The Bush administration's decision to imprison some seven hundred of the tens of thousands of prisoners captured in the war in Afghanistan at Guantánamo Bay Naval Base is not unprecedented. Although rarely, other liberal democratic governments have also held and mistreated populations of exceptional captives in spectacular isolation. Nevertheless, the Guantánamo decision *is* extraordinary and thus commands close analysis because it is a perfect "anti-scandal." Political scandals reveal hidden wrongdoing by politicians or their staff members to the public, which then joins rival politicians or opposition parties in moral condemnation of the wrongful acts. Anti-scandals, by contrast, involve proclamations of what would normally be understood as wrongdoing in a manner that disarms rival politicians and aborts the public's moral condemnation.

Widely acknowledged as being ineffective or counterproductive as counterterrorism policy, the Guantánamo decision is unrecognized for what it achieved: hiding in plain sight that which is morally repugnant. No more impressive exercise of power is possible.

While the story of the prisoners at Guantánamo is familiar, what is less well-known to the American public—and the reason why their moral condemnation has been curtailed—is that the official explanation for isolating these prisoners, torturing them, and maintaining them in legal limbo is not supported by facts. Yet the official explanation survives intact. The three rationales offered by senior figures in the Bush administration for the Guantánamo decision are almost unchallenged even by critics of the decision and remain the basis for public policy making about the affected prisoners. The official explanation for the Guantánamo decision is as monolithic as it is empty.

Official explanations for government policies do more than merely satisfy public curiosity. They legitimate decisions already made by government officials. When unchallenged by the press or public, those same officials treat the success of official explanations for decisions as license for more of the same. That can have important implications, but none more so than when the rights and welfare of persons in government custody are at stake. Consider the exchange during the January 15, 2007, interview of the commanding officer of Guantánamo Bay Naval Base, Admiral Harry Harris, by CNN anchor Kyra Phillips that aired on *CNN Newsroom*.[1] After a fawning description of Harris as being "in charge but not out of touch," Phillips listened as he asserted that the force-feeding of hunger-striking prisoners by nasogastric tubes was neither painful nor torturous by comparing their experience with his own voluntary submission to the same procedure. What she neglected to ask was whether the absence of patient consent had transformed a medical procedure into physical torture under the guise of medical treatment. Rather than pursue that obvious line of questioning, Phillips instead prompted Harris to restate elements of the official explanation for the Bush administration's Guantánamo decision.

"But isn't the point to get good intelligence and keep terrorists off the street?" she asked.

Taking his cue, Harris hastened to agree that "strategic intelligence gathering" and "detention" were indeed part of the mission, but so too was prosecution for "war crimes."

As the exchange between Phillips and Harris illustrates, despite five years of revelations that had exposed the official explanation as false or improbable, as either illogical or supported by exaggeration, the same three rationales were still being repeated without challenge by the media whose normal responsibility it is to reveal government deception. Journalists, pundits, politicians, and academics with rather less at stake in its faithful recitation than Bush administration officials joined in repeating the official explanation, and some continue to do so. Indeed, even as this book goes to press, one of the three rationales—the supposed extraordinary threat posed by the prisoners—continues to be deployed by opponents of the Obama administration's proposal to close Guantánamo.

The rhetorical power of the official explanation is interesting as a phenomenon and certainly deserves the examination it receives in this book, but it is hardly mysterious. Why was it successful? Consistent repetition and absence of challenge provide a sufficient account. However, there is a more important and more difficult question to ask: What motivated the Guantánamo decision? As I contend in this book, purposes other than the three rationales identified in the official explanation probably lie behind its flaking façade. Understanding those other purposes is vital, because political success is usually emulated. Mimesis is important to decision makers not simply for the manipulation of audiences but also for the selection of possible decisions. The Guantánamo decision was a success, although not in the sense that its apologists defend. If anything, it probably inspired more acts of terrorism than it helped prevent. Instead, the decision may be counted a success because it achieved unannounced purposes that motivated the decision.

While these other purposes cannot be proven because the decision-making process took place behind closed doors, they may be inferred.

This book marshals the logic and evidence for doing so in eleven chapters organized in three parts.

Part 1 outlines the decision, surveys its reception, and then presents comparable cases. Chapter 1 unpacks the language of the official explanation and sets it in its international and domestic political context. Chapter 2 surveys how other authors, including journalists, pundits, lawyers, academics, interpreters, and even prisoners released from the camp, have largely failed to challenge the official explanation for the Guantánamo decision. Chapter 3 examines three cases of internment of special classes of prisoners that help to make sense of such decisions by liberal democratic governments. The next three chapters examine the three rationales of the official explanation for discrepancies of logic and fact. Chapter 4 examines the threat rationale that the Guantánamo prisoners are unusually dangerous, an idea captured in the much repeated description of them as "the worst of the worst." The intelligence rationale that the prisoners are especially valuable sources of tactical or strategic intelligence is examined in chapter 5. The prosecution rationale that the prisoners might be tried for acts of terrorism and war crimes is examined in chapter 6.

The core argument of this book is then elaborated in part 2. Chapters 7, 8, and 9 articulate three rationales that comprise an alternative explanation that fits seamlessly both the domestic and international contexts and what is known about such decisions from other, comparable historical cases. The spectacle rationale, that prisoners taken in the war in Afghanistan were transferred to Guantánamo to serve as evidence of quick military victory in that conflict, is developed in chapter 7. The punishment rationale, that the prisoners transferred to Guantánamo were substitutes punished because the principal al-Qaeda and Taliban leaders responsible for the September 11, 2001, terrorist attacks were not in custody, is developed in chapter 8. The announcement rationale, that treating the prisoners as "illegal combatants" rather than "prisoners of war" under the Geneva Conventions was a signal that the United States intended to reconstruct the international order with the United States as global hegemon, is developed in chapter 9.

Part 3 explores the near- and long-term repercussions of the Guantánamo decision. The attempt to fulfill the campaign pledge to close Guantánamo has proved one of the longest and most difficult passages for the Obama administration. Chapter 10 presents an analysis of the constraints that have foiled the effort. How that fits with subsequent developments is explained in chapter 11, the conclusion.

A note on terminology is in order because the language typically used to describe the wars waged by the United States after September 11, 2001, is so heavily freighted with ideological and emotional connotation. As historian Jill Lepore noted in the preface to her brilliant account of King Philip's War, war threatens to cultivate language not only as description but also as justification.[2] Warfare extends even to struggles over the choice of nouns identifying the enemy in government pronouncements and news coverage.[3] Consider the many nouns commonly used in press releases and news reports to describe persons who employ violence to challenge a political regime. The favorites among press officers and journalists include "combatants," "fighters," "guerrillas," "insurgents," "rebels," "revolutionaries," and "terrorists." However, "assassins," "attackers," "bombers," "cadres," "commandoes," "forces," "gunmen," "killers," "militants," "separatists," "snipers," "troops," and "warriors" are also used. Even this longer second list fails to exhaust the possibilities. The choice of noun matters because the emotional connotation varies with each term. Less opprobrium attaches to "guerrilla" than to "terrorist," and less opprobrium attaches to "combatant" than to "guerrilla." What news audiences come to understand about the identities of the persons described is the product of the mixture of terms used—multiple nouns are typically used to name participants in news reports about political violence—and how frequently individual nouns are used.[4] Although some of the variation in terminology is attributable to an understandable and inescapable desire for variety in word selection by government officials and journalists, rather more may be attributable to an intention to shape the subjective interpretation of events by news audiences.

Propaganda often involves nothing more sophisticated than the attempt to sculpt public opinion through the selection of identifying nouns. An obvious example was the effort by the Bush White House and media magnate Rupert Murdoch's News Corporation to replace the consensus terms "suicide bomber" and "suicide bombing" with the presumably more threatening "homicide bomber" and "homicide bombing" beginning in April 2002. Apparently offered to blunt any connotation of honorable martyrdom that might be coded in the consensus terms, the effort "bombed."[5] Newspapers and television channels not affiliated with News Corporation failed to adopt the new terms not only because the terms seemed less descriptive but also because their sudden appearance seemed an altogether too Orwellian exercise in the manipulation of language to shape public opinion. In time even the Bush White House and Murdoch news sources reverted to the regular use of "suicide bomber" and "suicide bombing." Ironically, the militant Islamists of Hamas also object to the term "suicide bombing," preferring instead the euphemistic phrase "act of martyrdom."[6]

Given the difficulty and perhaps impossibility of demonstrating genuine neutrality in language, the terminology used in this book was selected for precision of description and the midrange in emotional connotation. Thus "guerrilla" and "fighter" rather than "terrorist" or "combatant" are used to refer to armed al-Qaeda and the Taliban members. Consistent with the practice of comparative politics and international relations scholars, "Islamism" and "Islamist" are used, respectively, to refer to the political movements, and their adherents, espousing an Islamic theocratic politics rather than "Islamic extremism" and "Islamic extremist" or "Islamic fundamentalism" and "Islamic fundamentalist."

Where useful to offer greater specificity, "Salafiyya" or "those who follow," rather than "Wahhabi," which is still commonly used in English-language news, will be used to designate adherents of the most puritanical and fundamentalist school of Sunni Islam. Encompassed by the terms are "Wahhabism" and "Deobandism." Wahhabism has its roots in the teachings of the eighteenth-century Arab scholar Muhammad bin Abd al-Wahhab. Deobandism is the product of Deoband, a town north of Delhi where Islamist scholars organized an influential anti-British madrassa, or religious school, in 1867 as a reaction to the failure of the Moghul dynasty to reestablish its authority during the

Indian Mutiny.[7] Parallels drawn between theological schools or religious sects in different religions are fraught with imprecision, but the
theological relationship between contemporary Salafiyya and Deobandism in Sunni Islam may be likened to that between Calvinism
and Lutheranism in Protestant Christianity: adherents recognize one
another as close allies in struggles to purify their faiths of corruption,
perhaps by seizing state power to impose their visions of a just moral
order. While they seek to return the faithful to what they believe to be
core tenets of their faiths, they willingly employ modern technologies.

The most difficult choice of terms is that used to name the individuals in custody at Guantánamo. Referring to them as "detainees," as was
the consistent practice of the White House, Pentagon, State Department, and Justice Department as well as mainstream American news
sources during the Bush administration, would endorse by implication
the controversial position that they were not "prisoners of war" under the terms of the Geneva Conventions. Alternatively, referring to
them as "prisoners of war" would ignore that interpretation of international law while threatening to confuse readers because few others
who have written on this topic have used such language. Faced with
this dilemma, I choose to punt. The term used most frequently in this
book is "prisoner," which is sufficiently precise for effective communication of the concept and both neutral and midrange in connotation.
The propositions in this book are challenging enough to the consensus about Guantánamo without insisting upon new language to grasp
them. Note, however, that "prisoner of war" is the appropriate term to
use for soldiers fighting in the same manner in other conflicts, such as
the war in Vietnam. So that term is used for the sake of simplicity and
familiarity when referring to the captured in those conflicts. For the
sake of consistency and neutrality, the term "prison" is used instead
of the strangely clinical "detention facility" or "prisoner-of-war camp"
with its implicit contested international legal interpretation.

Different presidential administrations are identified in the text
rather than by reference to the "United States government" because
their foreign and domestic policies differ significantly, and those differences are a crucial part of this interrogation. The terms "administration" and "Bush administration" are used throughout the book to

identify the administration of George W. Bush, to distinguish it from that of the predecessor Clinton and George H. W. Bush administrations. Several previous wars are discussed in this text, and conventional references are adopted in each case. Thus the American wars waged in Vietnam, Laos, and Cambodia are subsumed in the "war in Vietnam" or "Vietnam War," while the Soviet invasion and occupation of Afghanistan is the "Soviet-Afghan War." Whether to use the phrase "War on Terror" to designate the wars and several smaller military and intelligence operations conducted by the United States since September 11, 2001, poses a greater problem. That it was ever more than a public relations construct was widely challenged by many critics who made the case that the Bush administration's decision makers cynically exploited public fear and outrage after 9/11 to pursue unrelated war aims in the Middle East.[8] Beyond installing a client government, the war in Afghanistan initially bore very little resemblance to the war in Iraq. Where the former toppled an almost medieval theocracy, the latter toppled one of the most modern, if terrifyingly authoritarian, regimes in the Middle East. What the two wars shared were geographic borders with Iran, a country on the neoconservative wish list for regime change by invasion or subversion, and protracted counterinsurgency campaigns conducted to establish political control over less than completely defeated enemies. Despite these similarities, the legal designation and treatment of the captured in Afghanistan and Iraq differed from the beginning. Where prisoners captured in Afghanistan, including Afghan nationals fighting as soldiers in the Afghan army, were deemed "illegal combatants," those captured in Iraq were deemed prisoners of war under international law.

For the sake of clarity, the 2002 invasion and occupation of Afghanistan is the "war in Afghanistan" while the 2003 invasion and occupation of Iraq is the "war in Iraq." Despite the obvious reification, for the sake of brevity the term "War on Terror" is used when necessary to discuss all other American and Allied military or covert operations undertaken against Salafi insurgents and insurgencies outside Afghanistan and Iraq.

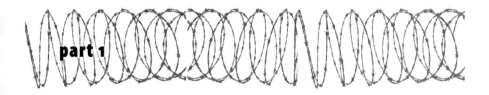

part 1

THE OFFICIAL
EXPLANATION

1 Framing the Decision

The world first learned that some of the Afghan and foreign nationals taken prisoner in Afghanistan were being transported to the United States Naval Base at Guantánamo Bay in news reports of their arrival on January 11, 2002. Although well covered by the press, the decision to use the military base as a prison initially encountered more interest than opposition in the United States. Previous administrations had used the base as a location to detain refugees from Haiti and Cuba. Ongoing combat operations in Afghanistan and pervasive anxiety about new terrorist attacks within the United States meant that the decision was initially understood as little more than a stopgap, a reasonable response to the exigencies of wartime. Prompted by both the press and politicians, public opinion viewed the September 11, 2001, terrorist attacks as comparable to the December 7, 1941, Japanese attack on Pearl Harbor.[1] In his address to the nation on September 20, 2001, President George W. Bush referenced Pearl Harbor directly with the phrase "one Sunday in 1941," and Jon Bridgman developed the parallel in a December 2001 newspaper article, "Lessons Learned from Two Days of Infamy."[2] National security crises of such magnitude are typically thought to require immediate and decisive action.[3] Captured enemies must be held in custody somewhere, and the number taken captive in Afghanistan was expected to be large. Airlifting prisoners captured on battlefields and at roadblocks in South Asia halfway around the planet to a prison camp in the Caribbean might seem excessive, but Washington knew that the American public was inured to immense waste and secrecy in everything involving national security. After the terrifying events of September 11, 2001, with the images of passenger airliners smashing into the Twin Towers of the World Trade Center replayed again and again on television news, few Americans would balk at the high price tag. Only four months after the most traumatic public event in their lives, most Americans were persuaded that they wanted security and they wanted it now.

The first indication that the Guantánamo decision involved something more than a ready-made location for a military prison camp emerged during a lengthy January 22, 2002, news briefing by Secretary of Defense Donald H. Rumsfeld.[4] A former Nixon and Ford administration political appointee given to military bureaucratic doublespeak delivered while executing inscrutable chopping motions with his hands and arms, Rumsfeld offered three rationales for the Guantánamo decision: threat, intelligence, and prosecution.

Holding the captured at Guantánamo was necessary, Rumsfeld explained, to prevent them from being released to commit further terrorism. Using the sort of language that American politicians use when promising to "get tough" on violent crime, he painted a picture of the prisoners as veritable terrorist supermen.[5] The principal problem with the threat rationale is that the hundreds of prisoners transferred to Guantánamo were no more dangerous than the tens of thousands of other prisoners then being held in prison camps in Afghanistan. The most dangerous of the lot were no more capable of violent acts than any other captured soldier in a Third World army. Nor were there any important figures in al-Qaeda or the Taliban. Most of the senior al-Qaeda and Taliban figures at the start of the war escaped capture by slipping across the border into northern Pakistan. The most promising middle-rank al-Qaeda figures taken captive were being held by the CIA in "black sites," an archipelago of secret prisons from Poland to Thailand, rather than by the United States military. The agency would do its part to provide a post hoc justification for the Guantánamo decision by transferring a handful of its more valuable prisoners to the naval base, but that was years in the future. Although the invasion of Afghanistan managed to topple the Taliban from power, it largely failed in its other political and military objectives. The overwhelming majority of Guantánamo prisoners would be repatriated and released, while most of those who remained at the base would be there because there was, effectively, no place to send them.

Rumsfeld's second and "most important" rationale for the Guantánamo decision was to collect intelligence that might be used to prevent terrorist attacks in the future. The secretary of defense and his fellow neoconservatives in the Bush administration were still smarting because they had been caught napping on September 11, 2001. That such a successful and preventable terrorist attack had been conducted on American soil was a stain on the pretension among conservatives of all stripes that they possessed greater competence in national security issues. Beyond deflecting public attention to avoid accountability, they were determined to find some justification, any justification, for preemptive military action against Iraq. Using the 9/11 terrorist attack to justify war against Iraq was a recurring theme in both the September 15–18, 2001, meetings of Bush's war council and in the September 19–20, 2001, meetings of Rumsfeld's Defense Policy Board.[6] The road to Baghdad obviously lay through Kabul, but getting from Kabul to Baghdad was going to require creativity in constructing the Iraqi threat. Information extracted through interrogation of the prisoners might be used to justify the second war that was already being planned. Any information that connected Baghdad to 9/11 would have been welcomed, even trumpeted, by the administration. In the months after their transfer to Guantánamo, the proposition that the prisoners could provide intelligence valuable for preventing future terrorist attacks would have seemed reasonable to an American public that was more frightened than skeptical.

The idea that the prisoners would be tortured for this intelligence was casually shrugged off. Two years before the sickening photos of prisoner abuse at Abu Ghraib in Iraq revealed depravity in United States military prisons, there was scope for laughter about the subject of torture during Rumsfeld's news briefing, with the secretary of defense bantering with one reporter about the possibility that the absence of air-conditioning at Guantánamo might constitute torture. The exchange both dismissed the possibility and diminished the moral gravity of the practice of torture while also allowing Rumsfeld to posture as tough because of his indifference to the suffering of others.

Several years later Rumsfeld and other Pentagon officials would express feigned surprise about the brutality at Abu Ghraib prison in Iraq. Laughter about torture would no longer be possible.

An even stranger note was that Rumsfeld dismissed questions about the legality of the designation of the prisoners as unlawful combatants as a problem for lawyers but then couldn't resist the temptation to offer a legal theory for that designation. In the months that followed, it became clear that other decision makers in the administration had already thought through the international legal issues relating to the law of war and wanted to postpone that part of the controversy attending the Guantánamo decision. However, the chance to demonstrate intellectual command of the issue proved too much for the secretary of defense. Revisiting the poorly informed legal interpretation of the Geneva Conventions he had articulated during a February 8, 2002, news conference with Chairman of the Joint Chiefs of Staff General Richard Myers, Rumsfeld proceeded to explain that the agreements require that soldiers wear uniforms that distinguish them from civilians because a central purpose of the agreements was to protect innocent civilians.[7] In reality, the Geneva Conventions were drafted, and then redrafted after World War II, to reflect increased humanitarian concern for the welfare of all persons, civilian or not, innocent of war crimes or not, taken into custody during war. The defense secretary's grasp of both the spirit and the content of international humanitarian law was thus shaky.

Rumsfeld's third and last rationale for the Guantánamo decision was that "some" of the prisoners might be processed "through the criminal justice system" and "some" might be tried before "military commissions." If the intention to prosecute cannot be dismissed, it may be doubted. What is now clear is that at the time of the announcement, the White House and the Pentagon were unprepared to conduct prosecutions before military tribunals. Nor does it appear that they were in any haste to do so. Habeas corpus and due-process challenges would inevitably slow proceedings, but the leisurely pace in mounting these prosecutions suggests something important about their likely purpose. Rather than proceeding rapidly with prosecutions, the administration was instead apparently intent upon being—and content to appear—"in control" of a crisis situation and willing to take whatever "tough measures" might be necessary to respond to threats to national security. Apologists for the Guantánamo decision invoked the example of the 1942 prosecution of German and German-American saboteurs in military commissions established by the Roosevelt administration. However, the two events are meaningfully different. Where the Roosevelt administration tried, convicted, and executed the saboteurs within three months of their being captured, the Bush administration appears to have been content to let the preparation for prosecution languish once the announcement was made. The speed with which the prosecutions were prepared and conducted is important in judging whether they were perceived by decision makers to be responses to actual wartime emergencies.

That senior administration officials sensed the immense political opportunity in cultivating a continuing crisis atmosphere after September 11, 2001, is probable. This was a political moment in which aggressive posturing not only was permitted but might be handsomely rewarded. The necessary administrative and legal planning for the military tribunals was eventually undertaken, and a handful of trials begun in August 2004, long after their announcement affected news coverage and public opinion.[8] Partially obscured by the controversy over the military commissions was the important question of the status of the Guantánamo prisoners under international law, the Geneva Conventions, to which the United States is a signatory. When not calling them "detainees," official Washington insisted on describing them as "unlawful combatants" rather than as "prisoners of war." That latter designation imposes unambiguous obligations on captor states, and the treatment meted out at Guantánamo violated the most important of them. The argument made by the Bush administration was that the captured did not merit "prisoner-of-war" status because they had not carried weapons openly, worn identifying uniforms, or operated under a chain of command. Thus they were "unlawful combatants" and by implication could be dealt with in any manner that their captors pleased. If they were accorded any rights, then that should be taken as evidence of American generosity. The problem for both the administration and mainstream American news sources is that this is a complex story to tell and vulnerable to further examination if compared with the treatment of captives in other conflicts.

As may have been Rumsfeld's intention, the apparent threat of drumhead trials before military commissions emerged as the immediate focus of international and domestic political controversy. The furor caused by the Guantánamo decision certainly developed less as a consequence of the administration's insistence that the captured were not "prisoners of war" under the law of war but rather "unlawful combatants" than in response to its announcement that some of them might be tried before military tribunals. News commentary supporting and opposing the idea of prosecution shifted the focus of attention from the status of the prisoners under international law to public policy questions about the most appropriate means for dealing with the security threats that the prisoners were believed to pose, especially with their compatriots still at large. To an anxious American public at the time, al-Qaeda's operatives appeared to lurk everywhere from the mountains of southern Afghanistan to the local shopping mall. Even a year later, 80 percent of the respondents in an August Gallup/CNN/ USA Today poll of Americans expressed their belief that "terrorists associated with Osama bin Laden" were then in the United States and possessed the means to launch another major attack.[9] Fear of terrorist attack would remain a constant in public opinion thereafter. The percentage of poll respondents reporting that they were either "very worried" or "somewhat worried" about another attack was 59 percent in November 2010, a decline from 71 percent in October 2001 but still impressive.[10]

For American journalists, military tribunals proved not only an easier but also a safer news story to report than the status of the prisoners under the Geneva Conventions. They know that their news audiences often reveal remarkable impatience and ignorance.[11] Unsurprisingly, then, reporters and their editors prefer to cover less complex stories. That offering intellectually less challenging fare has accustomed their news audiences to demand more of the same, in a tragic positive-feedback loop, makes it no less a fact of life for journalists. Reporters and editors also prefer stories that carry less risk of being accused of a liberal or even leftist ideological slant, something almost guaranteed when reporting government decisions involving national security. That accusations of the much more probable conservative or rightist slant are heard so infrequently is a tribute to the conservatives' disciplined repetition of claims of liberal or leftist editorial bias. The crisis atmosphere cultivated after September 11, 2001, further discouraged journalists from taking up stories that might result in accusations of being "soft on terrorism."[12] With news coverage focused on the military tribunals, the legal status of the prisoners under the Geneva Conventions was marginalized and their indefinite and incommunicado imprisonment largely obscured. Perhaps that reflected nothing more than chance favoring the Bush administration during a moment of disorienting crisis, but an equally convincing interpretation is that it was the product of a mass media strategy disguised as wartime exigency.

Problems with the official explanation for the Guantánamo decision notwithstanding, senior administration officials demonstrated remarkable public relations discipline by remaining "on message" just as they did with explanations for the decisions to invade Iraq, withdraw from the Kyoto Protocol, and renounce the 1988 Rome Statute that established the International Criminal Court. In each instance, world public opinion was defied and American public opinion further polarized. Although it impoverishes political exchange, consistently repeating the same message in similar or identical language so as not to offer critics any leverage is deemed best practice in contemporary American politics. Disciplined repetition was made possible by "the use of talking points, the rarity of unauthorized leaks from members of the administration, the use of off-the-record background briefings, and the lack of press conferences."[13] Indeed, the first serious crack in the wall of denial would come during a press conference.

Four years into the War on Terror, a global struggle evoked in moralistic language but with war aims as poorly defined as those of the Cold War, President George W. Bush was still relying heavily on two of Rumsfeld's three justifications. In a January 12, 2006, joint press conference with newly elected German chancellor Angela Merkel, Bush defended the Guantánamo decision in the mangled syntax and truck stop grammar that were his rhetorical trademarks:

[T]here's some misperceptions about Guantánamo. First of all I urge any journalist to go down there and look at how the folks that are being detained there are treated. These are people picked up off the battlefield who want to do harm. . . . The way forward, of course, is ultimately through a court system. I think the best way for the court system is through our military tribunals, which is now being adjudicated in our courts of law to determine whether or not this is appropriate path for a country that bases itself on rule of law, to adjudicate those held in Guantánamo.[14]

What Bush did not mention in this passage is more important than what he did mention. Although the threat and prosecution rationales were repeated, he said nothing about intelligence gathering. The reason is obvious. Among the Guantánamo prisoners was German national Murat Kurnaz, and German news coverage would have highlighted any statements made by Bush in Merkel's presence that implied interrogation under torture or any other form of mistreatment. Nor did Bush mention the prisoners taken captive in extraordinary renditions, covert operations in which terrorist suspects were kidnapped far from any battlefield and then transferred to distant prisons. Germany was one of the older European Union (EU) member states, whose citizens had been outraged to learn that the CIA was operating secret prisons in new EU member state Poland and candidate EU member state Romania. Beyond their own tragic historical experience with police state terror, the German public was aware of the Kafkaesque nightmare of Khaled al-Masri, a forty-two-year-old German citizen of Lebanese origin from the German city of Ulm who was abducted by the CIA in Macedonia on December 31, 2003, held incommunicado, and tortured in a squalid secret prison in Afghanistan called the Salt Pit for five months before being released in an abandoned area in Albania. Someone named Khaled el-Masri had helped recruit some of the 9/11 hijackers, but the agency had bagged the wrong Khaled el-Masri. Bush obviously had to say something about Guantánamo during this press conference, but in this instance saying less was clearly preferable to saying more.

Bush's responses to questions during the June 14, 2006, press conference in the White House Rose Garden suggest that he had settled on the threat and prosecution justifications but abandoned the intelligence gathering justification. "I'd like to close Guantánamo," said the president, "but I also recognize that we're holding some people there that are darn dangerous and that we better have a plan to deal with them in our courts."[15] The reference to the courts probably reflected his awareness of the anticipated June 30, 2006, Supreme Court ruling in *Hamdan v. Rumsfeld* on the constitutionality of presidential authority to order military tribunals. Bush also used the press conference to justify continuing to hold the prisoners at Guantánamo:

> Part of closing Guantánamo is to send some folks back home, like we've been doing. And the State Department is in the process of encouraging countries to take the folks back. Of course, sometimes we get criticized for sending some people out of Guantánamo back to their home country because of the nature of the home country. It's a little bit of a Catch-22. But we're working through this.[16]

The argument he made was that continued custody of the prisoners at Guantánamo was necessary because a decision had already been made to imprison them at that location. Here was the equivalent of painting everyone into a corner and then insisting that they remain patient while the paint dried. Beyond its patent absurdity, the problem with his response is that it failed to account for many of the missing pieces of the puzzle in the Guantánamo decision. Why were prisoners captured in distant Afghanistan not being held in that country or recognized as prisoners of war under the Geneva Conventions? Why had they been hauled from the other side of the planet for incommunicado and indefinite imprisonment in what was believed by many to be an international legal lacuna? Rather than provide answers, what Bush offered was a sunk costs argument to justify continued execution of the original decision. Sunk costs arguments are normally assumed to be illogical. The only exception to that generalization occurs when benefits from continuing to execute a decision outweigh the costs of changing the decision. However, here the costs seemed to outweigh the benefits. If the threat, intelligence, and prosecution rationales were essentially empty, as it appears, then keeping the camp open damaged the national reputation without any resulting benefit.

The solution to this puzzle is that a different calculation was probably made in the Bush administration. As has been true of every other administration, decision makers would deny that any of its foreign policies was mistaken. If denial ultimately failed, then perhaps eventual admission of error might be deferred until the American public either lost interest or accepted that it was too late to reconsider the decision. Considered against the distortion of collective historical memory about Vietnam and Contragate, time was clearly on their side.[17] Moreover, other benefits from the Guantánamo decision are likely to have been weighed in the calculation. That the Bush administration could realize those benefits was a function of the uncritical acceptance of the official explanation.

2 Strange Consensus

As the report of an investigation into the motives of a presidential administration for a major decision that is widely viewed as morally reprehensible, this book is akin to the report of an interrogation of a criminal suspect. Here the analogy is not to encounters where questioning is merely the excuse to inflict punishment. Instead the analogy is to encounters where an interrogator attempts to solve some puzzle involving the subject. Interrogators often question their subjects to develop a convincing narrative about motive that accounts for criminal behavior. Understanding the context in which the interrogation subject acted is essential for correctly interpreting that information. In the end, what makes an interrogator's narrative superior to that of the interrogation subject is that it does a better job of accounting for motive.

The problem facing the guilty interrogation subject is well known: every answer surrendered to an interrogator's questioning risks exposure of some damning fact or logical contradiction in previous statements that causes the subject's story to unravel. Veteran revolutionary Victor Serge advised fellow revolutionaries held in custody by the authorities to respond with silence or, if that was impossible, to respond with simple declarations affirming or denying responsibility. Once arrested, he recommended:

Don't be intimidated by the eternal threat: "You'll pay for this!" What you'll pay for is a confession, or a clumsy explanation, or falling for tricks and moments of panic; but whatever the situation of the accused, a hermetically sealed defense, built on much silence and a few definite affirmations, or denials, can only help.[1]

Consistently offering the same brief answer is a strategy employed not only by criminal suspects but also by those who speak for governments. The steely discipline with which officials of the Bush administration repeated the official explanation for the Guantánamo decision is an example. Every generation in a liberal democracy learns through experience that claims made by public officials should be treated with a measure of skepticism. That remains true despite the contemporary sophistication with which information is consumed and easy access to alternative sources of news. Although once common, outright fabrications in public pronouncements have been replaced by sophisticated tools such as the redirection of attention through emphasis or omission and the dilution or subversion of meaning. Decoding sense and nonsense through the close reading and fact checking of statements issued by the government is an attractive analytic approach because it may reveal the concealed motivations of decision making. However, it has the drawback of potentially confining the scope of the interrogation to the categories of thought and perception found in such communications. The risk is that the unwary interrogator may end up endorsing, whether explicitly or implicitly, the narrative that is offered by the interrogation subject. That is how even the harshest critics of the decision ended up accepting all or part of the Bush administration's explanation. Again and again they made the mistake of analyzing the Guantánamo decision and its execution in isolation from other comparable events. Like the larger public discourse on the topic, their treatments were impoverished because they ignored the many historical precedents. In the chapters to follow, I show that, far from being unique, the Guantánamo decision and its execution followed a familiar arc of decisions by liberal democracies to intern special classes of prisoners, while the treatment of the Guantánamo prisoners is tragically similar to that in other asymmetric conflicts. These comparisons help to make sense of the many discrepancies of logic and fact surrounding Guantánamo that otherwise seem to be nothing more than the random noise of international and domestic American politics.

In principle, the responsibility for detecting and denouncing deception perpetrated by elected and appointed public officials lies with the citizenry. In practice, real citizens are too uninformed, inattentive, and apathetic to perform that role with any consistency. Instead, that responsibility is borne by rival elected and appointed officials, activists, journalists, and academics. While criticism is the background noise of American politics, denunciation of wrongdoing is less common and depends on the detection of deception. Although there was plenty of criticism directed at the Guantánamo decision, it failed to develop into denunciation of the obvious wrongdoing. There was no scandal, because the deception was never detected.

What is striking about the sizable literature of books and documentary films about Guantánamo produced by journalists, academics, soldiers, attorneys for prisoners, and the prisoners themselves is the consensus that exists among apologists and critics about the purposes for the decision. They endorse all or part of the official explanation. Those whose responsibility it is to detect and denounce failed to do so.

Consider ten books written by serious journalists—Jane Mayer, David Rose, Karen Greenberg, Michael Otterman, Bradley Graham, Stephen Grey, Michelle Shephard, Benjamin Wittes, Jonathan Mahler, and Viveca Novak (who coauthored the memoir of U.S. Army interpreter Erik Saar).

Jane Mayer's 2008 *The Dark Side: The Inside Story of How the War on Terror Turned into a War on American Ideals* locates the Guantánamo decision in the broader context of Bush administration policy on the treatment of prisoners taken in its War on Terror. Her narrative characterizes the decision as a regrettable deviation from an otherwise proud tradition of morally superior past practice:

The distinction—between killing an enemy as the result of a legitimate legal process (including warfare) and torturing a defenseless enemy captive—was woven deeply into the fabric of America's military history and sense of honor.[2]

To support this sweeping generalization she offers a tidy capsule history of American treatment of prisoners of war obviously intended to evoke patriotic pride. The brutal indifference of the British Army to the captured American soldiers is contrasted with the humane treatment of British soldiers in American custody during the Revolutionary War; the Lieber Code drafted during the American Civil War blazes the high road in the humane treatment of the captured; unlike the Japanese, the United States scrupulously adheres to the provisions of the 1929 Geneva Convention during the Second World War; and the United States helps to close loopholes in the 1929 agreement in the 1949 Geneva Convention. Missing from this inspiring story is the difference between the treatment of "civilized" and "savage" enemies. From the slaughter of Narragansett women and children by Puritans in the 1675 Battle of the Great Swamp in King Philip's War to the drumhead military tribunals and mass execution of captured Santee Sioux warriors following the 1862 Sioux War, and on to the indefinite imprisonment of Geronimo and his Chiricahua Apache warriors, Americans have often treated much less humanely those enemies who fail the standard of waging what they considered to be civilized warfare.[3]

That distinction was expressed in the 1863 Lieber Code, the regulations to govern operations of the Union Army more formally titled the *Instructions for the Government of Armies of the United States in the Field*, drafted by Columbia College (today's Columbia University) professor of law, ardent abolitionist, and liberal Prussian exile Francis Lieber. Under these regulations, captured combatants enjoy the protections of a prisoner of war only if they obey commanding officers, wear distinctive emblems, and carry arms openly, three requirements incorporated in the later Geneva Conventions. That was the source for the claim by Rumsfeld during the February 8, 2002, news conference that the captured enemies in Afghanistan were not entitled to treatment as prisoners of war under international law.[4]

Captured native warriors, spies, saboteurs, and insurgents had sometimes, but not always, been denied the protections of prisoner-of-war status in America's wars during the previous 150 years. Inconsistency makes for a more complex history. Mayer neglects to note the one major conflict in which the U.S. military chose to treat captured insurgents, even if they did not wear distinctive emblems or carry arms openly, as prisoners of war: the war in Vietnam. For all the many horrors of that long conflict, National Liberation Front guerrillas and other personnel, commonly named the Viet Cong in the American news coverage, who were captured in South Vietnam were accorded prisoner-of-war status. That historical fact and U.S. military defeat were perhaps too poor a fit in Mayer's otherwise happy historical account to merit close attention.

For Mayer, the Guantánamo decision was nothing more than a component of the Bush administration's objective of collecting intelligence about an unanticipated and frightening terrorist enemy through "flexible" interrogation, the obvious euphemism for questioning under torture.[5] She accepts that senior administration officials believed that such interrogations would yield valuable intelligence and might uncover information useful for criminal prosecutions. Rivalry with the CIA, which claimed success using "enhanced" interrogation techniques, caused the Department of Defense to order its interrogators at Guantánamo to redouble their efforts, which resulted in prisoners being subjected to even greater abuse. Mayer condemns torture but does not challenge the proposition that it and/or the Guantánamo decision were for any purpose other than intelligence collection.

David Rose's 2004 *Guantánamo: America's War on Human Rights* is a forthright criticism of the practice of torture and more specifically of the Guantánamo decision that nonetheless accepts that intelligence collection was the primary purpose for both.[6] After challenging the quality of the intelligence collected through interrogations under torture and after entertaining the possibility that another purpose for interrogation under torture was to produce evidence of complicity in terrorism as post hoc justification for the Guantánamo decision itself, he endorses intelligence collection as the original purpose. Rose is skeptical only of the prosecution rationale, noting that none of the prisoners had been tried before the military commissions by the time his book had gone to press. That the analysis short-circuits, becoming a critique of the execution of the decision rather than an examination of the reasons for making the decision, is all the more regrettable because Rose searches for explanation in the ideological enthusiasms of decision makers. In his account, President George W. Bush and Attorney General John Ashcroft and other senior administration decision makers embraced a millennial evangelical Christian vision of the United States as a world power with a redemptive mission that is actually the mirror image of the violent Islamism they claim to battle. As evidence Rose offers the ranting nonsense of Deputy Undersecretary of Defense Lieutenant General William G. "Jerry" Boykin.[7] In several speeches delivered in 2002 and 2003 the general revealed a medieval worldview in which Christendom wages holy war against the Islamic world. However disquieting, both because such ideas are patently irrational and because some other officers in the armed forces embrace them, this is at best only a partial explanation of the ideological motivation for the Guantánamo decision. Better represented in the administration were other figures whose foreign policy perspectives were derived not from their millennial religious beliefs but instead from their shared political philosophy: neoconservatism.

Karen Greenberg's 2009 microhistory *The Least Worst Place: Guantanamo's First 100 Days* charts the first three months of implementing the Guantánamo decision, which she describes as being driven by the wartime necessities of imprisoning and interrogating the captured enemy. The United States Department of Defense failed to plan appropriately for the large numbers of prisoners taken in Afghanistan, she explains, and the deplorable conditions in the prisoner camps in Afghanistan required that other locations be found to avoid a humanitarian catastrophe.[8] Greenberg concludes that Guantánamo was selected as a location only after rejecting U.S. military bases in Germany, on Guam, and in the continental United States and after reaching the conclusion that the Cuban base offered a unique international legal environment. Missing from her "just so" story is that only a small number of the prisoners captured in Afghanistan were transferred to Guantánamo. The vast majority remained in the deplorable conditions of the Afghan prisoner camps.

Greenberg creates a measure of dramatic tension with a sympathetic portrayal of the military personnel initially responsible for executing the Guantánamo decision and a decidedly unsympathetic though less detailed portrayal of the Bush administration's lawyers in the U.S.

Department of Justice's Office of Legal Counsel, who are described as working within the "secretive corridors of executive power."[9] The result plays to the military patriotism of readers by absolving military decision makers nearest the execution of the decision. "Telling individuals in the military that the rules—in this case, the Geneva Conventions—do not apply is tantamount to saying: You have entered a place in which you are not trained to function."[10] The apology extends to blaming the prisoners for their own mistreatment, for daring to provoke their guards. Although Greenberg is critical of the intelligence gathering effort for conflating tactical with strategic intelligence, she does not challenge the assumption that it was the primary purpose for interrogations. Interestingly, her discussion of the dilatory nature of preparing for a war crimes tribunal could be read as expressing doubt that prosecution was an actual purpose for the Guantánamo decision.

Freelance journalist and documentary filmmaker Michael Otterman's 2008 book *American Torture* is a straightforward condemnation of torture by the United States. The first half of his book summarizes the development of expertise in torture for interrogation by the U.S. military and the CIA under the transparent guise of training military and intelligence personnel to resist it in the Survival, Evasion, Resistance and Escape or SERE program. Otterman's chapter on Guantánamo (Bagram Air Base in Afghanistan and the Abu Ghraib military prison in Iraq are given their own chapters) describes it as a convenient location for interrogation under torture of prisoners held in the custody of the U.S. military rather than the CIA. For Otterman, the primary purpose of torture in all of these prisons is to collect intelligence from the interrogation subject. That is the reason for technical sophistication in torture such as the use of the Behavioral Science Consultation Team, typically reduced to BSCT and pronounced "Biscuit Team." Only secondarily is the purpose of torture to punish, and this appears as the motivation of individual decision makers and torturers rather than a reflection of institutional mission or design. Thus Otterman describes Major General Geoffrey Miller, the second commander in charge of the prison at Guantánamo, as being motivated by revenge to punish prisoners. Miller, it seems, lost friends in the 9/11 terrorist attack on the Pentagon.[11]

Bradley Graham's 2009 biography of Donald Rumsfeld, *By His Own Rules*, describes the Guantánamo decision as the result of pressure to find a location to hold some of the large number captured in the war in Afghanistan and the necessity of intelligence gathering.[12] In this the book offers the same apology as Greenberg. Biographers, even veteran *Washington Post* reporters, often fall prey to the temptation to minimize or excuse the mistakes of their subjects, which explains why Graham's narrative shifts so much responsibility for the choice of Guantánamo as a prison camp and approval of brutal treatment during interrogation from the secretary of defense to his legal counsel, William J. "Jim" Haynes. "Rumsfeld was ill served by Haynes," writes Graham, and explains that Haynes acted in the interests of the White House rather than the Pentagon.[13] Citing Mayer's *The Dark Side*, Graham is at best only mildly critical of Rumsfeld for his reluctance to allow diplomatic representatives of America's allies to visit their nationals held at the base.

Stephen Grey's 2006 *Ghost Plane*, a history of extraordinary renditions conducted by the CIA, devotes only a few pages to the Guantánamo decision.[14] That makes sense because most of those who were abducted were actually held in locations other than the Cuban base. Grey's narrative explores the legal basis for the abductions and torture, and discusses the relative effectiveness of CIA and military interrogations, yet never seriously challenges the assumption that torture was conducted for the collection of intelligence. Guantánamo is thus reduced to a location for interrogation.

Canadian journalist Michelle Shephard's 2008 *Guantanamo's Child* is the sympathetic biography of Omar Khadr, the youngest of the prisoners transferred to the Cuban base after the war in Afghanistan, and also one of the few Canadian nationals to be held there. Her narrative describes callous, even brutal, intelligence gathering at Bagram Air Base and Guantánamo.[15] Although critical of torture to collect intelligence, Shephard fails to challenge the conclusion that torture and imprisonment at Guantánamo served any purpose other than intelligence gathering. Such is the persuasive strength of the official explanation.

Benjamin Wittes's 2008 *Law and the Long War* is an extensive apology for the Guantánamo decision and other major Bush administration foreign policy decisions thinly veiled in criticism of their execution. The analysis is driven by the public policy and legal problem presented by the capture of irregular combatants who "transcend their theater of conflict" because they are engaged in a "global struggle with the United States."[16] Should the "international jihadis" who are a threat not only as members of an armed force but also in their "individual capacity" be treated as criminal suspects under domestic law or as prisoners of war under international law when they have the characteristics of both? Whatever answer is given, posing the problem in this manner, with the assumption that the prisoners held at Guantánamo are as dangerous as portrayed, endorses both the prosecution and threat rationales in the official explanation.

Wittes's unsurprising answer is that the Bush administration's Guantánamo decision was an appropriate if poorly crafted response to the conjured dilemma. He contends that preventive detention is warranted in the War on Terror and that the traditional law of war and past practice of the United States supports prosecutions before military tribunals. Offered as evidence of past practice is the 1942 trial by military tribunal and execution of German and German-American saboteurs by the administration of Franklin Delano Roosevelt. His choice of a historical example is rhetorically effective but possibly more instructive than he may have intended. The blundering, and in several cases plainly halfhearted, saboteurs are now all but forgotten, but Nazi Germany represents the ultimate in evil for many Americans. "Fascist" has lost its name-calling punch in America, but "Nazi" still does the trick. Franklin Delano Roosevelt remains an iconic figure for American liberals, many of whom are critical of the Guantánamo decision. That the regular criminal justice system at the time was entirely competent to try the defendants is the obvious problem with the example. Less obvious is that trying them before a military tribunal was intended to give the Roosevelt administration a victory over its foreign enemies at a moment when it sorely needed one, which is the more important parallel to the Guantánamo decision. And as will be explained later, the United States also has a second and superior legal-political tradition that grew out the use of military tribunals, one in which the 1942 trial stands out as an aberration.

To the extent that Wittes criticizes the Guantánamo decision, it is as an attempt by the Bush administration to move against the tide of American constitutional history. Asserting presidential power to establish slapdash military tribunals is contrary to what he characterizes as increased bureaucratization and congressional oversight. He argues that Bush should have used the power of his office to persuade the Congress to establish a new legal regime with new courts to try terrorist suspects. A mature legal architecture would have been more legitimate because it would have accorded defendants more procedural protections and imposed higher evidentiary burdens on the prosecution.

Jonathan Mahler's 2008 *The Challenge* describes the Guantánamo decision as a process of elimination in which senior Bush administration officials searched for a location to serve as the optimal venue for prosecuting prisoners for war crimes, with the prosecutions serving in turn to enhance formal and informal presidential power. Only secondarily was the decision about collecting intelligence. Focusing on Charles Swift and Neal Katyal, attorneys for Salim Ahmed Hamdan in the landmark *Hamdan v. Rumsfeld* Supreme Court decision, the book ignores the official threat rationale and any alternative explanations for the decision. When torture is discussed, it is framed in terms of intelligence collection. Mahler attributes the choice of Guantánamo to the decision by senior administration legal counsel, including Vice President Richard B. "Dick" Cheney's chief legal counsel David Addington, White House legal counsel Alberto Gonzalez and Timothy Flanagan, Department of Defense general counsel William J. Haynes, and Justice Department Office of Legal Counsel deputy assistant attorney general John Yoo, to try prisoners before military tribunals, which was followed by a search for the optimal geographic and legal venue for the trials. After U.S. military bases in Frankfurt, Germany, and the Marshall Islands were rejected as possible prison venues, "someone" suggested using Guantánamo.[17] Unfortunately, Mahler does not identify that someone. Although the Department of Defense approved, one wrinkle was that the naval base was also the intended location of an "interrogation battle-lab."[18] The illogic in this narrative is that if the decision to transfer prisoners to the Cuban base for interrogation had already been made, then its selection must have been driven at least as much by whatever purpose was thought to be served by interrogation as by prosecution for war crimes. The bulk of Mahler's book details the efforts to prosecute and defend Hamdan, a treatment that might persuade the unwary reader that prosecution was the primary purpose for the original Guantánamo decision.

The 2005 memoir of U.S. Army interpreter Erik Saar, coauthored by Viveca Novak, *Inside the Wire: A Military Intelligence Soldier's Eyewitness Account of Life at Guantánamo*, treats intelligence collection as the primary purpose for the decision, and the need to imprison "some of the world's most dangerous terrorists" as its secondary purpose.[19] This narrative of disillusionment, however, characterizes the mistreatment of prisoners as punishment meted out by military police guards acting out of hatred and ignorance of their charges. That the authors failed to do more with such observations is attributable to Saar's indoctrination in loyalty to his military service and acceptance of the legitimacy of higher authority.

Journalists were not the only elites to be taken in by the official explanation. Legal scholars and attorneys representing Guantánamo prisoners, professionals trained to analyze the logic and evidence of an argument, were also trapped. Consider then the books written by Laurel E. Fletcher and Eric Stover, Philippe Sands, Joseph Margulies, Clive Stafford Smith, and Mahvish Rukhsana Khan.

Philippe Sands's 2005 international legal-political analysis with the lengthy title *Lawless World: America and the Making and Breaking of Global Rules from FDR's Atlantic Charter to George W. Bush's Illegal War* is a sweeping condemnation of the Bush administration's foreign policy, including especially the Guantánamo decision. An old-school international relations idealist, Sands values international law as the crucial instrument for establishing a more just world order. His wrath is directed at the decisions such as Guantánamo that undermine international legal norms. Although Sands accepts the intelligence rationale of the official explanation for the decision, he dares to assert that another of its purposes was to supplant international humanitarian law. In support of that claim he quotes U.S. Deputy Assistant Attorney General John Yoo as saying that the Bush administration intended to "create a new legal regime."[20] Unfortunately that insight is never developed. Sands returned to the subject in a 2008 book with the rather less lengthy title *Torture Team: Rumsfeld's Memo and the Betrayal of American Values*, in which he examines the ethical and legal responsibilities of the Bush administration lawyers who were responsible for decisions involving torture at Guantánamo.

Legal scholars Laurel E. Fletcher and Eric Stover's 2009 book, *The Guantánamo Effect: Exposing the Consequences of U.S. Detention and Interrogation Practices*, criticizes the mistreatment of the Guantánamo prisoners before, during, and after their captivity in language that expresses academic precision, yet seethes with moral indignation. Although they report that a quantitative analysis establishes that few of the prisoners selected for transfer to Guantánamo could be accurately described as anything like "the worst of the worst" and that a qualitative analysis based on interviews shows that the regimens in the camps caused some prisoners lasting physical and psychological damage, they nonetheless accept that the primary purpose of the Guantánamo decision was to collect intelligence. The following passage is illustrative:

In Guantánamo, military commanders explicitly subordinated camp administration and procedures to the priorities of interrogation and thus created an atmosphere of constant surveillance and intrusion in the cellblocks that dehumanized detainees. The operating assumption was that camp conditions should serve to weaken the defenses of detainees and enable interrogators to break them down psychologically. Indeed, each component of the camp system—from the use of numbers to identify detainees to solitary confinement—was designed to increase the authority and power of camp interrogators while compounding the detainees' sense of isolation, powerlessness, and uncertainty.[21]

Lawyers by training, and thus indoctrinated to accept the authority of the state and its official pronouncements, the authors adopt that part of the official explanation that says the prisoners, whom the authors dutifully describe as "detainees," are being held in custody for the purpose of interrogation. They fail to consider the plausible alternative reading: that the dehumanizing camp regimen is designed to punish the prisoners and that the needs of interrogation are simply a rationalization.

Joseph Margulies's 2006 *Guantánamo and the Abuse of Presidential Power* characterizes the Guantánamo decision as a plot to make the presidency more powerful and thereby redistribute constitutional authority in the United States. A law school professor and respected champion of civil liberties, Margulies served as legal counsel for the three British Muslim prisoners who became known in the press as the Tipton Three: Ruhel Ahmed, Asif Iqbal, and Shafiq Rasul. Their habeas corpus challenge to their detention resulted in the enormously important *Rasul v. Bush* decision by the U.S. Supreme Court.

Despite anxiety that the Bush administration was attempting to increase the power of the executive branch vis-à-vis the other branches of the U.S. government, Margulies nonetheless endorses the proposition that the Guantánamo decision was made to facilitate intelligence collection. He accepts that the decision was made so that interrogations of numerous prisoners could be conducted to extract the information needed to construct piece by piece a mosaic of a secretive enemy the U.S. government hardly understood. Information collected from the prisoners held in prolonged custody would be of some use even over the long term. Although Margulies described the brutal treatment of his clients in disturbing detail, made a point of referring to the release of the infamous photographs of shackled prisoners clad in orange jumpsuits and blackened goggles, and noted that the Guantánamo decision moved the United States to the margins of international behavior, he failed to suggest alternative purposes such as punishing the prisoners as representatives, staging a spectacle of victory, or undermining international law and international order.

Clive Stafford Smith's 2007 *Eight O'Clock Ferry to the Windward Side* is another memoir by an attorney. Much of the narrative is devoted to the horrific experience of his client Binyam Ahmed Mohammed. An Ethiopian national, British resident, and convert to Islam, Mohammed reported being subjected to interrogation under very brutal torture in Rabat, Morocco, after his extraordinary rendition from Islamabad,

Pakistan. Subsequently transferred to Kabul, Afghanistan, and then to Guantánamo, the prisoner received an abortive trial before a military commission. Smith recounts the Kafkaesque absurdity of the hearing for that trial in exquisite detail.

Eight O'Clock Ferry to the Windward Side challenges some of the rationales of the official explanation and begins to suggest alternatives. Smith puts the lie to the claim that torture is primarily for intelligence collection rather than punishment by quoting from an interview with philosophy professor Michael Levin. An academic apologist for interrogation under torture who invokes the ticking-time-bomb scenario, Levin tells Smith that "torture's not a punishment, right? It's not a punishment, it's to prevent harm."[22] Yet, as Smith relates throughout the book, torture was used to punish prisoners like Binyam Mohammed but failed to elicit useful intelligence from them. Later he asserts that the prisoners held at Guantánamo were far from terrorist supermen and that few of them could be deemed terrorists of any kind.

Mahvish Rukhsana Khan's 2008 *My Guantánamo Diary* is yet another memoir by an attorney. Khan describes several of the prisoners that she represented in highly sympathetic terms, including Ali Shah Mousovi, an Afghan pediatrician arrested by American soldiers in Gardez, Afghanistan. Before being transferred to Guantánamo, Mousovi first spent twenty-two days in a makeshift prison in Gardez, a period during which he was humiliated by being denied permission to bathe, and was then transferred to Bagram Air Base, where he was subjected to a month of beatings, drugging, and forced nudity. Unlike most of the other prisoners held there, Mousovi was an adherent of Shi'a Islam, an identity that made him an especially unlikely recruit for the Taliban or al-Qaeda. The stories Khan tells about the other prisoners also suggest that they were something less than dangerous terrorist suspects. In describing the experience of Sudanese journalist Sami al-Haj at Guantánamo, she characterizes force-feeding with gastro-nasal tubes as punishment imposed to break his and the other hunger-striking prisoners' will to resist.

If the accounts written by the critics are incomplete because of failure to interpret, those written by the apologists—who include Kyndra

Miller Rotunda, Larry C. James, and Gordon Cucullu—are ultimately implausible. Rotunda's 2008 *Honor Bound: Inside the Guantanamo Trials* is a memoir of her career to date as a military lawyer, an officer in the Judge Advocate General's Corps (JAG), and a straightforward defense of the Guantánamo decision that indirectly or directly endorses all three rationales comprising the official explanation. Rather than address the rationale that the prisoners were brought to the navy base in Cuba to collect intelligence through interrogation rather than for punishment, she challenges the claims that prisoners were mistreated by repeating conclusions drawn in an investigation conducted by Vice Admiral Albert Church. "In Guantanamo Bay," Rotunda writes, "where there had been over 24,000 interrogation sessions, the investigators found *only three* cases of substantiated interrogation-based abuse."[23] The italics in the quote are Rotunda's. Her assertion need not be read closely to identify the effect of the important qualifying phrase "interrogation-based." The memoirs of released prisoners report that abuse also took place outside the interrogation rooms. Moreover, even a cursory familiarity with internal investigations conducted by bureaucratic organizations, especially those of organizations that demand extraordinary loyalty from their members and exercise nearly complete control over information about the sensitive subject matter of the investigation, would elicit suspicion that the conclusion might not reflect an entirely accurate account of events.

Rotunda also appears to endorse the threat rationale of the official explanation when she describes the prisoners as "over 800 detained terrorist enemies."[24] That many were less dangerous than her description may be inferred from the fact that a majority were eventually transferred to the custody of the governments of their home countries and then promptly released. Anticipating that weakness in her defense of the Guantánamo decision, Rotunda writes that 5 to 10 percent of the released prisoners "*return to the battle* against the U.S. and coalition forces."[25] The underlining in the quote is again by Rotunda. The actual figure from the Department of Defense is 6 percent, which is in fact between 5 percent and 10 percent, yet seems less impressive in its single-digit precision.

There are three serious problems with the 6 percent recidivism rate claimed by the Department of Defense. The first is the lack of any basis for comparison. Is 6 percent high? Comparison with prisoner releases in Northern Ireland provides an answer. Despite the dire predictions that large numbers of Irish Republican and Irish Loyalist prisoners held by the British in Northern Ireland would return to terrorism after their release, fewer than 10 percent were rearrested for either political or ordinary crimes.[26] That rate is well below the 48 percent and 58 percent recidivism rates for ordinary prisoners in Northern Ireland and the rest of Britain, respectively. By implication, a recidivism rate for the released Guantánamo prisoners of only 6 percent would indicate an outstanding policy success.

The second problem is that many of the prisoners may never have been guerrillas. The prisoner memoirs suggest that many were taken into custody because they seemed suspiciously foreign and thus could be sold by Afghan or Pakistani authorities to their American counterparts, who were in the market for prisoners to interrogate. Logically, they could not "return" because they had never been in "the battle" to begin with.

The third problem is that their "return" to battle was in some cases nothing more than verbal criticism of U.S. foreign policy.[27] Even if released prisoners had taken up arms before their capture, public condemnation of the conditions of their imprisonment at Guantánamo could hardly constitute doing battle with the U.S. military. Moreover, public criticism of either the Guantánamo decision or the wars in Afghanistan and Iraq was extraordinarily common during the Bush administration. Even if one was traveling abroad in the uniform of one of the U.S. military services, it would have been impossible to miss.

Rotunda appears to endorse the rationale that the prisoners were brought to Guantánamo for prosecution for war crimes, with a lengthy defense of the basis for such prosecution—she praises the 1942 Supreme Court decision in *Ex Parte Quirin* approving the decision of the military tribunal to execute a group of rather hapless German saboteurs—and a criticism of what she deems overly generous due process rights accorded prisoners in the Combatant Status Review Tribunals. Denunciation of actions characterized as appeasement, for example ending deployment of female interrogators in the name of cultural sensitivity, is a principal theme running through the memoir. While professional courtesy appears to have prevented Rotunda from joining Cucullu in criticism of the attorneys representing prisoners, that did not shield representatives of the International Committee of the Red Cross.

There are several possible reasons for the almost Manichean dualism that characterizes the Rotunda narrative. Perhaps it was the product of a calculation that arguing for the Guantánamo decision as a stark choice between "them and us" offered the best and perhaps the only possible way to persuade readers. Perhaps successful arguments made by military lawyers generally lack the subtlety of those made by civilian lawyers because military courts are generally more arbitrary in asserting authority. Perhaps Rotunda was compensating for feelings of inadequacy for serving a noncombat role in what may be the most important military conflict of her generation. Whatever the reason, her account was neither complete nor convincing.

Larry C. James's 2008 memoir, *Fixing Hell: An Army Psychologist Confronts Abu Ghraib*, is a defense of the military personnel, and in particular of the psychologists in mufti, who served at Guantánamo and at Abu Ghraib prison in Iraq. In the first few pages of the book, the author positions readers to identify with military personnel rather than their prisoners by describing an interrogation he observed at Abu Ghraib in which a twenty-two-year-old American soldier is reduced to tears and slumped over in her chair, emotionally defeated by a shackled forty-year-old "hardcore, killer terrorist."[28] He heaps praise on military personnel for their stoicism in the face of vile behavior by prisoners. He also deflects responsibility for the use of "harsh and abusive interrogation tactics," unmistakable code for torture, away from the military interrogators and psychologists with whom he identifies, and instead toward CIA contract psychologists at the base. However, that attempted redirection of attention is muddied by his description of an organizational culture at Guantánamo in which popular rage over the 9/11 terrorist attacks is projected onto prisoners, not only by the CIA contact interrogators but also by the military personnel.

Although the purpose of the Guantánamo decision is not directly discussed, the twin focuses on interrogation and on the dangerous nature of the prisoners carry the unmistakable implication that its purposes were to collect intelligence and to keep especially dangerous captives in continuing custody. Thus James describes Guantánamo as being "home to the military prison that housed some of the worst terrorists in the world."[29] The three teenage Guantánamo prisoners that he was tasked to interrogate are described as "far from innocent."[30] He does, however, grant them the status of victims. In his account they are the products of indoctrination into fanaticism inspired by ancient religious hatreds. Given the seeming shallowness of the observations that he makes about his prisoners/patients, perhaps it is not surprising that he subscribes to a simplistic but popular account of Islamist terrorism. Despite assistance from his cowriter, James nonetheless stumbles across the terminological minefield. Where the word "terrorist" is used to describe prisoners held both at Guantánamo and at Abu Ghraib, the word "torture" is used in connection with Abu Ghraib and "abuse" in connection with Guantánamo.

Approximately one-fifth of the narrative is devoted to an account of the author's tour of duty as chief psychologist at Guantánamo. The remainder offers descriptions of the author's tour of duty at Abu Ghraib and his subsequent emotional struggle, and an outraged defense of all military psychologists, including the individual most important in his narrative: Larry C. James. Even for a memoir, this seems rather too narcissistic.

The story does not end with the publication of *Fixing Hell*. On January 26, 2011, the Ohio State Board of Psychology announced its decision not to sanction James, who was then dean of the School of Professional Psychology at Wright State University in Dayton. In a newspaper interview two years earlier, James expressed his understanding of the case that had been leveled against him:

No matter what third party, objective review board or person, they've all come to the same conclusion—there's no probable cause. There's no detainee, there's no guard, there's no psychologist who's come forward and said, "With my own eyes, I've seen Dr. James do X, Y or Z."[31]

Resorting to such legalism when accusations involve violations of professional ethics suggests the sort of evasion common to the classic defense mechanism known as denial.

Gordon Cucullu's 2009 *Inside Gitmo: The True Story Behind the Myths of Guantánamo Bay* is a defense of the Guantánamo decision and the military personnel charged with its execution. Apparently written primarily for a reading audience of American conservatives, the book praises the stoicism of guards serving at Guantánamo in the weepy language of old soldiers, and denounces both the journalists covering the story for their hostility to the military mission and the attorneys representing the prisoners for their disloyalty, as for example by organizing prisoner hunger strikes. Cucullu also charges that legal "machinations" of the attorneys were responsible for keeping prisoners confined longer.[32]

Cucullu relies on the threat and intelligence rationales for his defense of the Guantánamo decision. Prisoners are described as being physical threats to their guards and likely to return to terrorism after their release. Cucullu denies that prisoners were tortured at Guantánamo, offering as evidence the observation that he did not witness acts of torture being committed during his visit to the base as a private citizen, albeit one who was there as "part of a government-sponsored media outreach program."[33] The idea that a writer with a book project whose object was defending the Guantánamo decision would have been given the opportunity to observe acts of torture is patently silly. So too is Cucullu's statement that "the public may never know the extent and magnitude of the actionable intelligence that has been extracted in Guantánamo,"[34] an assertion that could be correct whether the intelligence collected from the prisoners was of enormous value, of limited value, or of absolutely no value at all in fighting terrorism. If either of the latter two characterizations is correct, then there are good bureaucratic reasons for preventing the public from learning how much useful information was, or was not, extracted from the prisoners. Indeed, there may be more interest in maintaining secrecy about having collected intelligence of limited or absolutely no value.

Prison memoirs written by prisoners released from Guantánamo come closest to identifying punishment as an important reason for the decision. Murat Kurnaz's 2007 *Five Years of My Life: An Innocent Man in Guantanamo* details his experience of indefinite imprisonment and interrogation under torture. A Turkish national who had spent most of his life in Germany, Kurnaz described himself as a *tablighi*, a religious student wandering from madrassa to madrassa, who was taken into custody in Peshawar, Pakistan, at a police checkpoint in December 2001. Choosing the life of a religious scholar and pilgrim appears decidedly suspicious to North Americans and Europeans in the early twenty-first century. However, it is a respected life path of the religious traditions not only in Islam but also in Orthodox Christianity, Hinduism, and Buddhism. Indeed, in centuries past it would have seemed less alien in Roman Catholicism and Protestantism. After a few days spent in Pakistani custody, Kurnaz was transferred to American custody, after which he was imprisoned and tortured for two months in Kandahar, Afghanistan, and then in Guantánamo for the next five years. What he relates is harrowing in the extreme. His mistreatment appears to have been designed to punish and to elicit false confessions rather than to extract useful information. In addition to the punitive intent that may be inferred from gratuitous physical torture, Kurnaz recounts statements made by guards and interrogators indicating their determination to punish. He writes about an interrogation session in Kandahar: "I can still remember the words he kept repeating. 'You're a terrorist! We know that. We're going to keep you forever. You're never going home.'"[35] Contradicting the claims of the apologists, that is language expressing not an individual but a collective and perhaps institutional punitive intent. Using "we" puts the lie to the defense that individuals in the military overstepped their authority.

Moazzam Begg's 2006 *Enemy Combatant: My Imprisonment at Guantánamo, Baghram, and Kandahar* details the experience of the author's imprisonment and interrogation under torture. While not presenting an explicit explanation for the Guantánamo decision, his blow-by-blow description of his mistreatment in custody strongly suggests that its purpose was as much punishment as it was intelligence collection, at least for the military personnel and intelligence officers responsible for executing policy. During his captivity in Kandahar, for example, he and other prisoners were held in cells designated by the most salient terrorist events perpetrated by al-Qaeda and its affiliates.

On the way back from interrogation, I noticed something else: each cell had its own name, written in bold white marker: Somalia, Lebanon, USS *Cole*, Nairobi, Twin Towers, and Pentagon. I wondered what all these names and places had in common. Was the USA unleashing pent-up rage, seeking vengeance for every military engagement it had lost or terrorist act that it had suffered?[36]

Two documentary films explore the topic by focusing on the specific prisoners. The 2006 film *The Road to Guantánamo* describes the experiences of the Tipton Three, who were captured in Afghanistan and held in Guantánamo from its opening as a prison camp in 2001 until their release in 2004. Using recorded statements and re-created scenes, the film refers to the intelligence collection rationale twenty-three times and to the threat rationale four times, but makes no reference to the war crimes prosecution rationale. What is evident in the events portrayed in the film, however, is that the trio's captors, both Afghan and American, intended to punish their prisoners. The extraordinary measures taken by military personnel in Afghanistan and at Guantánamo to control the physical bodies, behavior, and communication of the prisoners were ineffective in eliciting information that might be useful as political military intelligence or for war crimes prosecutions, and were instead effective only in causing discomfort, pain, and mental anguish. There the film stops. The film does not convey the impression that the Guantánamo decision reflected an intention on the part of Bush administration officials to punish. Nor does it convey the impression that they made the Guantánamo decision to conduct a spectacle of victory for American and world public opinion or that they intended it as a means of undermining existing international law and international order.

The 2007 documentary film *Taxi to the Dark Side* by director Alex Gibney describes the death under torture of the Afghan national Dilawar, which will be discussed in chapter 4, as a vehicle for denouncing the interrogation by torture that became ubiquitous in the Bush administration's War on Terror. Where Dilawar and other prisoners held at Bagram Air Base were tortured using methods like those of the Spanish Inquisition, the prisoners at Guantánamo were subjected to more sophisticated tortures. The Cuban base is described as a laboratory for breaking the will of prisoners, using such methods as prolonged sensory deprivation, as part of an effort to collect intelligence. The film denounces senior Bush administration officials and military officers for giving untrained interrogators at Bagram Air Base tacit approval for using torture to extract intelligence, which served as license for enlisted soldiers to act out their anger, frustration, or sadism against prisoners.

These books and films suggest the decision making of the proverbial committee of the blind tasked with identifying an elephant. While the committee members are said to touch different parts of the animal and then disagree in their inaccurate conclusions, here they agree on an inaccurate identification provided by a mendacious sighted observer.

Despite obvious discrepancies of logic and fact that would have exposed the mendacity, none of the authors or producers directly challenged all three of the rationales comprising the official explanation. Most challenged none. The apologists accepted them all, while the critics spun critiques around, rather than in opposition to, the rationales. If the world had never seen the mass internment of special classes of prisoners in a geographically remote location that drew attention for that very reason, then it might be understandable. But the world has seen it before.

3 Three Comparable Historical Cases

Attempting to understand the reasons for the Bush administration's Guantánamo decision in isolation from other historical cases of internment of special classes of prisoners runs two major risks. The first is failing to distinguish putative from actual purposes. The second is failing to understand what makes the present case truly different.

Comparison with three historical cases provides some crucial insight into the reasons for the Bush administration's Guantánamo decision and identifies why it is in fact unique: the internment of the Chiricahua Apache at Fort Pickens and in Saint Augustine, Florida, in 1885–87, the internment of the British fascists on the Isle of Man in 1940–44, and the internment of Haitian "boat people" at Guantánamo in 1986–91. Each case involved a decision by a liberal democracy to hold a special class of prisoners, who symbolically represented security or political threats greater than they actually presented in the flesh, in indefinite custody in geographically remote yet very public locations.

These three cases were not selected because the actions of either those in custody or those at large that they symbolically represented were morally equivalent to those of the prisoners transferred to Guantánamo beginning in 2002 or members of al-Qaeda and the Taliban. For the Chiricahua Apache to wage a guerrilla war against the U.S. Army for the right to live off the reservation and according to their traditions of migration and raiding is not the moral equivalent of the Taliban waging a guerrilla war against the U.S. military for the right to govern Afghanistan as an Islamic state and a base for al-Qaeda's international terrorism. For the British fascists to engage in pacifist agitation or, worse, to engage in suspected espionage and sabotage, is not the moral equivalent of young Muslims traveling to Afghanistan before the U.S. military attack to express solidarity with fellow Muslims by working in specifically Islamic humanitarian aid projects or by joining the Taliban as soldiers. For Haitian refugees to protest and riot after fleeing misery and oppression in their homeland is not the moral equivalent of prisoners hurling verbal abuse or feces at their guards. If the inquiry is about the reasons for decisions such as these, then moral equivalence is irrelevant.

Instead, the real equivalence is between the emotional responses of the American and British publics to bodies of prisoners and those that they represent. Most Americans living along the Mexican-American border in the 1880s were alarmed about the possibility of raids by the Chiricahua Apache. They feared and hated the Chiricahua much as contemporary Americans feared and hated members of al-Qaeda after September 11, 2001. Most Britons living in the early 1940s felt at least as betrayed by the British fascists with their aristocratic leader as did most Americans by the young middle-class Saudis who had been living in their midst before becoming airline suicide hijackers. Many Americans in the 1980s, alarmed by the new HIV/AIDS contagion that they associated with the Haitian refugees, reacted to the idea of their arrival in the United States in large numbers with a degree of panic comparable to that expressed by some present-day Americans about the transfer of the remaining Guantánamo prisoners to federal prisons in the continental United States. Only selfishness and ignorance rival fear and its offspring hatred as emotions that may be exploited by ambitious leaders. Fear of violence, betrayal, and contamination are likely to tempt mass publics to demand demonstrations of coercive might rather than measured responses from their government.

Chiricahua Apache

By the late twentieth and early twenty-first century, most Americans viewed the conquest of North American native peoples and resettlement of the continent by descendants of European immigrants as

unambiguously shameful. In a historical narrative that gained ascen-
dancy beginning in the 1960s, the native peoples of the continent became the objects of sympathy as the victims of violence that amounted
to slow-motion genocide. Such thinking, however, was not the norm
for much of the history of the United States. Instead, public opinion
about the "Indian problem" among the majority white population was
often divided. Those living farthest from the frontier of settlement
were often the most sympathetic to the plight of Native Americans.
Those living closest to the frontier often hated Native Americans because they feared being attacked. Policies of both assimilation and
extermination found advocates across most of the eighteenth and
nineteenth centuries. The last episode of this tragic history was an
atrocity committed against largely unarmed Sioux on December 29,
1890, that is now remembered as the Massacre at Wounded Knee. That
was followed on January 16, 1891, by the surrender of the remaining
"hostiles," who were then herded onto the Pine Ridge reservation. The
general officer responsible for that campaign was Brigadier General
Nelson A. Miles, who had also been responsible for the final stage of
the campaign against the Chiricahua Apache five years before.

When the Chiricahua Apache were settled on the San Carlos Apache
Reservation in 1882, the American Southwest appeared to many to
have been finally pacified. Although it sounds like an Orwellian euphemism to contemporary ears, "pacified" was the verb most often
employed to describe the military defeat and subsequent relocation
on reservations of Native Americans. The eleven years of fighting from
1861 to 1872 between the Chiricahua Apache under the leadership of
Cochise and the U.S. Army was one of the longest, most expensive Indian wars in American history. With the peace agreement that ended
that war, three centuries of endemic raid, reprisal, and massacre between nomadic and settled Native Americans, the Spanish, later the
Mexicans, and finally the Americans in the Southwest seemed to
all observers to have been brought to a conclusion. The Chiricahua
Apache were the last of the ethnically related tribes speaking Athabas-
can languages in the region to be subjugated. The Navajo and the other
Apache tribes—Kiowa, Lipan, Jicarilla, and Mescalero—had already
accepted the limitations of reservation life. Only a band of Chiricahua

on the other side of the border in the mountains of northern Mexico were still "at large."

However, there was one last martial spasm in the Chiricahua: a final eruption of raiding on both sides of the border between the United States and Mexico by the Bedonkohe or Enemy People band. Leading them was Geronimo, an aging shaman who proved just as adept a guerrilla leader as Cochise and Mangas Coloradas. Miserable on their Arizona reservation, the Bedonkohe were ready to follow Geronimo across the border to join the last free Apache band in the Sierra Madre Mountains of Mexico in April 1882. After they joined, they suffered an attack by the Mexican Army at Casas Grandes that resulted in hundreds of Apache dead and dozens of Apache women and children in captivity. Subsequent captures in Mexico by the U.S. Army led by Apache scouts left Geronimo with a force of only thirty-six warriors. This remnant warrior band would double in size while on the run in the arid mountains of northern Mexico, and that small force would be sufficient to keep thousands of American troops on patrol on both sides of the border and guarding the bulk of the Chiricahua population still living on the reservation. Commanding the Arizona Territory, General Nelson Miles sought to solve the regional security problem by removing the Bedonkohe, Chihenne, and Chokonen bands of the Chiricahua to a reservation in the Indian Territory of Oklahoma where the Kiowa Apache (or Plains Apache), the Kiowa, and the Comanche had already been successfully relocated.[1] Instead, President Grover Cleveland and General Philip Henry Sheridan decided that they would be removed east of the Mississippi to Florida, where a humid lowland environment very different from their arid, mountainous homeland would work its malign magic on their numbers. Forced population movements and relocation to unfamiliar environments is a recurring feature of the subjugation of indigenous peoples and ethnic minorities by governments. Where the voluntary migration by modern populations in search of economic opportunity often results in individual achievement, involuntary transfers of native populations that are executed by governments to exert political control often result in the opposite. Passivity born of disorientation and depression are common psychological responses to the predicament of becoming a refugee, and passivity was what Washington wanted from Native Americans.

By 1885, Geronimo and his band of exhausted followers were ready to surrender. The Apache leader later claimed that he had been promised ranch land and livestock as a quid pro quo during the negotiations that took place in Skeleton Canyon. General Miles probably promised that Geronimo and the Chiricahua would spend at most two years in exile before being allowed to return to their homeland. Instead, they would spend eighteen years in exile.

After a hundred-mile trek to the railhead at Holbrook, Arizona, 381 Apaches were loaded onto railcars for a long journey to internment in Florida. Six decades before the deportations to internal exile of the Chechens, Ingush, and Crimean Tartars in the Soviet Union, the idea of forcing an entire ethnic group onto railcars for relocation must have seemed much less ominous. Yet the outcome was similar. Geronimo and 16 of his warriors were imprisoned at Fort Pickens, on Santa Rosa Island near Pensacola, while the remaining Chiricahua, including 103 children and the Chiricahua scouts who had been instrumental in helping the U.S. Army pursue Geronimo and his rebel band, were interned at Fort Marion in Saint Augustine.[2] The prisoners held at both locations were made available for public viewing by tourists, living proof that the U.S. Army had indeed, at long last, been victorious over the wily Apache.

Fort Marion had been used to imprison Native Americans before. Seventy-two Cheyenne, Kiowa, Arapaho, Comanche, and Caddo warriors captured during the 1874 Red River War were transferred to Fort Marion from Fort Sill in Oklahoma for internment without trial. The administration of Ulysses S. Grant rejected proposals to conduct trials of the warriors before either military tribunals or civilian courts.[3] The seventy-one prisoners who completed the journey—one having been killed in an escape attempt—were subjected to four years of involuntary cultural assimilation, including the evangelizing efforts of Protestant Christian clergy. In 1878 the older prisoners in this population were shipped back west for release, while the youngest prisoners were sent to Indian boarding schools.

Most of the Chiricahua exiles left Florida in 1887, but not for their homeland. The children of the exiles were taken from their parents and sent to an Indian boarding school in Carlisle, Pennsylvania. Herbert Welsh, corresponding secretary of the Indian Rights Association, toured the school shortly after they arrived and concluded:

> Those Chiricahua Apache children who are not at Carlisle should in every way be encouraged to remain, and their parents, where these are still living, should be shown that this course is in the best interests of their children. There is no better place for them than Carlisle.[4]

Events would prove him very wrong. Death from disease, psychological wounds of abuse, and alienation from their traditional culture took their terrible toll, just as it did with other Native Americans. By late 1889, 30 of the 100 children who had been sent to the boarding school in Carlisle had died. Among them was Geronimo's son Chappo. Most of the adults in Florida were moved to Mount Vernon Barracks in Alabama, where they continued to experience a disproportionately high death rate. Imprisonment far from their homeland, first in Florida and later in Pennsylvania and Alabama, thus proved an effective means both for staging a spectacle demonstrating military victory and for inflicting indirect punishment on the prisoners. Like the Chechen, Ingush, and Crimean Tartars in the Soviet Union, they would be made to suffer before the surviving remnant were allowed to return to their homeland. In 1894 the Chiricahua Apache were relocated to Fort Sill, then part of the Indian Territory. Not until 1913 were a minority allowed to move onto the Mescalero Apache Reservation in Ruidoso, New Mexico. By then, neither the Chiricahua Apache nor any other group of Native Americans were much feared by the majority white population. By the early twentieth century other national security threats had been found, including Mexican revolutionaries in the mountains of northern Mexico that had been familiar to the Apache. The Native Americans of the American West had become objects of curiosity or even sympathy, thanks to the efforts of Hollywood and Madison Avenue. The first national security threats to the United States were thus successfully transformed into victims of ethnocentric ignorance and noble guardians of the natural environment. Enemies are usually respected only long after they are defeated.

British Fascists

The constitutional relationship between the Isle of Man and the British Crown renders the island simultaneously both British and not British. Like the Channel Islands, it is not formally part of the territory of the United Kingdom of Great Britain and Northern Ireland, but is instead a "crown dependency." As detailed in appendix 2, relative physical isolation in the form of distance and water barrier makes islands especially attractive locations for the imprisonment of special categories of prisoners. Isolation from the jurisdiction of British courts also made them attractive to the British government in the seventeenth century. In one early historical parallel to the decision of the Bush administration to exploit the anomalous international legal status of Guantánamo some three and half centuries later, the Restoration English government used both Jersey in the Channel Islands and the Isle of Man to imprison antiroyalist political prisoners indefinitely because the Writ of Habeas Corpus did not obtain there. That obvious subterfuge caused Parliament to give the Habeas Corpus Act extraterritorial effect in 1679.[5] Notwithstanding that restraint on executive authority, the Isle of Man continued to be an attractive location for British governments intent upon imprisoning special categories of prisoners into the mid-twentieth century. During both of the world wars, tens of thousands of prisoners of war and civilian enemy aliens and, most controversially, British nationals administratively designated as politically disloyal were held in camps on the island.

When Germany replaced France as the primary challenger to British naval and colonial dominance in the last decade of the nineteenth century, British imperialists began to encourage anti-German sentiment in British public opinion through the dissemination of warnings about German naval shipbuilding in the press and the publication of fiction depicting sabotage and secret invasion plans. The May 1915 sinking of the passenger liner *Lusitania* off the coast of Ireland by a German U-boat sparked a popular hysteria that caused the government of Prime

Minister Herbert Henry Asquith to introduce the mass internment of all Central Powers nationals, Germans and Austrians for the most part, as enemy aliens. In passing the Defence of the Realm Acts of 1914, Parliament had granted the legal authority to the King's Council to issue regulations necessary to protect national security. Although it violated the spirit of individual liberty celebrated in English common law, this transfer of authority from the legislature to the executive to hold persons in custody without a hearing in civil court was consistent with responses to previous and subsequent internal security emergencies in British possessions from Jamaica to New Zealand.[6] Civil liberties are frequently sacrificed in reaction to perceived internal security threats.

The specific legal authority for the mass internment of enemy aliens in Britain took the form of Regulation 14B. Notwithstanding the reputation of Britain as a society in which the state was less intrusive than on the Continent, enforcement was thorough. Fully 32,440 enemy aliens had been interned by November 1915.[7] In 1917, even after two years of brutal combat on the Western Front and large numbers of German soldiers taken prisoner, enemy aliens still comprised more than one-third of all German nationals in British custody. During the early stages of the conflict, the civilian internees and military prisoners were held in the same camps, though typically in separate housing. Many were held in the multiple camps on the Isle of Man, the largest of which was Knockaloe Camp.

Peace eventually allows for more dispassionate reflection on the conduct of war. During the *interbellum* of the 1920s and 1930s, the consensus emerged that the mass internment of enemy aliens in the First World War had been an expensive mistake. Many of those interned had posed no security threat, and their internment had deprived the economy of useful labor. When the enemy-aliens issue arose again at the beginning of the Second World War, London's first impulse was to avoid repeating the mistake.[8] Given the larger number and political identities of the enemy alien population in Britain, mass internment made even less sense in the Second World War than it did during the First World War. However, that initial cautious, proportional impulse soon evaporated. The mass internment decision in May 1940 was the product of elite and mass hysteria produced by news of the unexpectedly rapid German military victory over the Dutch, Belgian, French, and British armies defending the Low Countries. British decision makers were reduced to panic as the evacuation at Dunkirk of the British Expeditionary Force without their artillery and armored vehicles convinced many that an invasion of the British Isles might succeed. Ordinary Britons responded to press reports that exaggerated the security threat of espionage, sabotage, or advance scouting posed by German, Austrian, and Italian nationals resident in Britain. News coverage of the threat reached hysterical proportions in the newspapers owned by Lord Rothermere, the most conservative of the British press lords. Anxiety about being condemned for his prewar sympathies for fascism and the two fascist dictators was the likely motivation for the eruption of superpatriotism in his newspapers, which included the influential *Daily Mail*. One critical observer pulled no punches in making the accusation:

One is struck by the fact that the newspapers which were loudest in the agitation against refugees were those which, before the war, were the most assiduous in their advocacy of appeasement and of kowtowing to dictators. Many of the signed articles in these papers were written by publicists who in peace-time had become generally regarded, not as British journalists, but almost as English mouthpieces of Goering and Goebbels.[9]

That same observer also speculated that the decision to intern antifascist and Jewish refugees in Britain actually pleased the German and Italian governments. By implication, Rothermere succeeded in saving himself from the accusation of disloyalty even while acting in the interests of the fascist regimes during the war. Whether true or not, more than 26,000 German, Austrian, and Italian nationals were soon interned.[10]

The legal fate of each enemy alien was in the hands of tribunals empowered to consider any evidence, including hearsay and information in intelligence reports not available to the individual whose fate was being decided. Individuals facing internment were not allowed to bring attorneys, but might instead bring a "friend" as an advisor.[11] Many reportedly had to contend not only with the inability to respond to evidence against them but also with the lack of political sophistication or even prejudice of many tribunal members. Some of the refugees seemed suspect because of their leftist politics and others because they were Jews.

Far more controversial during the Second World War than the internment of enemy aliens was the decision to intern large numbers of Britons who were suspected of political disloyalty. In mid-1940 anxiety was running high among British decision makers that a domestic British "fifth column" loyal to the two fascist powers would assist an invasion of the island that seemed imminent. Fascist fifth columns were assisting the German and Italian military occupations of countries across the Continent. MI5, the chief British counterintelligence body, was acutely aware that Sir Oswald Mosley, leader of the British Union of Fascists (BUF), was on familiar terms with many of the then current political elites not only of Britain and the United States but also of Italy and Germany. They knew that the BUF had received generous subsidies from the Italian government to finance its operations. Like its counterparts on the Continent, the BUF had its own paramilitary corps. Rather than a discredited movement on the very eve of war, as late as July 1939 the BUF could still attract 20,000 supporters to a rally. Reasonable minds could conceive of the BUF leadership and paramilitary corps, as well as many of its rank-and-file members, as serious security threats.

On May 22, 1940, the War Cabinet decided to neutralize the perceived threat by adopting an amendment to Defence Regulation 18B (1A) permitting internment of British nationals determined to be sympathetic to the two fascist powers. As with the enemy aliens, tribunals decided the fate of those in custody without permitting them access to the evidence or legal representation. Within two months, 753 British fascists had been taken into custody. Dozens of senior leaders, including Mosley, were separated from one another and from their followers in prisons in England and Scotland. The most ideologically committed ordinary members of the BUF joined thousands of enemy aliens in the internment camps on the Isle of Man. The perverse result of this decision was that British fascists were held in close proximity to Jewish and antifascist political refugees.

Interrogations of the internees by MI5 revealed that most of them were sincerely committed to fascism, and the experience of internment hardened their ideological commitment, which included intense personal loyalty to Mosley. The leader principle is as basic an element of fascist ideology as anything else. Also in common with the Continental fascisms, the British version exploited the theme of martyrdom by portraying internment as a collective Golgotha.[12] In reality, the fascist prisoners were treated well by comparison with many of the interned antifascist and Jewish enemy aliens.[13] They were allowed to wear civilian clothing, provided with varied meals and health care, granted mail privileges and some entertainment. One of their camps even featured a tennis court. The prisoners were also allowed to conduct political meetings. Unsurprisingly, none of that would be mentioned when they elaborated narratives of their political martyrdom.

Befitting a society where social class still determined privilege and privation, the prison regimen varied according to the status of the prisoner. A wealthy aristocrat and former member of Parliament, Mosley was imprisoned under a regimen that was more comfortable than the life of much of the working class in wartime Britain. He was held at Holloway Prison in a large two-bedroom flat with a small garden and servants. Despite popular antipathy, he was released from custody in September 1943 with the explanation that he was suffering from phlebitis. Most of the other British fascists had to wait until victory was more certain. Perhaps unfair, but other British elites who had displayed fascist sympathies before the Second World War were not threatened with internment because of their social status and their fervent if recent wartime antifascist patriotism.

Haitian and Cuban Refugees

In February 1986 the Duvalier dynasty—François "Papa Doc" Duvalier and Jean-Claude "Baby Doc" Duvalier—that had ruled Haiti for three decades fell to a military coup amid widespread political and social unrest. Five years of political crisis would follow before the election of Jean-Bertrand Aristide in February 1991. With the support of a populist social movement that had been embraced by most Haitians and convictions expressed in the rhetoric of liberation theology, this first democratically elected president of Haiti promised social reform and intended to deliver on his promises. That brought him into conflict with the Haitian economic and military elites, who waited all of eight months before overthrowing him. The brutal repression of the protests against the military coup generated a new wave of refugees.[14]

By 1991, Washington had more than a decade of experience in dealing with waves of boat people. The first modern tragedy of this kind had come in 1979, when as many as 500,000 Vietnamese had been allowed to leave postwar Vietnam to seek asylum elsewhere. Initial efforts by the governments of Thailand, Malaysia, Indonesia, the Philippines, and Hong Kong to deny the refugees first asylum were discouraged by the United States, which ultimately granted asylum to the bulk of the refugees. Unpopular with many Americans as a reminder of the bitter failure in the Vietnam War that culminated in the collapse of the government of South Vietnam in 1976, the influx of Vietnamese refugees helped to launch a new anti-immigration movement that gained momentum with anxiety about the Mariel Boatlift in 1980. During that chaotic event, some 124,000 Cubans fled their homeland for the United States after the Cuban government granted permission. Much of the anxiety was focused on the presumed poverty and criminality of the Marielitos. Unspoken but obvious to most observers was discomfort with the fact that, unlike the previous wave of Cuban refugees arriving from 1960 to 1974, many in this wave of refugees were nonwhite and from the poorest segments of Cuban society.[15]

If the waves of Vietnamese and Cuban refugees aroused opposition, the Haitian refugees elicited something close to panic in Washington. Between 1986 and 1991 the U.S. Coast Guard interdicted numerous small ships carrying Haitian refugees fleeing the political violence in their impoverished country for the safety of the United States and repatriated many of their unlucky passengers. Under international law and relevant implementing statutory law, refugees who manage to set foot in the United States are entitled to a formal hearing before an administrative law judge about their status as political refugees before possible deportation. Those who fail to reach the shores of the United States are entitled to far fewer legal rights under international law.

The unfortunate Haitians who attempted to reach the U.S. mainland in small boats embodied much that white middle-class Americans found threatening in the early 1980s. Poor, black, and many speaking only Haitian French patois, they were perceived by much of the American public as carriers of the HIV virus at precisely the time when anxiety and ignorance about the pandemic were greatest.[16] Conservative pundits had a field day stoking fear of an invasion by the dark-skinned, the desperate, and the diseased. Anti-immigrant interest groups joined in sounding the alarm.[17] Taking custody of the refugees while they were still on open water thus made perfect sense, legally, bureaucratically, and politically, to the Reagan and George H. W. Bush administrations.

As would be true of decision making by the administration of George W. Bush two decades later, decision makers in the two Republican administrations considered internment of these "undesirables" in impressively remote locations. One possibility given serious consideration was to intern the Haitian refugees who succeeded in reaching U.S. soil at the Glasgow Air Force Base in Montana, reputedly one of the coldest places in the lower forty-eight states.[18] Although the deterrent effect of that choice of location was probably foremost in their minds, it seems likely that some took satisfaction in the prospect of the suffering it would cause. Despite that temptation, the obvious inhumanity of relocating refugees who had spent their lives in the tropics and who were physically vulnerable because of the stress of refugee flight, and in some cases illness and malnutrition, to a distant, frigid air base close to the Canadian-American border must have occurred to some, because that location was not selected. If nothing else, they may have been dissuaded by the public relations damage that could result from demonstrating such meanness of spirit.

Another wrinkle was the anxiety that if large numbers of Haitian refugees were granted asylum in the United States, others fleeing noncommunist authoritarian states might emulate their example. Throughout the Cold War the practice of the United States was to accept most asylum seekers from communist states but reject most asylum seekers from noncommunist states.[19] What mattered in the decision on asylum applications was less the severity of oppression experienced by victims than the political identity of the state that oppressed them. Although this was consistent with Washington's foreign policy goals, it left people who feared persecution for their political beliefs in noncommunist authoritarian regimes without an exit option comparable to those in communist regimes. This notorious double standard was part of the calculations being made by political refugees and states across the Caribbean.

Interdiction began with President Ronald Reagan's Executive Order 12324, which authorized the Coast Guard to stop vessels and repatriate passengers intent on violating U.S. immigration laws. When the scale of the Haitian humanitarian crisis grew, President George H. W. Bush reinforced the interdiction policy by issuing the Kennebunkport Order, creating what was characterized at the time as a "floating Berlin Wall" around Haiti that prevented refugees from fleeing for any country by sea."[20] When the presidential order was successfully challenged in the federal courts as a violation of the Refugee Convention and roundly criticized as inhumane by 1992 Democratic presidential nominee William Jefferson "Bill" Clinton, the administration responded by temporarily suspending the repatriation of Haitian refugees and instead interning them at Guantánamo. There they were housed in cinder block quarters at Camp Bulkeley at the eastern side of the base or in a tent city that was erected on McCalla Field, an inactive airfield.

Internment at Guantánamo made political sense to conservatives because it was outside the sovereign territory of the United States, and thus asylum seekers could be denied the full range of legal rights, such as the presence of an attorney, that would have been required if their hearings had been conducted in the United States. The Cuban base thus served as a useful legal limbo—or, more appropriately, a legal purgatory—a full decade before the war in Afghanistan. Dismayed by their failure to reach the U.S. mainland, the refugees demonstrated and engaged in minor rioting, which led to further apprehension in American public opinion and the segregation of demonstration and riot organizers in a separate camp that was "a cross between a holding facility and a brig."[21]

Of the 34,624 Haitian refugees who were interned at the naval base, 10,791, or fewer than one-third, were ultimately granted political asylum in the United States. The remaining 23,833 were repatriated to Haiti. Repatriations of more than one thousand refugees per month were effected using Coast Guard vessels. Promises that no reprisals would be conducted in Haiti were made by U.S. embassy and Haitian government officials, backed up by the threat of force by U.S. Marines.

Trapped at Guantánamo for the longest time were the 310 prisoners who had tested HIV-positive and their family members. Immigration and Naturalization Service regulations explicitly denied entrance into the United States to anyone who was HIV-positive. The same irrational fear that generated that regulation also prompted the authorities to confine this subpopulation of refugees to a separate camp.

Campaign promises are easily broken. Even before taking office, president-elect Clinton changed his mind and decided not to admit the Haitian refugees to the United States but instead to maintain the Bush policy of interning the HIV-positive refugees in a new guise. In a foreshadowing of the experience of the captives transferred from Afghanistan and Pakistan beginning in 2002, some of the most desperate prisoners attempted suicide.[22] Demonstrations in the United States that drew press attention because they included several Hollywood celebrities and Yale University law students denounced "America's first HIV-concentration camp."[23] Aware that they were now losing control over the issue in American public opinion, Clinton administration officials conceded defeat after U.S. Circuit Court of Appeals judge Sterling Johnson Jr. ruled that the Haitians possessed due process rights under the U.S. Constitution that had been violated and also that the First Amendment rights of their attorneys had been violated by denying them access to their clients.

A second humanitarian crisis involving boat people emerged even as the other was still maturing. The more sympathetic reception given to Cuban than to Haitian refugees after they had arrived in the United States reflected the greater geographic proximity of southern Florida to Cuba than to Haiti, and the different legal treatment accorded Cuban and Haitian refugees who were picked up in U.S. waters encouraged several waves of *balseros* or rafters to attempt the crossing from Cuba. The perverse incentive for Cubans to attempt the journey was the fact that while the American government would grant only a handful of entry visas through its United States Interests Section at the Swiss embassy in Havana, which undertook consular duties in the absence of regular diplomatic relations, Cubans were granted automatic asylum if they were taken into custody in U.S. waters. In contrast, Haitians who were taken into custody under the same circumstances were hauled to Guantánamo. This perverse incentive for Cubans appears to have been constructed not only as a humanitarian gesture but also to embarrass Havana. International news coverage of citizens so desperate to flee a country that they attempt to cross the open ocean in flimsy boats is obviously bad publicity for a regime that presents itself as committed to social development.

As the increasing numbers of *balseros* making the voyage from 1991 onward threatened to become a third wave, there was increasing alarm in Washington about the additional burden on social services and adverse public reaction. The administration of George H. W. Bush responded by adopting the approach taken to Haitian refugees: arrest and/or rescue on the high seas and then transfer to Guantánamo for incarceration. No doubt sensing a political opportunity to return the insult by embarrassing Washington, in early 1994 the Cuban government announced that it would relax its restrictive migration policy. Just as with the Haitian refugees, the Clinton administration continued to follow the policy of the predecessor administration toward the threatened new wave of Cuban refugees. Automatic asylum for the Cubans was suspended, and they were held at Guantánamo under the same conditions as the Haitians.[24]

The Clinton administration also considered but rejected another proposal for internment at Guantánamo, this time in response to the 1999 humanitarian crisis presented by the 100,000 Kosovars who fled from the Yugoslav (Serbian) Army across the border into neighboring Macedonia. Painful memories of the casualties and refugee flight during the war in Bosnia were fresh. Just as with the prisoners taken in

Afghanistan, Anderson Air Force Base in Guam was also considered as a possible location for interning the Kosovar refugees. The official proposal was to airlift 20,000 of the 100,000 Kosovars to Guantánamo rather than to the United States, "if only to demonstrate to President Slobodan Milosevic of Yugoslavia that the relocation is temporary and his campaign of 'ethnic cleansing' in Kosovo will not succeed."[25]

What These Three Historical Cases Tell Us

Some of the parallels between specific facets of the Guantánamo decision and each of the three cases outlined above are obvious. Transferring hundreds of prisoners in custody in Afghanistan and Pakistan to Guantánamo, many because they were suspect when first taken into custody, echoes the transfer of hundreds of Chiricahua Apache women and children together with the U.S. Army scouts to Fort Marion. The denial of legal counsel or the right to view evidence from intelligence reports and the use of hearsay evidence in the internment hearings of the British fascists clearly echo the denials of due process in the hearings to determine whether the Guantánamo prisoners should be deemed "unlawful combatants" and thus require continued custody. The search for remote locations such as an uninhabited island in Lake Kariba in Zambia to hold the prisoners captured in Afghanistan and Pakistan who would eventually be held in Guantánamo echoes the consideration given to interning the Haitian refugees at Glasgow Air Force Base in Montana before they were interned at Guantánamo.[26]

However much these obvious specific parallels may tell us about the purposes of the Guantánamo decision, the arc of events that they share tells us more. To the American and British publics of their historical moments, the Chiricahua Apache, the British fascists, and the Haitian refugees symbolized daunting unresolved problems, even as the nature of the security threat that they posed was exaggerated.

Whether at large or in custody, the Chiricahua Apache represented the unsettled legal status of Native Americans and the lawless nature of the border between the United States and Mexico. Moreover, if further armed rebellion by Native Americans seemed unlikely by the 1880s, it took little foresight to imagine there would be native peoples in other lands to be pacified in the future. U.S. Army officers who participated in the last of the Indian wars would still be serving by the time of the Spanish-American War and Philippine-American War.

The British fascists represented more than a body of traitors who would betray the country. They also represented the forbidden illiberal solution to class conflict in Britain: the coercion practiced in Britain's colonies. Vigorous challenges to capitalism and inherited social privilege were expressed in demands for social reform in election campaigns and in work stoppages called by trade unions. The old Tory urge to employ police violence and harsh prison sentences to enforce familiar social hierarchy attracted nervous members of the middle and upper classes. Although largely restrained by the rule of law, public opinion, and general elections in Britain, the coercive power of the state was used freely in the colonies. For example, under the Defence of India Act, British colonial courts in India convicted no fewer than 25,000 people of sedition in 1941. That hundreds of Britons could be interned on the Isle of Man simply because of their political affiliations, albeit a generally despised political ideology, was a message that many more could be locked up if British elites felt sufficiently threatened.

Haitian refugees embodied the demographic, racial, and public health anxieties of white Americans. Impoverished, numerous, nonwhite, and in many cases infected with a poorly understood and still deadly virus, they posed a challenge that overwhelmed the instinct to help those in greatest need. That most of them spoke Haitian French patois and that Haiti conjured images of an exoticized voodoo only increased the cultural distance. Following the recent waves of Vietnamese and Cuban refugees, they portended a flood from the Third World that might leave America unrecognizable. Holding the Haitians and the subsequent wave of Cubans in custody offshore signaled Washington's willingness to use whatever coercive instrument was necessary to prevent even the perception of such a transformation.

The arc of events thus begins in the public spectacle of a special class of prisoners representing present and future security threats who are transferred to confinement in a location emphasizing physical isolation. There they are punished in a manner befitting the security threat that they symbolize for public opinion in the liberal democracy that holds them captive, and also in each case by the emotional stress of uncertainty about their individual and collective fates. Their captivity in turn heralds a new state of affairs, a declaration of change in a power relationship. In each of these cases the arc of events ends in anticlimax. The public then ignores the transfer to other locations or the release of prisoners from custody months or years after the initial imprisonment has lost its power to impress. It is precisely here that the contemporary case differs. Rather than anticlimax, the Bush administration's Guantánamo decision acquired a life of its own. Many Americans are fearful of the remaining prisoners and oppose closing the prison. Although the willingness of ambitious political elites to stoke those irrational fears has exacerbated the problem, they have been able to do so only because the original message was so effective.

4 Extraordinary Threat

The "worst elements of al-Qaeda and the Taliban" was how Brigadier General Michael Lehnert, the U.S. Marines officer in command of the prison, described the prisoners as they began to arrive at the base.[1] Not to be outdone by a subordinate posturing for the press, Joint Chiefs of Staff chairman General Richard Myers promoted them as terrorist supermen during a joint press briefing with Secretary Rumsfeld on January 11, 2002. "These are people who would gnaw through hydraulic lines in the back of a C-17 to bring it down . . . these are very, very dangerous people."[2] By the end of the press briefing, Myers and Rumsfeld were backtracking on that absurd claim, but it nonetheless revealed something important about the thinking current at the highest levels of the Pentagon. The press and public were to be presented with the image of an irrational enemy extraordinarily dangerous even in captivity.

Behind the scenes there were less histrionics. During a White House meeting a week later on the legal status of the captives, Myers argued that failing to treat the captured as if they were prisoners of war might result in the mistreatment of captured American military personnel.[3] This argument for the primitive calculus of mutual deterrence that long predated the development of international humanitarian law was successful, if only in part. Others at the meeting wanted all of the captives to be treated like international outlaws. The result was a compromise. Prisoners identified as members of al-Qaeda would be deemed "unlawful combatants." Prisoners identified as members of the Taliban would not be formally designated as prisoners of war under the Geneva Conventions but would still be accorded some of the rights associated with that status.

Three observations should be made about this exchange. First, the timing of the debate about their legal status—a week after they had already begun arriving at Guantánamo—indicates ad hoc decision making. Important determinations were being made on the fly. Second, the assumption that the Taliban would reciprocate the treatment of the captured suggests that they were not seen as irrational fanatics with whom one could never expect to negotiate. People so ferocious that they would attempt to bring down aircraft by gnawing through hydraulic lines are hardly capable of reciprocity. Third, the decision makers were determined to select at least some from among the prisoners for harsher treatment. The urge to punish was close to the surface of their thinking.

For public consumption, however, the prisoners were still being cast in the role of extraordinarily dangerous enemy. Rumsfeld described them as "extremely dangerous" and justified their transfer to Guantánamo as necessary to prevent their release "back out on the street to engage in further terrorist attacks" during a January 22, 2002, press conference at the Pentagon.[4] His choice of words is revealing. When prisoners in police custody are ordered released by the courts because criminal charges against them have been dismissed for lack of evidence, procedural irregularity, acquittal, or parole, American politicians who want to posture as tough on crime describe them as having been released "back out on the streets." Although most of the prisoners arriving in Guantánamo were captured in rural Afghanistan, a world away from urban America, Rumsfeld employed the phraseology of aggressive crime fighters contemptuous of the civil rights of the accused. "Back on the streets" is code for a punitive approach to crime. Implied in the phrase is the idea that the guilty have escaped proper punishment because of excessive concern for their legal rights. Perhaps Rumsfeld subconsciously associated the Guantánamo prisoners with street criminals in custody because they were presented to the television and print press elaborately shackled and dressed in prison-orange jumpsuits. More probably, he or his advisors selected those words to evoke the threatening image of the African American or

Hispanic violent criminal that has haunted the psyches of white middle-class Americans at least since the 1960s. Using the singular "street" rather than "streets" also succeeded in connecting the familiar domestic threat with that of "the Arab street," a reference to public opinion in the Arab world. Two generations of conservative American intellectuals have instructed one another in what Arabs think or might think in language scarcely different from that used by British and French colonial officials in the 1920s. Whether it was habit or calculation that prompted his choice of words, the image that he conjured was more in keeping with domestic law enforcement than with international counterterrorism operations. Later during the same press conference, Rumsfeld's description of the prisoners merged the image of the thuggish criminal with that of the politically motivated terrorist. "These people are committed terrorists," he said. "We are keeping them off the street and out of the airlines and out of nuclear power plants and out of ports across this country and across other countries."

The rhetorical outbidding escalated that weekend during the appearance on *Fox News Sunday* of Vice President Dick Cheney. "These are the worst of a very bad lot. They are dangerous. They are devoted to killing millions of Americans, innocent Americans, if they can, and they are perfectly prepared to die in the effort."[5] So not only were the prisoners irrational fanatics, but if permitted to do so, they would kill on a scale that was heretofore only dreamed of by war planners in the major powers. With this, the vice president reminded viewers of the weapons of mass destruction that might be possessed by the Baathist regime in Iraq as well as a possible link between Baghdad and the September 11, 2001, hijackers. Neither ever materialized. Nor would the prisoners live up to their billing as terrorist supermen.

That the Pentagon was aware that the captives were not living up to their billing is suggested by an April 20, 2003, memorandum written by Major Jeff Bovarnick for Secretary of Defense Rumsfeld that specified the categories of those captured who were to be screened for transfer to Guantánamo.[6] The categories include "all al Qaeda personnel," "all Taliban leaders," and "anyone with special skills of education, such as those with 'professor' or 'engineer.'" The memorandum also instructs that "it is essential to understand that US forces are not authorized to detain 'common criminals' that have no connection to combat activity." The inescapable implication is that some of the prisoners who arrived at Guantánamo were not who they were supposed to be. Classified merely as Secret rather than being given a higher classification, and produced more than a year after a majority of the prisoners who would ever be held at the camp were already there, the memorandum looks like an exercise in producing a post hoc paper trail.

If more accurate information about the prisoners eventually worked its way up through channels to the Pentagon, that did not stop other Bush administration officials and congressional Republicans from insisting that they were more dangerous than the sort of prisoners captured in other wars that the United States has waged. During the debate in the U.S. Senate on the Military Commissions Act of 2006, Republican majority leader Bill Frist of Tennessee spoke in almost hysterical language about both the war and the prisoners before a painstaking recitation of the three rationales of the official explanation for the Guantánamo decision:

> Mr. President, for 5 years we have been a nation at war. It is a war unlike any we have ever before fought. It is an ideological war against radicals and zealots. We are fighting a different kind of enemy—an enemy who seeks to destroy our values, to destroy our freedom, and to destroy our way of life, people who will kill and who will actually stop at nothing to bring America to its knees. It is a war against an enemy that won't back down, ever, telling interrogators: I will never forget your face. I will kill you. I will kill your brothers, your mother, your sisters. It is a war against an enemy who undertakes years of psychological training to consciously resist interrogation to withhold information that could be critical to thwarting future threats, future attacks. . . . That is why over the last month we have focused the Senate agenda on security, and that is why today we address our Nation's security by debating one of the most serious and most urgent security issues facing the Nation: the detaining, questioning, and prosecution of enemy combatants—terrorists captured on the battlefield.[7]

Exaggerating the prowess of the enemy was not confined to the upper echelons of the Department of Defense. In his 2006 prison memoir, Moazzam Begg used the mistake made by U.S. Army military police guards in thinking that Feroz Abbassi had been trained by the British Special Air Service, or SAS, before joining al-Qaeda to illustrate what he observed as "the American mentality . . . geared to the creation of heroes and anti-heroes, so their enemies had to be the very worst characters possible, but highly trained, committed, and effective enemies."[8] The determination with which the captors sought to convince themselves that their captives were more than ordinary soldiers or bewildered civilians is illustrated by the suspicion that attached to the possession of Casio digital watches.[9] For eight of the prisoners, wearing a Casio digital watch when taken into custody was considered evidence of al-Qaeda membership, because such watches—which cost less than $30—had been used in the past as the timers for bombs.

Reality proved much more prosaic. Far from being the cream of the Taliban and al-Qaeda fighting elite captured by U.S. armed forces on the battlefield in Afghanistan, many of the men who were flown the roughly 8,000 miles from Bagram Air Base to Guantánamo were prisoners in the custody of Northern Alliance militia warlords or of Pakistani Army or police officers who were purchased by the U.S. armed forces and the CIA with generous bounties. Given the incentives of the participants in the exchanges, it is not surprising that most of the prisoners were not so much dangerous as simply unlucky. Why quality was sacrificed for quantity in the exchange is obvious.

For all the nonsense spoken about honor in Afghanistan, expecting honest dealing from warlords who live by looting, extortion, and bribery is absurd. Little better could be expected of underpaid Pakistani security officers. Then there were the high prices being offered for individual prisoners, with the more interesting non-Afghan captives fetching as much as $5,000 each.[10] Add to that the usually nonrecurring nature of the transaction, which meant that the seller need not worry about his reputation for honesty, and it was inevitable that sellers would attempt to deceive buyers about the identity of the goods being offered.

Buyer ignorance, haste, and irresponsibility fitted seller cupidity perfectly. Operating in an alien culture, often at the mercy of their interpreters, and under pressure from their distant superiors to produce quick results in the form of live captives, the American intelligence officers acted in the same manner that agents always act when spending an unobservant principal's money, by gambling that they would not be held accountable for mistakes. If the purpose was to produce live bodies for display rather than proper subjects for interrogation and prosecution, then the process made a sort of perverse sense. The altogether unsurprising result of the process was a population of several hundred prisoners, most of whom were not very dangerous, not capable of providing useful intelligence, and not sufficiently responsible to be worth subjecting to proceedings in a war crimes tribunal.

The large number and impressive regularity of the repatriations from Guantánamo to home countries that began in 2004 testifies to the ordinariness of most of the prisoners. Release and repatriation of prisoners of war at the end of hostilities is normal practice in international law. Although the prisoners at Guantánamo were supposed to be anything but ordinary, that is exactly how most of them were treated after they were transferred to the custody of the governments in their countries of origin. As of 2006, only 40 of 245 prisoners who had been tracked after being released and repatriated still remained in the custody of their governments.[11] The other 205 were freed shortly after the governments of their countries of origin were given custody. All 83 of the prisoners transferred to Afghanistan and all 29 of the prisoners transferred to Australia, Bahrain, Britain, Denmark, Germany, the Maldives, Russia, Spain, and Turkey were released. Only 3 of the 70 Pakistani prisoners who were transferred remained in custody. Of the 14 prisoners who had been tried after their repatriation, 8 were acquitted and another 6 were awaiting judgment. What this process of custody transfer and release more clearly resembled was not the treatment of captured terrorists but the treatment of repatriated prisoners of war or perhaps of nonviolent political prisoners. Whatever might be said by the United States or other governments about the nature of the prisoners from Guantánamo, the goods simply did not measure up to the advertising.

Most of the repatriated prisoners disappeared from public view, as is true of most prisoners of war after their release. There were exceptions. A handful of the repatriated either rejoined or joined the fight. Russian national Ruslan Odizhev appears to have rejoined Chechen separatist comrades after his release with six other Chechens in 2004. On June 27, 2007, he was killed in a shootout with Russian authorities in Nalchik, capital of the north Caucasus autonomous republic of Kabardino-Balkaria.[12] That Washington was reluctant to link Moscow's struggle against the Islamist and nationalist Chechens with its own struggles in the Middle East and Southeast Asia makes inclusion of the Odizhev case and similar cases odd.

Apologists for the Guantánamo decision like Gordon Cucullu have made much of the claim made by the Department of Defense that many released prisoners returned to the fight. However, as Fletcher and Stover cautioned, such figures are inflated by the inclusion of individuals such as the Tipton Three who merely expressed opinions thought to be anti-American after release.

If the potential for released prisoners to return to the fight has been exaggerated, the difficulty of persuading countries to accept custody of released prisoners has been underestimated. Under international law, states are normally expected to accept the repatriation of their own nationals who are released at the end of hostilities. Indeed, delayed repatriation is likely to emerge as an important domestic political issue and primary diplomatic interest of governments, as happened in Germany and Japan after the Second World War and in Pakistan after the Bangladesh War of Independence. However, the Bush administration insisted upon designating the Guantánamo prisoners as something other than prisoners of war. That gave their home countries an argument for declining immediate repatriation. Although the government of Afghanistan accepted repatriation of many of its nationals, it was reluctant to accept all of them without extracting further generous infusions of U.S. economic aid. If it is absurd that the liberated should demand and receive payment from their liberators to act responsibly, it is also understandable in this case. The regime of President Hamid Karzai that was installed in Kabul by the Bush administration and its NATO allies is entirely dependent on foreign aid. Indeed, foreign aid and the opium trade comprise the bulk of the Afghan economy.

Some of the released prisoners were unwilling to be repatriated to their home countries, and third countries were reluctant to accept custody of released prisoners who were not their own nationals. This is most clearly illustrated by the "orphan" Uighurs, the twenty-two ethnic Uighur Chinese nationals whose departures from Guantánamo were obstructed by a pair of political taboos. Uighurs are an Islamic and Turkic ethnic minority living in Xinjiang, China's restive western province. From the perspective of Beijing, the Uighur prisoners at Guantánamo were terrorists and separatists. From the perspective of Washington, they were potential victims of communist oppression. The almost instinctive anticommunism developed during the Cold War thus prevented their repatriation to the People's Republic of China.[13] Washington could hand over unwilling prisoners to noncommunist authoritarian governments with grim human rights records such as Algeria, but it was politically unacceptable to hand over unwilling prisoners to communist governments with comparably grim human rights records. Resettling them anywhere in the United States was also politically unacceptable because of the inevitable furor that could erupt after the probably inevitable accusation that the government had brought terrorists to America. With this second obstacle the Bush administration was constrained by the disproportional anxiety about terrorism that it had done so much to cultivate. After being rejected by the governments of more than a hundred countries, five of the Uighur prisoners were offloaded onto Albania. The reasons why the Albanian government proved so accommodating had more to do with the positive feelings many Albanians had for the United States because of the 1999 Kosovo War than the U.S. foreign aid that accompanied the five Uighurs or their shared religious identity. In that most recent of Balkan wars, the Clinton administration had helped to liberate the breakaway Yugoslav province. The population of Albania is predominantly if only nominally Muslim, as is the population of Kosovo. Resettlement of the Uighurs proved less than smooth, and Albanian authorities refused to accept any of the others, leaving them stranded in Guantánamo until other takers could be found.

Further evidence for the proposition that many Guantánamo prisoners were not especially dangerous is that a majority of them were eventually moved from a regime of extraordinary isolation and constant monitoring in individual maximum security cells to housing in prison dormitories.[14] While the Level 4 prisoners, those believed dangerous or observed to be incorrigible, were given prison-orange uniforms, denied privileges, and held in individual cells, the larger population of more compliant Level 1 prisoners were given white uniforms, permitted communal eating and limited recreation, and held in dormitories with small exercise yards.

The majority of prisoners were eventually transferred to the new prison regime because the Department of Defense eventually concluded, from the interrogations of prisoners and the corroborations of the information gathered from other intelligence sources, that most of the remaining prisoners at Guantánamo failed to live up to their billing as terrorist supermen. Unclassified portions of the transcripts of hearings conducted by Combatant Status Review Tribunals reveal a prisoner population composed primarily of ordinary foot soldiers, among them non-Afghan, largely Arab recruits to al-Qaeda or its affiliated organizations and Afghan Taliban recruits and conscriptees, together with non-Afghan civilians claiming to be humanitarian volunteers inspired by Islamism or hapless Afghan peasants probably arrested because they were in the wrong place at the wrong time. Nearly all of the prisoners are alleged to have received small-arms training in Afghanistan, and many are alleged to have fought with the Taliban against the Northern Alliance. Even if this is accepted as true in each case—and many of the prisoners deny both allegations—the hearing transcripts reveal that most of the prisoners were no more dangerous than other prisoners captured in the aftermath of any contemporary war in a less developed country. In particular, the questions that they were asked fail to suggest that they posed any unusual potential threat.

Mohammed Yacoub, a thirty-year-old ethnic Pashtun, is typical of many of the Afghan nationals. After losing a leg in a mortar attack in Kabul, this member of the Taliban was captured by the Northern

Alliance and held in the notorious Sheberghan prison in Mazar-i-Sharif before being handed over to the U.S. military. He was then transferred to Bagram Air Base for a month and half before being flown to Guantánamo Bay. What makes his testimony before the Combatant Status Review Tribunal exceptional is how he describes his motivations in fighting with the Taliban:

TRIBUNAL PRESIDENT: Is there any other information that you feel would be important to help us determine if you have been properly classified as an enemy combatant?

YACOUB: You are accusing me of joining the Taliban. At that time, the Taliban was the government of Afghanistan. Even if I were in Afghanistan now, I'd join the government, if any government came. You have to support the government. . . . It was for my country. I was for Afghanistan and whatever I did, I did it in my country.

Here is the voice of any ordinary soldier in any war in history. From the perspective of external observers, his participation in wars is not laudable and his simple political beliefs are not inspiring, but that could be said of most soldiers in most wars.

The testimony of most of the prisoners found in the tribunal transcripts is nothing more than a succession of assertions of innocence of any wrongdoing, assertions of religiosity that seem excessively fervent from the perspective of citizens of secular advanced industrial societies, denials of alleged membership in terrorist organizations, and denials of any terrorist motivation for traveling to and from Afghanistan. Afghan prisoners assert that they entered Afghanistan as returning refugees and hoping only to help rebuild their country. Non-Afghans assert that they intended only to volunteer in Islamic charities.

The voice of outright defiance is also heard. In a brief statement read by his personal representative (the prisoners were denied representation by an attorney at these hearings), then thirty-nine-year-old Saudi Arabian national Mohammad bin Abdul Rahman al-Shamrani rejects the hearing tribunal and everything associated with it.

I tell you I don't believe in the American Justice Department and your Supreme Court. So judge me the way you like. I'm looking for god to judge between me and you.

The threat justification for the Guantánamo decision also rings hollow because of the U.S. military's experience in successfully operating prisoner-of-war camps, experience that includes dealing with much larger numbers of prisoners and with prisoners at least as fanatical and highly trained as any held at Guantánamo. The historical record of the U.S. military in treating large numbers of captives was little different from that of other major international powers in the nineteenth and early twentieth centuries. Conditions in the Union and Confederate prison camps in the American Civil War ranged from poor to horrific. Combatants and noncombatants were sometimes summarily executed during the Indian wars and the Philippine-American War. However, the historical record during much of the rest of the twentieth century was markedly better. During the First World War, a small population consisting of 1,356 German sailors, approximately 2,300 German merchant seamen, and approximately 2,300 German and Austrian civilians was interned in four camps in the continental United States with only a handful of violations of international law.[15] Indeed, their treatment was so good that 173 of the German sailors applied for permission to remain in the United States as immigrants after the war. During the Second World War, 425,871 Axis prisoners of war were held in 511 camps scattered across the country.[16] The only four states without a prisoner-of-war camp were Montana, Nevada, North Dakota, and Vermont. This vast prisoner population included 371,683 Germans and 54,188 Italians. (Few Japanese were taken prisoner before the end of hostilities, and most of those were interned in camps in the insular Pacific and Australia rather than in the continental United States.) Many of the German and Italian prisoners were the elites of their armed forces. The Germans included captured airmen, U-boat crewmen, and members of Erwin Rommel's Afrika Korps. The most fanatical of the Nazis, approximately 4,500 in number, were isolated in a camp in Alva, Oklahoma. Many of the German prisoners in the other camps exhibited sufficiently intense fascist or patriotic loyalties to make them dangerous. Technical educations gave many of them the ability to engineer sophisticated escape plans and improvise weapons. Many of the prison camps were located in states with large ethnic German populations—eleven camps in Missouri and thirty-two in Texas—which might have increased the temptation to escape.[17] Nor were the camps always guarded by the cream of the U.S. armed forces. The best military units and soldiers were serving overseas rather than on guard duty in the continental United States. Despite circumstances that would seem to have invited repeated demonstrations, riots, and escapes, there were few problems. There were a handful of successful escapes from camps located near the Mexican and Canadian borders, and instances of ideologically motivated violence and intimidation committed by some German prisoners of war against fellow prisoners. Generally, however, the prisoners posed little threat to one another, their guards, or civilians living near the camps. Such success was attributable in large part to the understanding between captors and captives that their interaction was bound by international legal norms. Other important factors include the cultural proximity of the Germans and Americans and the food and housing conditions in the American camps. During the early 1940s, at least, the U.S. military knew how to intern vast numbers of prisoners, all of them potentially dangerous and some of them actively so, without violating international law.

As the threat justification for the Guantánamo decision began to crumble because of information about the prisoners in news coverage and published prisoner memoirs, public relations officers at the Pentagon responded by emphasizing the threat posed by the prisoners to their military guards. In a March 11, 2005, article for the American Forces Press Service, Kathleen T. Rhem wrote that U.S. service personnel were forced to "cover their nameplates and never call one another by their real names while they're near detainees," because they "never forget that some of the men they are guarding have sworn to kill their countrymen."[18] The same could be said of any population in any prisoner-of-war camp.

The Bush administration also employed the CIA to buttress the threat justification for the Guantánamo decision. If the prisoners already there were deficiently dangerous, then other prisoners could be found to better meet those specifications. In mid-2006, small numbers of the more important prisoners from CIA "black sites"—secret prisons in Poland, Romania, Thailand, Chad, and elsewhere—were transferred to Guantánamo to meet the pressing need. That served a dual purpose: defusing criticism by human rights activists and political elites in the European Union of the CIA's extraordinary renditions and secret prisons on the territory of the EU, and justifying the Guantánamo decision. Among this new group of prisoners were some individuals who, if released, might present more threat than an ordinary prisoner of war. However, the original Guantánamo decision was hardly necessary to hold this recent population of prisoners. Had it been necessary, they would have been transferred to Guantánamo soon after their capture, rather than awaiting transfer there for several years.

5 Intelligence Collection

The initial emphasis on the threat rationale was supported and then supplanted by the intelligence rationale, the notion that the Guantánamo decision was necessary so as to exploit prisoners as sources of information necessary to prevent future terrorist attacks. "The most important thing for us from our standpoint is gathering intelligence," claimed Rumsfeld. "[W]e feel not just entitled but an obligation to try to gather intelligence about future terrorist attacks and how the network functions. And that is what we're doing."[1]

Stephen Kenny, the attorney who represented Australian national David Hicks, points up the discrepancy between the intelligence rationale that Rumsfeld articulated and the actual practice of interrogations:

> On average, prisoners were interviewed 20 to 30 times. . . . Often they were interviewed by different people who had no idea and hadn't read the previous interrogations or if they did it certainly wasn't obvious because they continued to ask very basic questions. The interrogations were also conducted by people who were obviously poorly trained or incompetent. For example, they had no idea of the geography of Pakistan and Afghanistan or how to spell the names of the main cities. In the interrogation documents that I saw, there was nothing that could have been called reasonable intelligence. Most of it was aimed at getting prisoners to implicate others usually by some form of incentive.[2]

Consider the logic of the Guantánamo decision. Rumsfeld's explicit claim was that the Bush administration was hauling hundreds of prisoners from the other side of the planet because they were members of a terrorist network and possessed information that could be used to foil the terrorist attacks their network would launch. His implicit claim was that Guantánamo would be a better location for extracting intelligence through interrogation than other locations such as Bagram Air Base in Afghanistan. Was either of these even remotely plausible?

Intelligence obtained from prisoners through interrogation takes two basic forms. The first is "actionable intelligence," or information that might be used in planning counterinsurgency operations in Afghanistan or counterterrorism operations elsewhere. The second is background political intelligence, in this case information about the organization, resources, and personnel of al-Qaeda and its affiliates. The former appeared to be the priority when the policy was first announced. Rumsfeld, answering questions during his press briefing on January 11, 2002, repeatedly stressed the urgency of intelligence collection through interrogations to prevent future attacks. At one point he stated, "I mean, if you think about the September 11th event here and in New York, and the value of that information, and the extent we can put this thing together even a day or two or five days faster, by putting great effort on it, we may very well prevent a terrorist attack involving thousands but more than thousands."[3] Responding to a follow-up question, Rumsfeld also appears to hint at the use of torture. "The faster we can interrogate these people and identify them, and get what they have in them out of them, in as graceful a way as is possible—needless to say, we have a better chance of saving some people's lives." Only eleven days later, during a January 22 news briefing, however, Rumsfeld shifted the purpose of interrogation at Guantánamo to include both actionable intelligence and background political intelligence when he explained that the goals included information about "future terrorist attacks and how the network functions."[4] Perhaps in the interim the secretary was briefed about the actual value of the prisoners, but it is more likely that he had begun to worry about the holes in his story.

The obvious problem with holding prisoners in Guantánamo to obtain urgent "actionable intelligence" is that it increases the distance and time between collection and use of the information. Commanders in the field frequently move their assets, precisely to defeat efforts by the enemy to exploit intelligence about their location and capability. Such mobility is especially important for insurgent units because of the greater firepower possessed by counterinsurgent units. The Taliban or al-Qaeda are therefore unlikely to leave their forces in the same location for very long, once they have been detected, for fear of air strikes. That puts a premium on communicating the location and capability of insurgents learned through interrogation of prisoners as soon as possible. The contradiction is inescapable. If the prisoners moved to Guantánamo possessed information of immediate value to commanders in the field in Afghanistan, then why locate them on opposite sides of the planet? That so many prisoners were retained at Bagram for interrogation rather than being transferred to Guantánamo indicates that at least some military intelligence officers understood the value of proximity between the sources of actionable intelligence and those who make use of it. Reinforcing this point, prisoners who were released from Guantánamo report that they were interrogated at length in Afghanistan before ever being transferred. Holding large numbers of prisoners for interrogation at both Guantánamo and Bagram would also complicate the exchange of information among interrogators and intelligence analysts. The sophistication of communications technology notwithstanding, the escapable facts of physical separation and opposing sleep cycles reduce the effectiveness of communications, a burden difficult to square with the claims about urgency.

If transferring several hundred of the thousands of prisoners who were taken in Afghanistan and Pakistan to Guantánamo to obtain actionable intelligence is improbable as a purpose, then that leaves only background political intelligence. There are three problems with accepting that purpose as well. The first and most important is that many of the prisoners would have had little or nothing to offer. The large number of Afghan prisoners who were the first to be released and repatriated attests to their basic uselessness as sources of even political background intelligence. Their departures left a smaller population, including several hundred Arab nationals and small numbers of European, Russian, and Chinese nationals. Before their specific individual identities were determined, the Pentagon could plausibly claim and perhaps also actually believe that the former were "Afghan Arabs," the designation given to volunteers from Arab states who were recruited to fight in Afghanistan, and that the others were members of Islamist terrorist groups hidden in Muslim immigrant or ethnic minority communities. Thousands of volunteers fought in the Soviet-Afghan War. That the CIA, working in cooperation with Pakistan's Inter-Services Intelligence, or ISI, encouraged their recruitment is perhaps the worst-kept secret from the last decade of the Cold War. What makes it controversial is that their recruitment resulted in the emergence of al-Qaeda as the Soviet-Afghan War wound down. American conservatives credit the Reagan administration with winning the Cold War single-handedly but ignore its role as midwife at the birth of al-Qaeda.

American military intelligence and CIA officers would have been aware of the genealogy of al-Qaeda even if they obeyed the taboo against speaking about it publicly. No doubt they hoped that interrogating the Arab nationals would shed light on al-Qaeda's structure and operations not only in Afghanistan but wherever its affiliates operated. Prisoners identified as citizens or residents of Western countries would have been of interest to interrogators for comparable reasons. Several 9/11 hijackers had lived in Hamburg, Germany, home to one of the largest Muslim immigrant communities in Europe. Interrogations might ferret out information that would be useful in the surveillance of the Islamist networks in Western Europe, Canada, and Australia. Another terrorist attack on the scale of September 11, 2001, still seemed likely in 2002. Frustratingly for the interrogators, most of the non-Afghans in custody at Guantánamo appear to have been as much nonentities as the Afghans. Rather than grilling the worst of the worst, they found themselves trying to extract information from a cast of sullen or disoriented nobodies. The bulk were either not members of al-Qaeda or were merely al-Qaeda's ordinary foot soldiers. They were distressingly uninteresting, unimportant, and unable to provide the sort of information sought. With that disappointment came recognition that the Pentagon and the Bush administration faced a potential public relations fiasco.

The second problem with interrogating prisoners at Guantánamo to elicit background political information is that, after months and then years in captivity, most of the information that could be extracted from them would have grown stale. Given their clandestine activities and the knowledge that some of their compatriots had been captured, members of al-Qaeda and its affiliate organizations would have changed locations and operating procedures in response to possible breaches in security. In effect, the minority of prisoners held at Guantánamo Bay who would have known anything of value became wasting assets soon after their arrival. Despite assertions like that of General Jay Hood that every week "we learn something that assists in piecing together the strategic mosaic of international terrorism,"[5] the reality is that the value of much of the information extracted from them would have declined with each day they were held in custody.

The third problem with interrogating prisoners at Guantánamo for background political intelligence is that the CIA appears to have taken custody of many of the most important prisoners in its High Value Terrorist Detainee Program. Although fourteen of the approximately one hundred high-value prisoners were later transferred to Guantánamo in 2006 from "black sites" in Poland, Romania, Thailand, and Chad in an apparent effort to justify the original Guantánamo decision and to assuage criticism in the European Union about extraordinary renditions and about secret flights across and secret prisons in the territory of European Union member states, they appear to have provided whatever valuable background political intelligence they possessed before being transferred to the Cuban base.[6] If the prisoners with real value as interrogation subjects were in the custody of the CIA elsewhere, then why were any of the remaining population of prisoners in Afghanistan and Pakistan transferred to Guantánamo?

Public acceptance of the intelligence rationale for the Guantánamo decision has been reinforced by its continuous association in news coverage with the controversy surrounding the use of torture in interrogation. Bush administration officials have been vigorous in publicly defending the proposition that intelligence officers must have the option to use every method in the seeming liminal zone between ordinary questioning and torture. One of the reasons for their enthusiasm for such methods and for dropping broad hints about them was its effect on public opinion: rather than being practiced to extract intelligence, torture was practiced and talked about to reinforce public belief in the intelligence rationale.

Another reason for their enthusiasm was the urge to utilize the latest technology, in this case increasingly sophisticated interrogation techniques. Intelligence collection from war captives has been part of normal military operations since ancient times and is clearly permissible under international law if it is not coercive. Explicitly prohibited in the Geneva Conventions of 1929 was the use of violence or threat of violence during the interrogation of prisoners. Moral outrage expressed at the threatened torture of prisoners for information by the German military during the Second World War was repeated so often in Anglo-American popular culture that it became a comedic cliché by the 1960s.

The Geneva Conventions of 1949, which were negotiated to deal with shortcomings of the Geneva Conventions of 1929 revealed during the Second World War, reproduced the prohibition of the torture of prisoners while also requiring the humane treatment of other persons in war zones. The Universal Declaration of Human Rights of 1948 prohibited torture by civil authorities. In response to the horrors evident in the wars of national liberation, the 1977 Additional Protocols to the Geneva Conventions extended the protection of the Geneva Conventions to persons involved in those conflicts as well. The International Covenant on Civil and Political Rights of 1976 also prohibited torture. With the 1984 United Nations Convention against Torture and Other Forms of Cruel, Inhuman or Degrading Treatment or Punishment, the prohibition of the practice was made even more unambiguous.

Faced with the conflict between the desire to preserve international reputations and the desire to torture select prisoners, Washington and London threaded the needle, circumventing the prohibition with abusive medical and psychological treatments that were deniable as torture, and subcontracting the services of the intelligence agencies in client states less concerned with international reputation. Although a number of prisoners taken in the war in Afghanistan and elsewhere in the War on Terror were subjected to torture by client states like Morocco, abusive medical and psychological treatment was the experience of many more of the captives at Guantánamo.

To the lessons learned by American military and civilian intelligence officers in the Korean War and Vietnam War, and by their British counterparts in colonial wars in Kenya, Malaya, Cyprus, and Northern Ireland and other foreign deployments, have been added a growing literature of relevant medical and psychological research findings.[7] Together these helped transform the art of interrogation into a science of interrogation. Highly trained interrogators now have an excellent chance of extracting any information possessed by interrogation subjects. Controlling the physical and mental environment of even well-trained and highly motivated captives renders them vulnerable to manipulation. When interrogators employ violence, it is often to establish the sense of weakness that results in the disclosure of information.

Unfortunately, the same highly trained interrogators using the same techniques also have an excellent chance of extracting information not possessed by their subjects. Immense efforts may be expended to extract nonsense from subjects without realizing it. That disoriented or desperate prisoners sometimes respond by giving false information to their interrogators, including false confessions of their own responsibility, is inevitable. For decades, psychologists have understood that techniques such as sensory deprivation, denial of food and water, and long interviews break the will of most people, at least temporarily, causing them to reveal any information they possess.[8] The same methods also cause some interrogation subjects to fabricate information.

Resignation or a desire to satisfy powerful and insistent interrogators causes some prisoners to lie. According to the case notes taken by American attorney Tom Wilner, the legal counsel for eleven Kuwaiti nationals imprisoned at Guantánamo, one of his clients recounted: "The American soldiers kept saying, 'Are you Taliban or are you al-Qaeda?' 'Are you Taliban or al-Qaeda!' They kept hitting me, so eventually I said that I was a member of the Taliban."[9] Given the potential for retaliation in the form of corporal punishment by his captors, it is unsurprising that Wilner's client declined to be named in the news story.

Other interrogation subjects may offer false information to their interrogators out of a spirit of resistance. Deceiving authority is a weapon of the weak. Persuading interrogators to squander their energies pursuing phantoms is an inevitable temptation for interrogation subjects. Clever and daring prisoners understand that detecting such deceptions is anything but automatic. Weeks or months might elapse before the nonsense in tales spun by prisoners is detected. Before that, official alarms might sound in cities, military bases, and embassies around the planet as military and civil authorities prepare for attacks that never arrive. Successfully hoodwinking the agents of a jittery superpower would no doubt give prisoners immense satisfaction.

Still other interrogation subjects may reveal information that they do possess, only after resisting for months, because they conclude that it is too dated or too unimportant to be of value as actionable intelligence. Two-thirds of the U.S. Air Force personnel captured during the Korean War admitted to giving information to their North Korean and Chinese interrogators but described it as being of little military significance.[10]

Naturally, among the hundreds of prisoners transferred to Guantánamo there must have been some who merited exploiting as sources of background political intelligence, and they may have provided some of that information. However, that fails to save the intelligence rationale from its fundamental flaw. Their captivity at Guantánamo was unnecessary because their interrogation at Guantánamo was unnecessary. They could have been interrogated at Bagram or elsewhere, as in many cases they were before being transferred to Guantánamo. Nor does the transfer of fourteen "high-value" prisoners to Guantánamo in 2006 save the intelligence rationale. Indeed, it strengthens the critique, because they had in each case already been thoroughly interrogated elsewhere.

6 Prosecution

"We undoubtedly will end up processing some through the criminal justice system," explained Rumsfeld in his news briefing on January 22, 2002. "I wouldn't be surprised if we did some through the Uniform Code of Military Justice, and I suspect there will be some military commissions."[1] That simple, almost offhand comment ignited a controversy that would dominate much of the discussion about Guantánamo. As perhaps intended, the threat of drumhead trials before military commissions emerged as a focus of international and domestic political furor, deflecting attention from the administration's insistence that the captured were "unlawful combatants" rather than prisoners of war under the Geneva Conventions.

The domestic political context here is important to understanding the reception of the prosecution rationale. By the time that the Guantánamo decision was made, it was widely understood that al-Qaeda operated not only as a terrorist or guerrilla group in its own right but also as an international umbrella organization for a dozen affiliated groups. In the months following September 11, 2001, anxious Americans suspected that Osama bin Laden's fanatical minions were everywhere from international airports to local shopping malls, and Washington was in no hurry to disabuse them of the belief that the security threat was general. That terrorists might attack anywhere and at any time fed a sense of collective powerlessness that soon stirred an urge to punish. Muslims, Muslim-owned businesses, and mosques were attacked in a spasm of xenophobic scapegoating that left the American Muslim community shaken. For the vast majority of Americans unwilling to turn on their Muslim neighbors, those already in military custody seemed more appropriate objects of collective hatred, and trials before military commissions would offer the requisite legitimacy. News commentary supporting and opposing the idea of prosecutions before military commissions shifted the focus of public attention from the status of the prisoners under international law to the more general public-policy question of the most effective means for dealing with the security threat posed by al-Qaeda.

There are two obvious flaws in the prosecution rationale. The first is that the Bush administration was unprepared to conduct prosecutions for war crimes when the announcement was made, and then demonstrated no haste in preparing prosecution cases. The second is that few if any of the prisoners who were transferred to the Cuban base before 2006 appear to have committed acts that would merit prosecution as war crimes. Where the first objection is straightforward, the second objection requires consideration not only of the prisoners themselves but also of their acts in the light of application of the law of war in American history. Only then can sense be made of the series of Supreme Court decisions that helped unravel the administration's story.

Perhaps it was inevitable that American news coverage and commentary would focus more on the prosecution rationale than on the threat or intelligence rationale. American popular culture is suffused with courtroom drama. Heroic intelligence officers might pursue and interrogate villainous terrorists in increasing numbers in film and television dramas after September 11, 2001, but they continued to be outnumbered by police officers, detectives, prosecutors bringing criminals to justice, and attorneys fighting for their clients in civil cases. So although the Bush administration was unprepared to actually conduct war crimes prosecutions when the announcement was made, and thereafter displayed less than intense interest in preparing such cases, the prosecution rationale never lost its thematic advantage for the attention of the press and the public. Prosecution progress might have been slowed by the challenges brought by the attorneys for Guantánamo prisoners, especially those eventually designated for prosecution, but all too obviously the administration was in no haste to carry out the threatened trials. The frequently cited model and accompanying historical precedent for the proposed military commissions were provided by the Roosevelt administration in 1942 with the prosecution of a handful of German and German-American saboteurs who had been landed by U-boat to attack industrial facilities on the East Coast. The saboteurs were taken into custody, tried, convicted, had their appeals heard and denied, and were executed all in the same year. In marked contrast, the prosecution of the Guantánamo prisoners proceeded at an almost leisurely pace. Although the chief prosecutor for the military commissions announced that the first trials were "imminent" in October 2003, preliminary hearings in the first four such trials did not begin until August 24, 2004.[2] By then the popular desire for vengeance that would have supported a prosecutorial march to the gallows had cooled. The Rules of Procedure for the military commissions were published in March 2002, but the Manual for Military Commissions, merely an abridged version of the Uniform Code of Military Justice, was not published until January 2007. The administration also neglected to pressure the intelligence agencies to cooperate with military prosecutors.[3] Rather than proceed with the prosecutions, the Bush White House and the Pentagon were content with having made the announcement that trials would be conducted—which suggests that it was the announcement itself and not actual prosecution that was deemed important.

What purpose was served by announcing prosecutions as a justification for the Guantánamo decision? In the febrile atmosphere immediately after September 11, 2001, officials at all levels of government in the United States sought to appear in control, a quality they could demonstrate by making statements evincing the willingness to take whatever tough measures were necessary to prevent further attacks and to punish those who were responsible. Decisive action is what the public expects of leaders during national security crises. Aggressive posturing is what the public more often receives and accepts as substitute. The appearance of decisive action by leaders during crises is often handsomely rewarded regardless of the severity of the threat or the effectiveness of the action taken. Since the dimensions of the national security threat after September 11, 2001, were still uncertain, official posturing was unrestrained by normal public skepticism. Many in the administration would have understood that there were political advantages in exaggerating the nature of the threat and prolonging the crisis atmosphere. Announcing prosecutions of prisoners helped to do that by drawing the historical parallel to the prosecutions in 1942. Instead of focusing on al-Qaeda, a fanatical network operating from Taliban-ruled Afghanistan that was capable of launching terrorist attacks but incapable of posing an existential threat to the United States, Americans were instructed that they were now engaged in an existential struggle for national survival comparable to the Second War World against forces that would be labeled with the unfortunate and ultimately unsuccessful neologism "Islamofascism." Waging the equivalent of the Second World War is more impressive than doing battle with one strain of Middle Eastern terrorism. Even if reality fell short, the reference to a period characterized by moral clarity promised greater national unity than Americans had experienced for decades.

Reinforcing the impression that the war was being waged against an especially dangerous enemy was the administration's insistence that the captured in Guantánamo must be denied prisoner-of-war status under the Geneva Conventions of 1949, which would otherwise be the controlling international law, and must instead be described and treated as unlawful combatants. The announcement of trials before military commissions and the resulting international controversy initially obscured the question of the legal status of all of the prisoners. News coverage focusing on the trials not only sidelined this weighty international legal issue but also reduced the sum of news coverage about the purposes served by indefinite and incommunicado imprisonment. This success in diverting the attention of the press and the public suggests that the original decision was more than the result of simple exigency, that it was instead the product of careful political calculation.

Although they were cast in the roles of superterrorists, the original population of Guantánamo prisoners instead proved to be an assortment of individuals selected largely because they seemed suspiciously different from the common run of prisoners collected in Afghanistan and Pakistan. Reading the allegations made against a majority of Guantánamo prisoners in the transcripts of their Combatant Status Review

Tribunal hearings shows only that they acted in the same manner as ordinary foot soldiers in any contemporary war. Most of today's armed conflicts differ radically from the conception of symmetric interstate war held by much of the American public, which dates from the middle of the twentieth century. Characteristically asymmetric, contemporary wars are protracted struggles between armed forces with markedly different capabilities and in which several noncombatants die for every combatant who dies. That asymmetry is reflected in the composition of armies that depend on stealth to counter the greater firepower of their enemy. They tend to vary greatly in experience, training, motivation, commitment, and nationality. Illiterate and poorly trained militia with parochial loyalties may serve alongside former soldiers in the national army and ideologically motivated foreign nationals. In that respect the army of the Taliban was nothing special. No matter how morally repugnant the regime fielding the army in which a particular soldier serves, the Geneva Conventions hold that mere service as a soldier in its armed forces is not in and of itself a war crime. The basic norm that being an enemy soldier is not criminal was well established in the customary law of war long before the development of the formal treaty-based law of war in the late nineteenth century. So membership in the armed forces of Taliban-ruled Afghanistan could not by itself constitute a war crime.

Before being supplemented in 2006 with fourteen additional candidates for prosecution from among the prisoners being held by the CIA in its secret prisons in other countries, the Guantánamo prison population offered slim pickings for prosecutors. However, ten of those prisoners managed to make the cut as prosecution defendants: Yemeni national Salim Ahmed Hamdan, Australian national David Matthew Hicks, Canadian national Omar Ahmed Khadr, Afghan national Abdul Zahir, Algerian national Sufyian Barhoumi, Sudanese national Ibrahim Ahmed Mahmoud al-Qosi, Saudi nationals Ghassan Abdallah al-Sharbi and Jabran Said bin al-Qahtani, Yemeni national Ali Hamza Ahmad Sulayman al-Bahlul, and Ethiopian national Binyam Ahmed Mohammed. To be precise, Binyam Ahmed Mohammed was arrested in April 2002 in Pakistan but not transferred to Guantánamo until September 2004. In the interim he was held in CIA custody in Afghanistan and in the custody of the Moroccan secret police. Unlike the majority of their fellow prisoners, who remained nameless in news coverage, several of these figures achieved international notoriety.

Accused of being Osama bin Laden's personal bodyguard and driver, and of delivering weapons and ammunition to other members of al-Qaeda, Salim Hamdan achieved a measure of name recognition because of the U.S. Supreme Court's 2004 landmark habeas corpus ruling in *Hamdan v. Rumsfeld*, which is discussed below.[4] Hamdan was captured by Afghan militia in November 2001 and handed over to the U.S. military, which then flew him to Guantánamo Bay, where he was confined with the ordinary prisoners in Camp Delta. At some point during the subsequent nineteen months it was concluded that he should be deemed an important figure in al-Qaeda. He was then transferred to solitary confinement in Camp Echo on July 3, 2003.

Accused of fighting against the U.S. and Northern Alliance forces, David Hicks, whose adopted Muslim names were Abu Muslim al Austraili and Muhammed Dawood, was one of two Australian nationals in Guantánamo. The other was Mamdouh Habib, an Egyptian immigrant who received far less coverage in either the Australian or international press despite being the subject of an extraordinary rendition by the United States and subsequent brutal torture by Egyptian authorities.[5] Hicks won the lion's share of press and public attention in Australia for the same reason that John Walker Lindh, the "American Taliban," received far more press and public attention in the United States than did Saudi-American Yaser Hamdi: he was a homegrown white Christian convert to Islam. The Australian public reacted to Hicks much as the American public reacted to Lindh, with initial fascination because of racial and/or religious identification followed quickly by revulsion at his defection in joining an alien and hostile culture. Americans and Australians seemed to catch themselves in feeling sympathy for one of the enemy.

Hicks had converted to Islam in 1999 after returning to Australia from Albania, where he served in the Kosovo Liberation Army. The insurgent KLA fought against the Serb/Yugoslav army in the last of the wars in which multinational Yugoslavia fragmented into six separate national states. Most of the population of Kosovo were ethnic

Albanians and thus at least nominally Muslim. Just as in Bosnia, the conflict in the breakaway province attracted foreign volunteers who wanted to help the underdogs. In 2000, Hicks traveled to Pakistan, where he joined Lashkar-e-Taiba, or Army of the Righteous, an Islamist insurgent organization sponsored by the Pakistani ISI that conducts its operations across the Pakistani-Indian line of control that bisects Kashmir. The predominantly Muslim province has been the object of three conventional wars between Pakistan and India since they won independence from Britain. The unification of Kashmir as a territory of Pakistan is a permanent foreign policy interest of Islamabad. Lashkar-e-Taiba recruited other Australians, including Willy Brigitte, who was later imprisoned in France. From Pakistan, Hicks next traveled in January 2001 to Afghanistan, where he received training at al-Qaeda camps. Thus during his two-year odyssey Hicks volunteered in three insurgencies to liberate Muslim territories from the armies of secular states. The difference between them lay in the foreign policy of Washington toward each conflict. Where the aspirations of the Kosovars were viewed sympathetically, and those of the Kashmiris with hostility but scant interest, the pan-Islamic aspirations of al-Qaeda were taken to be a major national security threat to be defeated.

Hicks was captured early in the war in Afghanistan. In December 2001 he was taken prisoner in the northern province of Baghlan. From there he was transported to a U.S. naval vessel and then transferred to Guantánamo. Hicks was held for five years before facing trial as the first defendant before a military commission. In a plea bargain that spared the U.S. government the embarrassment of trying and punishing him for engaging in acts like those committed by countless other foot soldiers, Hicks was found guilty of providing material support for terrorism and then released to Australian authorities to serve an additional nine-month prison sentence in Australia.[6]

The only one of these ten defendants accused of actually killing anyone is teenage Canadian national Omar Ahmed Khadr. He is accused of having killed one U.S. Army Special Forces soldier, Sergeant First Class Christopher Speer, with a grenade in a firefight in July 2002. Fifteen years old when he was transferred to Guantánamo Bay in 2002, Khadr was one of the ten minors who have been held there.[7] Born in the Toronto suburb of Scarborough and raised in the kind of intense religiosity that celebrates the ability to recite verses from the Koran at an early age, Khadr would have interested U.S. intelligence officers as an interrogation subject because of his family. His older brother, a former Guantánamo prisoner, Abdur Rahman Khadr, is a suspected CIA turncoat. Intelligence interest in the two Khadr brothers appears less a function of their own activities than that they are sons of Ahmad Said Khadr, an Egyptian-born Canadian computer engineer and Islamic charity director who was believed to be an al-Qaeda financier and close associate of Osama bin Laden. The elder Khadr was killed in a 2003 air attack on a house in Pakistan. In addition to being interrogated by U.S. military and civilian intelligence officers, Omar Khadr was questioned by officers of the Canadian Security Intelligence Service and the Canadian Department of Foreign Affairs.[8]

Where Hicks eventually won a limited measure of public sympathy in Australia due to racial and cultural affinity compounded by increasing hostility toward the foreign policy of the Bush administration because of the war in Iraq, Khadr eventually won a limited measure of public sympathy in Canada due to his youth compounded by a similar hostility toward the foreign policy of the Bush administration because of the war in Iraq. The case of Maher Arar, a Jordanian immigrant in Canada subjected to extraordinary rendition after he was taken into custody in New York, also soured many Canadians on the Bush administration.

What characterizes the remaining prisoners in the group? Their close association with senior figures in al-Qaeda, or their expertise in business or communications or in making bombs or in training others to make and use bombs, and their representative range of nationalities. Afghan national Abdul Zahir may have served as a translator and disbursed funds for al-Qaeda operations. Algerian national Sufyian Barhoumi may have served as a bomb-making instructor. Saudi national Jabran Said bin al-Qahtani may have made remote-controlled bombs and written a manual about making them. Saudi national Ghassan Abdullah al-Sharbi may have served as a bodyguard for Osama bin Laden and as a translator and may have trained others to make bombs.

Sudanese national Ibrahim Ahmed Mahmoud al-Qosi may have served as a bodyguard for Osama bin Laden as well as one of al-Qaeda's financial officers. Yemeni national Ali Hamza Ahmad Sulayman al-Bahlul may have served as a bodyguard for Osama bin Laden and may have made a recruitment video about the bombing of the USS *Cole*.

Finally, there is Ethiopian national Binyam Ahmed Mohammed, who converted to Islam while in political exile in Britain from his homeland. A late arrival in Guantánamo, he achieved notoriety comparable to that of Hamdan, Hicks, Khadr, the Tipton Three, and Moazzam Begg because he was tortured by the CIA and the Moroccan secret police.

Mohammed stands out from the other nine defendants for more than his horrific experience as the subject of extraordinary rendition in the CIA's secret prisons. He was accused of having proposed attacks on subways in American cities and of attempting to enter the United States to meet with al-Qaeda operatives in the country with the goal of constructing and detonating a "dirty bomb," a conventional explosive that would spread radioactive material. Beyond the initial casualties from the explosion of such a weapon, the fear of radioactive contamination would cause panic.

Another figure more frequently associated with the hypothesized dirty bomb was José Padilla, an American national who also converted to Islam. A dirty bomb plot was the headline accusation in the charges initially leveled against Padilla. That part of the case against Padilla was subsequently dropped for the same reason that doubts were voiced about Mohammed's participation. Neither Padilla nor Mohammed seemed capable of executing such a plot. At the time, however, the possibility that al-Qaeda could conduct a dirty bomb attack seemed all too plausible. In the wake of the bombings of the U.S. embassies in Nairobi and Dar es Salaam on August 7, 1998, the attack on the USS *Cole* on October 12, 2000, and the attacks on the World Trade Center and the Pentagon on September 11, 2001, al-Qaeda seemed a superbly effective international terrorist organization. The train bombings in Madrid on March 11, 2004, and the subway bombing in London on July 7, 2005, reinforced that perception. The insurgencies of two al-Qaeda affiliates, al-Qaeda in Iraq and al-Shaba in Somalia, added to its reputation. However, foiled terrorist attacks closer to home suggested something else about al-Qaeda. The attempted bombing of airliners by "shoe bomber" Richard Reid on December 22, 2001, and "underwear bomber" Umar Farouk Abdulmutallab on December 25, 2009, as well as the fizzled car bombing in Times Square on May 1, 2010, by Faisal Shahzad, indicated that it might be an organization crawling with incompetent hangers-on. High-profile causes attract individuals suffering from low self-esteem who hope to find meaning for their lives by participating in larger events. Some of them are pathological liars who spin fantasies in an effort to achieve validating praise. They may seek to join the entourages of entertainers, athletes, and politicians. Others gravitate to radical political or religious movements led by charismatic leaders. Combining those traits with the general tendency of religious novices to compensate for their thin knowledge of religious teachings—many of the recently radicalized Islamist youth and especially recent converts are unfamiliar with the complexities of the faith—with demonstrations of intense commitment, the hangers-on who attached themselves to al-Qaeda were extraordinarily vulnerable to self-deception.

The implication is that Mohammed and Padilla may have been far less dangerous than either the authorities or they themselves believed. Rather than being a highly trained terrorist who would have wrought havoc with a dirty bomb, Mohammed might have been nothing more than a self-destructive, attention-seeking fantasist.

As the first and in all probability the only indicted war crimes defendants from among the original population of hundreds of prisoners at Guantánamo, these ten are an unimpressive lot. Worse, the accusations against eight of them hardly seem the sort of war crimes that normally horrify observers. Rather than atrocities committed against civilians such as massacres or mutilations, the eight are accused of engaging in combat, building bombs, training others to build bombs, serving as a bodyguard, translating, and disbursing funds. These are not the actions that result in ordinary soldiers being accused of war crimes. Only the accusations made against Khadr and Mohammed would merit the "war crime" designation. Khadr was accused of wounding a journalist, and journalists are illegitimate targets of violence as noncombatants.

However, compared with the horrors that have been perpetrated against noncombatants in all wars, what Khadr was accused of doing is small potatoes. And Mohammed, who was originally suspected of planning much more serious violence against large numbers of noncombatants, did not actually carry it out. In sum, these ten failed in their assigned roles as the worst of the worst of the worst.

What makes a prisoner in military custody subject to war crimes prosecution? The answer lies in the complicated interrelationship between U.S. constitutional law on the writ of habeas corpus and the international law of war, a body of law that regulates the treatment of the captured. Understanding how they developed in tandem across the boundary of U.S. national sovereignty provides context crucial for making sense of the Guantánamo decision.

The development of U.S. constitutional law with respect to prisoners taken in war is largely the history of cases that begin as petitions to courts for writs of habeas corpus, or legal challenges to imprisonment by the authorities. Habeas corpus, which may be translated from the Latin as "you must present the body," had been established in English law and society as the proper legal remedy for persons denied their liberty for a century before Parliament legislated the writ and the right in the Habeas Corpus Act of 1679. That legislation failed to extend the writ to the American colonies, and with the sole exception of South Carolina the writ did not exist in formal legislation until after the American Revolution, when similarly worded legislation was passed by the new state legislatures. A right to petition courts for a writ of habeas corpus was also required for admission of new states under the Northwest Ordinance of 1781, the most significant legislation passed by Congress under the Articles of Confederation. The framers of the current U.S. Constitution did not include an explicit right to petition for a writ of habeas corpus, but it was assumed to be such a basic right that they limited the authority of Congress to suspend the privilege of the writ in Article 1, Section 9, to those times "when in Cases of Rebellion or Invasion the public Safety may require it." Moreover, the Judiciary Act of 1789 subsequently passed by Congress gave persons imprisoned under federal law the right to petition for a writ of habeas corpus.

How effective is the writ of habeas corpus as a constraint on executive power over prisoners of war? Generations of Americans have been indoctrinated to believe in the separation-of-powers doctrine as a description of the actual functioning of their national government. They are taught that the Constitution established three branches of government that are roughly coequal and interdependent, all of which limits potential abuses of authority by officials in any one of the three branches. Although it is splendid as an expression of popular support for the legitimacy of constitutional authority, it is poor political science. The reality is that the differences in formal constitutional authority, as well as the powers accumulated through legislation and practice, make the president, Congress, and Supreme Court decidedly unequal in power. Where the president has authority to direct the actions of millions of employees in national civil and military bureaucracies, and Congress has authority to enact legislation levying taxes and allocating spending, the Supreme Court has authority only to interpret the Constitution in the course of deciding legal cases. Thus, unlike the other two branches, the authority of the Supreme Court lies almost solely in the power to react rather than the power to initiate.

Where the political interests motivating the decisions made by the president and Congress are typically barely concealed or openly admitted, those motivating decisions made by the Supreme Court lie concealed beneath billows of legal reasoning impenetrable to laymen, which normally safeguards the legitimacy of both its individual decisions in cases and the institution as a branch of government. Although they are individually selected in patently political bargaining between the president and the U.S. Senate, and although their decisions on some cases may be immensely important for officeholders throughout the political system and for the making of public policy, Supreme Court justices are compelled to maintain the appearance of political impartiality to safeguard the legitimacy of both their decisions and their branch of government. Moreover, the justices understand the fundamental weakness of their judicial authority. Any refusal by a president supported by majorities in the Congress to treat the judgments of the Supreme Court as anything less than authoritative threatens a constitutional crisis of the first order, a breakdown in the constitutional order that would do more damage to the judicial than to the executive or legislative branch. The result is that the justices normally avoid challenging the authority of the other two branches. That is most true with respect to foreign policy, a domain in which the president is unmistakably strongest vis-à-vis both Congress and the Supreme Court. Research has shown that the Supreme Court is usually more deferential to the president in cases involving foreign policy and national security, and that justices appointed by Republican presidents are usually more deferential to the president than justices appointed by Democratic presidents.[9] The same is no doubt true of judges in federal circuit courts of appeal and federal district courts.

The image of a skittish, even pusillanimous Supreme Court deciding cases based upon the direction that the political wind is blowing was captured by turn-of-the-century humorist and newspaper columnist Finley Peter Dunne in the voice of his favorite fictional character, Chicago bartender Martin T. Dooley: "That is," said Mr. Dooley, "no matter whether th' constitution follows th' flag or not, th' supreme coort follows th' iliction returns."[10] The topic was one of the major issues in the 1900 presidential election between Democratic Party nominee William Jennings Bryan and Republican Party nominee William McKinley. Bryan argued that the Constitution should follow the flag, that Hawaii and the new island territories acquired in the Spanish-American War should be governed by the same constitutional principles as the continental mainland of the United States. McKinley adopted a more ambiguous position, arguing that they need not necessarily be governed under the same principles. McKinley won the election, and his policy prevailed in Supreme Court decisions. In 1901 the Court handed down controversial decisions in seven cases that became known as the Insular Cases, concluding that U.S. constitutional law did not necessarily apply to the new island possessions of Hawaii, the Philippines, Puerto Rico, and Cuba. Another seven decisions delivered between 1903 and 1922 and described as the progeny of the Insular Cases reinforced the boundary drawn. With the Insular Cases and their progeny the Supreme Court succeeded in demarcating an extensive liminal zone between the authority of domestic law and the authority of international law, one that was required for the operation of American colonial rule.

Although the cases principally involved the Philippines, Puerto Rico, and Hawaii, they were relevant to the exercise of U.S. authority over the newly acquired Guantánamo Bay Naval Base in eastern Cuba.

Since the shock of the Japanese surprise attack on Pearl Harbor in 1941 that precipitated American entry into the Second World War, the prevailing assumption among American political elites has been that the U.S. president requires almost unrestrained authority in military decision making to respond to imminent threats to national security, a perspective reinforced by the nuclear deterrence doctrine articulated during the Cold War. The ponderous workings of the Supreme Court seemed especially unsuited to participating in foreign policy decisions in this period. As an institution, the Supreme Court may defend itself against having to hear cases that threaten or appear to intrude on the war-making powers of the president by declining to take up an appeal of a lower court's decision. Four of the nine justices must vote in favor of a writ of certiorari before such an appeal will be heard.

Given such excellent political reasons and such strong institutional defenses against challenging the president with respect to the treatment of prisoners captured in war, the reasonable expectation is that the Supreme Court would fail to defend the writ of habeas corpus as a remedy for alleged abuses. At the very least, an inverse relationship between the strength of its defense of the writ and the severity of the national security threat ought to be evident. Instead, the history of such cases is more complex. The Supreme Court has sometimes demonstrated strength and at other times weakness, with no relationship between its response and the severity of the national security threat. This is most evident in the decisions on appeals from military tribunals and commissions.

Used in each of the republic's first three international wars, military tribunals were not treated as essential instruments of national authority during security crises until the 1860s with the American Civil War and the Sioux Uprising. Before that, Americans disagreed vociferously about the practical necessity and constitutionality of imposing martial law even during invasions and insurrections. In marked contrast to the hysteria gripping most Americans after September 11, 2001, civil liberties were privileged over national security in the republican tradition born in the American Revolution. The first generation of American decision makers understood that they were leading a struggle to establish what would later come to be called a liberal society. Integral to their conception of justice was the writ of habeas corpus as a limit on the exercise of arbitrary authority. Part of the English common law tradition that was cherished as a source of liberty by Americans, and encompassing cases involving military prisoners dating from the seventeenth century, habeas corpus was presumed essential to the legal protection of individual rights even in the midst of crises.[11] American decision makers also understood that their new government's international reputation would be affected by their treatment of the captured. That meant that British military prisoners were well treated by comparison with the American military prisoners in British custody during the Revolutionary War. So powerful was the republican tradition that the declaration of martial law suspending the writ of habeas corpus issued by then-general and future president Andrew Jackson during the 1814 Battle of New Orleans generated political controversy that would continue for three decades.[12]

The United States began developing its national law of war with the articulation of the Lieber Code during the American Civil War and the contemporaneous Sioux Uprising. The trials before military tribunals in those two conflicts and the seminal influence of the Lieber Code on the development of the international law of war help to explain why the Bush administration would announce its own military tribunals in Guantánamo. The fact that the United States established military tribunals to prosecute Confederate sympathizers in the northern states during the Civil War does not feature prominently in the American collective memory. They lack either the simplistic moral drama or the heroic bloodshed that is necessary to secure a place in America's civic sacralization of the conflict. For constitutional legal scholars, however, the tribunals matter because they resulted in the U.S. Supreme Court's landmark habeas corpus ruling in *Ex Parte Milligan*, a decision whose contested meaning continues to reverberate.[13]

On September 15, 1863, President Abraham Lincoln issued a proclamation suspending the writ everywhere in the territory of the United States for persons in military custody as captured enemy soldiers, as abettors of the enemy, or for other offenses committed during wartime. One of those arrested by the military and tried for conspiracy against the government, aiding the enemy, insurrection, disloyalty, and violating the laws of war was a Copperhead attorney in southern Indiana named Lamblin P. Milligan. "Copperhead" was the political epithet given to the Peace Democrats concentrated in the midwestern states who opposed the Civil War supported by Republicans and War Democrats. Milligan was arrested on October 6, 1864, on a warrant from Union general Alvin Hovey and tried before a military commission in Indianapolis for having joined and aided a secret society called the Order of American Knights or Sons of Liberty whose purpose was to overthrow the U.S. government, seize weapons in Union arsenals, and liberate captured Confederate soldiers. Secret societies might appear quaint or juvenile today, but in the eighteenth and nineteenth centuries they were recognized as important vehicles for conducting revolutionary agitation and insurrection. Oath-taking rituals were used to strengthen group loyalties in secret societies into the twentieth century, as evidenced by the Ku Klux Klan in the United States and the Mau Mau in British colonial Kenya. Although the practical political prospects for a local secessionist armed rebellion in the Midwest during the Civil War were remote, the large numbers of poorly guarded Confederate soldiers in Union Army prison camps in Indiana and Kentucky made mass escapes assisted by disaffected northerners a rather realistic possibility. Moreover, in the autumn of 1864, Union victory was still not certain. For many observers at the time, the idea of a Copperhead conspiracy led by Milligan was anything but farfetched. The military commission convicted him in October 1864, but set aside his execution by hanging until May 1865. In the interim, a federal grand jury declined to indict him in January 1865.

Milligan can only be considered extremely fortunate that the legal team arguing his appeal before the Supreme Court included both David Dudley Field, who was a former Union Army major general, current member of Congress, and the brother of Supreme Court justice Stephen Field, and the future twentieth president of the United States, Republican James A. Garfield.[14] In an oral argument that addressed not only the Court and public opinion of the time but also future generations, Garfield evoked the venerable and universal status of the writ of habeas corpus among Anglo-Saxons and then did what no politician of today would dare, making an unfavorable comparison with the practice of the recently defeated enemy:

These principles our fathers brought with them to the New World, and guarded with vigilance and devotion. During the late Rebellion, the Republic did not forget them. So completely have they been impressed on the minds of American lawyers, so thoroughly ingrained into the fibre of American character, that notwithstanding the citizens of eleven States went off into rebellion, broke their oaths of allegiance to the Constitution, and levied war against their country, yet with all their crimes upon them, there was still in the minds of those men, during all the struggle, so deep an impression on this great subject, that, even during their rebellion, the courts of the Southern States adjudicated causes, like the one now before you, in favor of the civil law, and against courts-martial established under military authority for the trial of citizens.

The Supreme Court found for Milligan unanimously. The opinion was written by one of Lincoln's five Supreme Court appointees, Justice David Davis, who also found it necessary to march through the history he thought relevant, relying on the intent of the framers of the Constitution, to condemn the threat to the privilege:

Time has proven the discernment of our ancestors; for even these provisions, expressed in such plain English words, that it would seem the ingenuity of man could not evade them, are now, after the lapse of more than seventy years, sought to be avoided. Those great and good men foresaw that troublous times would arise, when rules and people would become restive under restraint, and seek by sharp and decisive measures to accomplish ends deemed just and proper; and that the principles of constitutional liberty would be in peril, unless established by irrepealable law. The history of the world had taught them that what was done in the past might be attempted in the future. The Constitution of the United

States is a law for rulers and people, equally in war and in peace, and covers with the shield of its protection all classes of men, at all times, and under all circumstances.

The majority of justices were impressed that Milligan had been a comparatively long distance from the military front and that the federal and state courts in Indiana continued to function during the conflict. If civil courts continue to perform their duties, they concluded, those charged are entitled to a civil trial and all of its legal protections. This practical conclusion of the majority in *Ex Parte Milligan* and the evocation of commonly held beliefs about civil liberties made it a legal precedent exceedingly difficult to ignore or overcome in subsequent judicial decisions in cases challenging trials before military tribunals during the Second World War and in the as-yet-unnamed period after September 11, 2001.

Less well known even among legal scholars are the military tribunals conducted in 1862 in the aftermath of the Sioux Uprising, also referred to as the U.S.-Dakota War. Overshadowed by the Civil War raging to the east, the two-month-long Sioux Uprising on the Minnesota frontier resulted in the deaths of an estimated 500 American settlers and Dakota or Santee Sioux before it ended with the surrender of approximately 2,000 Dakota warriors and their dependents on September 29, 1862.[15] An unknown number of Dakota also fled north to Canada and escaped capture. Following the mass surrender, some 390 of the captured Dakota warriors were tried before a military tribunal of five officers established by Colonel Henry Sibley. President Abraham Lincoln would later approve the executions of 39 of the 303 prisoners who were convicted, of whom 38 would be hanged together on December 26, 1862. Rather than release the remaining 1,700 Dakota in custody, most of them women and children, Colonel Sibley ordered them held for the time at Fort Snelling in Saint Paul, Minnesota. In 1863, approximately 1,300 of these captives were transferred to a new reservation at Crow Creek on the Missouri River, where they experienced a high mortality rate.[16]

Although contemporary American public opinion recoils in horror at the treatment of the Native Americans in previous centuries, the idea that the U.S. government was justified in treating captured Dakota warriors as savages entitled to few legal rights was less controversial in the Victorian Era. Indeed, the treatment meted out by the great powers of the day to rebellious indigenes in colonies across the Americas, Africa, and Australasia was often extraordinarily violent. Conducting drumhead military trials for captured rebels rather than summary executions would have been understood as progress of sorts in the colonies of the European powers. During the 1857–59 Indian Mutiny, thousands of Indian prisoners were summarily executed by the British military by shooting, hanging, or, most horrifically, blowing them from the mouths of cannons. One British officer was congratulated by his superiors on his "energy and spirit" for having ordered the summary execution of 282 captured mutineers who had surrendered believing they would be given fair trials.[17] Conducting trials before executing captured anticolonial rebels did not become common in the British Empire until the next century. As an example of the steady but slow march of civilization, British authorities tried and convicted only 350 of the roughly 9,000 rebels who were captured in the 1930–31 Burmese Rebellion.[18] Of that number, 128 were hanged.

As important as the military tribunals for Confederate sympathizers were for the development of U.S. constitutional law, the trials of the Dakota warriors may be more relevant to the politics of the trials of the Guantánamo prisoners. The parallels between the treatment of the Dakota warriors and the Guantánamo prisoners—the denial of basic due process rights and the political-legal identities of the prisoners—speak to the political calculation of the responsible decision makers. Among the violations of due process by Colonel Sibley's military tribunal for the Dakota warriors were the denial of representation by legal counsel, the admission of hearsay testimony as evidence, the assumption of guilt unless proven innocent, and an assumption of collective guilt that resulted in some individual trials lasting no longer than five minutes. Compare that with the denial of representation by legal counsel, the denial of the right to see classified material presented against them as evidence, the admission of hearsay evidence and evidence obtained under torture, the requirement of only a majority vote rather than unanimity for panel decisions, and the use of the "preponderance of the evidence" legal standard rather than the more stringent "beyond a reasonable doubt" in two related forms of judicial proceeding at Guantánamo: the Combatant Status Review Tribunals, which determined whether prisoners were in fact unlawful combatants, and the follow-on Administrative Review Panels, which determined whether prisoners continued to be unlawful combatants.[19] Often confused with the military commissions established in 2001 to try selected prisoners for war crimes, these panels were instead established in 2004 by order of Deputy Secretary of Defense Paul Wolfowitz in response to administration losses in the U.S. Supreme Court decisions of *Rasul v. Bush* and *Al Odah v. United States*. Those selected for prosecution in trials before the military commissions at Guantánamo were accorded greater due process rights than they and fellow prisoners before the Combatant Status Review Tribunals and Administrative Review Panels, but then the consequences of judgments made by the military commissions would be weightier than those of the panels. Where decisions against prisoners in the Combatant Status Review Tribunals and Administrative Review Panels might result in continuing indefinite and incommunicado imprisonment, conviction by a military commission at Guantánamo, like conviction by the Minnesota military commission, might result in execution.

Although the original presidential order on military commissions issued in 2001 accorded prisoners few due process rights, the Military Commissions Act of 2006 granted more procedural rights while at the same time falling short of those given to defendants in ordinary criminal trials in civil courts. The legislation authorized the trials of unlawful combatants for offenses including murder, torture, and rape. Although the prisoners being tried would have been determined to be unlawful combatants in Combatant Status Review Tribunal hearings only in 2004, retroactive to September 11, 2001, all such prisoners were denied access to the civil courts for making habeas corpus challenges. Evidence obtained through torture was disallowed, but the judges were permitted to admit evidence obtained through coercion if under the totality of circumstances they deemed it reliable and probative. Prisoners might be denied access to the classified evidence introduced against them by the prosecution, but their legal counsel would be permitted access to summaries of the relevant facts. The law also allows appeals to a newly created Court of Military Commission Review and from there to the U.S. Court of Appeals for the District of Columbia Circuit.

The political-legal identities of the prisoners constituted the second important parallel between the Minnesota military commission and the three Guantánamo military panels and commissions. From the perspective of Washington in the mid-nineteenth century, the lands occupied by the Dakota were part of the sovereign territory of the United States, while the Dakota themselves were neither U.S. citizens nor nationals of any other civilized country. To most Americans and especially to the frightened, vengeful settlers on the Minnesota frontier, they were savages who respected none of the rules of war and were owed none of the obligations due to a civilized enemy. Those perspectives match those of Washington and most Americans in the immediate aftermath of 9/11. The members of al-Qaeda and the allied Taliban—the distinction between the two was largely lost on most Americans—were citizens of Middle Eastern states but, more important, were vicious terrorists motivated by a religious fanaticism that made them willing to commit appalling acts of violence against the innocent and were thus owed no consideration under the law of war. The idea that the political-legal identities of captured enemy determine their captors' obligations to them has its origins in the unwritten laws and customs of war that had been developing in Europe for centuries before they were formalized in international law at roughly the same historical moment that a military commission in Minnesota was condemning Dakota warriors to death by hanging.

The next landmark Supreme Court decisions on the rights of prisoners captured during war would be handed down eight decades later, during and immediately after the Second World War. Before then, however, events occurring on both sides of the Atlantic contemporaneous with the *Ex Parte Milligan* decision would give birth to the formal law of war detailed in the Geneva Conventions. Henri Dunant, a Swiss businessman who witnessed the carnage of the almost forgotten

1859 Battle of Solferino in the almost forgotten Franco-Austrian War, played a central role in its eventual emergence. In the immediate aftermath of the battle that claimed the lives of approximately 40,000 French, Italian, and Austrian soldiers, Dunant and a band of fellow humanitarians offered help to some of the wounded and dying. More important, Dunant went on to publish his influential memoir of the event, *A Memory of Solferino*, in 1862. His slender book produced an international humanitarian movement that in turn led to the establishment of both national relief committees and the International Committee of the Red Cross with the goals of limiting the violence of war, reducing subsequent suffering, and protecting military and political prisoners. The treaties known as the Geneva Conventions would grow out of its work.

On the other side of the Atlantic, Francis Lieber drafted a code of military law for a Union Army that had grown from a small frontier force of hundreds to an army of hundreds of thousands. His 1863 *Instructions for the Government of Armies of the United States in the Field*, now commonly called the Lieber Code, was adopted in similar form by other major powers of the day and informed international treaty law on the treatment of war captives.

The normative authority of the Lieber Code is attributable in great part to its context and purpose. First, it was written for a civil war and not an international war. The American Civil War was not internationalized because the British government of Prime Minister Benjamin Disraeli declined the invitation of the French government of Emperor Napoleon III to intervene on the side of the Confederate States of America. That decision not only made military victory for the Union more likely but also meant that the Lieber Code was developed in circumstances that had in the past resulted in the mistreatment of prisoners. One of the recurring problems in ending civil wars and reducing their brutality is the refusal of governments to recognize the status of captured rebel soldiers as captured soldiers rather than as captured traitors. Recognizing that status risks appearing to confer legitimacy on the rebels and their rebellion, which is inconsistent with the accusation of treason.[20] By definition, armed rebellion against the state is treason. The unfortunate consequence of making policy on the basis of such logical consistency is that rebels may continue to resist long after the hope of victory has faded, simply in order to avoid the punishment that would attend surrender. If the purpose of war is to force the enemy into submission, rather than to exterminate or to exact revenge, then refusing to recognize captured rebel soldiers as captured soldiers is unnecessarily costly and irrationally wasteful of human life and effort. Therefore the dispassionately rational principle of law for both international war and civil war is to protect anyone captured from reprisal in order to induce surrender.

Second, and perhaps more important, the Lieber Code was primarily written for a total war rather than a limited war. Total wars mobilize entire societies. States engaged in total wars extract more of the available human and material resources than states engaged in limited wars. In the process they create new roles that are neither clearly military nor civilian, including medical personnel and construction workers, reporters, spies, saboteurs, commandoes, militarized police, and members of irregular militias. Camp followers have accompanied armies into battle throughout recorded history, but the total wars waged by modern industrial societies were producing large numbers of people filling social roles in war that fell in the widening gray area between the unambiguously military and the unambiguously civilian. Deciding how to treat them in law was an important task. Administering justice requires that reasonable distinctions be made, and the Lieber Code offered exactly that, however arbitrary they might appear to later generations. Under the Lieber Code, both surrendering Confederate regulars and members of irregular militia units—those with officers, distinctive emblems, and arms carried openly—were recognized as prisoners of war. The modern acronym POW would come into universal use in later wars. Captured noncombatants who were legitimately attached to armies, such as construction workers and news reporters, were also recognized as protected species of prisoners of war. Among the categories of captured combatant not entitled to that status were saboteurs and spies, combatants who disguised themselves in the uniforms of their enemies or as noncombatant civilians, deserters who had changed sides to become enemy combatants, rebels in occupied territory, and common bandits. All these might be summarily executed or otherwise punished.

The Lieber Code, its sibling national military statutes, and subsequent international treaty law rationalized the law of war in a manner suited only to the needs of the great powers of the nineteenth century. Most of the available weapon technology could kill or wound over distances measured only in yards. Modern civilized states waged war on land against one another using enormous bureaucratically organized armies that faced one another in set-piece battles while wearing distinctive uniforms and firing easily recognizable weapons. Precise large-unit maneuver combined with massive if very imprecise firepower won battles. Such warfare required officers, distinctive uniforms, and arms carried openly, all of which permit surrendering combatants to be legally recognized as prisoners of war.

The negotiation of the Hague Regulations of 1899 was the first major effort to write the emerging formal rules and customs of war law into international treaty law, and most of their provisions concerning persons taken captive in war were either comparable to or inspired by those in the Lieber Code. The captured were accorded legal protection if they met three basic requirements: officers, distinctive emblems, and arms carried openly. One important elaboration was that noncombatants who spontaneously take up arms without having had time to organize themselves with formal command, distinctive emblems, and arms carried openly might still qualify for prisoner-of-war status. Thus a small fissure was opened in the legal barrier to recognizing captured guerrillas as prisoners of war. So even before the beginning of the previous century some observers clearly foresaw that the law of war would have to accommodate the sorts of change that would be inevitable because of advances in small arms, camouflage, and mass communications permitting the mobilization of armed popular resistance.

The Third Geneva Convention was negotiated in 1929 at a historical moment when international public opinion nervously sensed the possibility of another war on the scale of what was then known too hopefully as the Great War and is now known simply as the First World War.[21] Signed by forty-seven states, though not the Soviet Union and

Japan, the 1929 Geneva Convention introduced new responsibilities toward war captives in addition to those in the Hague Regulations. In particular, the treaty banned the transfer of prisoners without advance notification of their destination, the commingling of prisoners of different nationalities, and the use of coercion in the interrogation of prisoners. Repatriation of the captured must follow peace or perhaps the end of hostilities with the least possible delay. The importance of these four treaty obligations for the protection of the captured is highlighted by the experience of the prisoners taken in the war in Afghanistan who found themselves in Guantánamo. Each of the four obligations would have been violated if their status as prisoners of war had been recognized.

The Fourth Geneva Convention was negotiated in 1949 in response to weaknesses in the Third Geneva Convention of 1929 revealed during and immediately after the Second World War.[22] The revised treaty articulated the responsibilities of captor states in greater detail than had the 1929 treaty, particularly with respect to captured civilians and persons in between the categories of military and civilian. Common Article III, which was to figure prominently in the U.S. Supreme Court's 2006 *Hamdan* decision, required that states involved in civil wars or insurgencies refrain from a variety of acts against prisoners, including "cruel treatment or torture," "outrages against personal dignity, humiliating or degrading treatment," and the "passing of sentences and the carrying out of executions without previous judgment pronounced by a regularly constituted court."[23]

Patriotic rhetoric now almost invariably describes every U.S. military deployment as necessary to defend American freedom. That platitude, voiced so often by politicians and pundits to express their support for the service of members of the U.S. armed forces, disguises the happy fact that for most of its history the United States has been less vulnerable to the sort of military attack that threatens foreign conquest or change of regime than any of the other great powers. The geographic barriers presented by the Atlantic and Pacific Oceans and land borders with militarily and economically less powerful Canada and Mexico gave the United States a superbly favorable national security environment. Indeed, since the War of 1812, the United States has fought only two wars in which it faced an existential threat: the American Civil War and the Second World War. At the very least, defeat in either conflict would have weakened the United States as a world power and perhaps undermined its liberal democratic political institutions. Both wars resulted in important Supreme Court habeas corpus decisions. *Ex Parte Milligan* has already been discussed. The decisions handed down during and after the Second World War had strikingly different outcomes.

The first of the two major Second World War cases was *Ex Parte Quirin*, a challenge to the authority of the president to establish a military tribunal to try enemy saboteurs or spies captured in the United States.[24] The case involved a group of eight saboteurs who were landed by German U-boats on the coasts of Florida and of Long Island, New York, in mid-June 1942. They were arrested before they could do any damage, and it seemed less than clear that several actually intended to carry out their mission. All eight had lived in the United States prior to their training as saboteurs in Germany, and their behavior once ashore suggests they were relieved to be away from the privations and repression of wartime Germany and back in the United States. After burying their explosives on the beaches where they landed, the saboteurs went on personal spending sprees with the cash they had been given or visited family and friends. One of the eight, an emotionally unstable German national named George Dasch, provided the information necessary for the apprehension and prosecution of the other seven.

Their capture was followed by a July 2, 1942, proclamation by President Franklin Delano Roosevelt establishing a military tribunal with authority to try these captured and other similar captured in the future for offenses against the law of war. With an eye to both the precedent of *Ex Parte Milligan* and the state of American public opinion only seven months after the Japanese attack on Pearl Harbor, the proclamation explicitly denied anyone tried before these military tribunals access to the civil courts.

That the Supreme Court would find for the Roosevelt administration appears never to have been in doubt.[25] The unanimous decision was even rendered months before the written opinion, something that permitted the quick-march trial of the eight defendants before the military tribunal, and the execution of six of them. The opinion attempted to distinguish the case from the facts in *Ex Parte Milligan* with the argument that the defendants had not been charged with offenses for which the Constitution requires a trial by jury. It then found justification for its decision in an understanding of the law of war little different from that articulated in the Lieber Code.

By universal agreement and practice the law of war draws a distinction between the armed forces and the peaceful populations of belligerent nations and also between those who are lawful and unlawful combatants. Lawful combatants are subject to capture and detention as prisoners of war by opposing military forces. Unlawful combatants are likewise subject to capture and detention, but in addition they are subject to trial and punishment by military tribunals for acts which render their belligerency unlawful. The spy who secretly and without uniform passes the military lines of a belligerent in time of war, seeking to gather military information and communicate it to the enemy, or an enemy combatant who without uniform comes secretly through the lines for the purpose of waging war by destruction of life or property, are familiar examples of belligerents who are generally deemed not to be entitled to the status of prisoners of war, but to be offenders against the law of war subject to trial and punishment by military tribunals.

Nor did the American citizenship of one of the petitioners, the young Chicagoan named Herbie Haupt, suffice to win release by the military tribunal and trial in a civil court.

Citizenship in the United States of an enemy belligerent does not relieve him from the consequences of a belligerency which is unlawful because in violation of the law of war. Citizens who associate themselves with the military arm of the enemy government, and with its aid, guidance and direction enter this country bent on hostile acts are enemy belligerents within in the meaning of the Hague Convention and the law of war. It is as an enemy agent that petitioner Haupt is charged with entering the United

States, and unlawful belligerency is the gravamen of the offense of which he is accused.

Here was a conception of war less in keeping with the mid-twentieth century than the mid-nineteenth, an era before the advent of professional espionage agencies, military camouflage, aerial warfare, and state sponsorship of insurgent movements.

On June 5, 1950, the Supreme Court handed down another habeas corpus decision involving German nationals who were tried before a military commission. *Johnson v. Eisentrager* developed from a petition filed by twenty-one German nationals who had been tried before a United States military commission sitting in Shanghai.[26] There they had been convicted of violating the laws of war by continuing to undertake military intelligence activities for the Japanese military in China in the period between the unconditional surrender of Germany on May 8, 1945, and the Japanese surrender on September 2, 1945. Following their convictions they were sentenced to serve terms in Landsberg Prison in Germany. Their petition for a writ of habeas corpus was dismissed by the District Court for the District of Columbia, but the Court of Appeals for the District of Columbia Circuit reversed that decision, and then the Supreme Court reversed the D.C. Circuit in a 6-to-3 decision. The majority opinion of the Supreme Court declared that the federal courts lacked territorial jurisdiction over nonresident enemy aliens.

> We have pointed out that the privilege of litigation has been extended to aliens, whether friendly or enemy, only because permitting their presence in the country implied protection. No such basis can be invoked here, for these prisoners at no relevant time were within any territory over which the United States is sovereign, and the scenes of their offense, their capture, their trial and their punishment were all beyond the territorial jurisdiction of any court of the United States.

Although the majority opinion was based on the question of territorial jurisdiction, it also briefly touched on the difficult issue of whether the Geneva Convention of 1929 was a self-executing treaty, whether further congressional legislation was necessary to give it effect, and in particular whether the federal courts could enforce its provisions. The majority was careful to point out that the prisoners were entitled to the protections of the Geneva Convention of 1929, this despite the fact that they had continued to serve as intelligence officers after the government of Germany had unconditionally surrendered and had thus for all intents and purposes ceased to exist as a state. Five decades later, the Afghan and foreign soldiers who continued to fight following the flight of the Taliban government in Kabul and were then captured were in a roughly analogous position. The majority in *Eisentrager* concluded that these were rights that could be asserted "only through protests and intervention of protecting powers as the rights of our citizens against foreign governments are vindicated only by Presidential intervention." Here once again is a conception of war less in harmony with the twentieth century than the nineteenth, an era when states did not cease to exist through total war and were always therefore available to assert the rights of their own captured soldiers.

Where the court that decided *Ex Parte Milligan* was a body that took the long view and based its decision making on its understanding of the development and importance of the privilege of the writ, the court that decided *Ex Parte Quirin* and *Johnson v. Eisentrager* was a body more interested in "th' iliction returns." As such the decisions offer subsequent Supreme Courts very different models for responding to challenges from the executive branch to the protection, however slight, against unlawful imprisonment offered by the privilege of the writ of habeas corpus.

Among the most important unfinished business in the negotiations that produced the Fourth Geneva Convention of 1949 was determining the legal status and rights of combatants and noncombatants who were involved in "wars of national liberation." Fueled by the ideological and military competition between the United States and the Soviet Union in the 1950s through the 1980s that came to be called the Cold War, guerrilla wars erupted across Africa, Asia, and Latin America. Decolonization spawned numerous insurgencies in Southeast Asia and Africa. Extreme economic and social inequality in Latin America produced others. One of the problems for international humanitarian law was that many of those fighting in these struggles did so under the banners of organizations that were not yet and perhaps would never become recognized sovereign states. Another problem was that the insurgencies bore little resemblance to the kind of conventional warfare envisioned in the Geneva Conventions. Humanitarian concern about the treatment of both combatants and noncombatants in these conflicts was one of the reasons the International Committee of the Red Cross initiated the negotiations that in 1977 added two protocols to the Geneva Conventions of 1949.[27] Article 43 of Protocol I addressed the first problem by defining a combatant with the right to participate in hostilities as any member of the armed forces of a party—whether state or nonstate—in a conflict, including paramilitary and armed law enforcement incorporated into its military. Article 44 of Protocol I then extended the protections of prisoner-of-war status to any combatant taken captive, but muddied the conceptual waters by stipulating that combatants should distinguish themselves from noncombatants in some manner and bear arms openly. The end result was that captor states could find language in the treaty supporting decisions either to grant or refuse to grant prisoner-of-war status to insurgents who lacked officers, uniforms, or arms carried openly. The inevitable temptation was to accord captured insurgents some but not all of the rights that would be accorded the captured in one of the increasingly rare conventional, interstate wars.

When the U.S. Supreme Court of Chief Justice William Rehnquist agreed to hear habeas corpus appeals from the execution of the Guantánamo decision in 2004, it did so against the backdrop of precedents from comparable cases in previous wars and the international law of war. If there was a surfeit of case and treaty law for legal arguments, there were also excellent reasons for the Court to avoid hearing such cases. The two most obvious reasons for judicial discretion were that its decisions would have to be delivered during rather than after hostilities and that the Guantánamo decision had been endorsed by Republican legislative majorities attended by a contingent of conservative Democrats in both chambers of the U.S. Congress. Context matters. *Ex Parte Milligan* was not decided until the Confederacy had been defeated and there was political advantage in decisions that signaled sectional reconciliation. *Ex Parte Quirin* was decided when the United States was only seven months into the Second World War and an Allied victory was far from guaranteed. The Guantánamo decision was so popular with some U.S. senators and House members that they toured the prison to demonstrate their approval. Brief flight time from Washington, negligible physical danger, and the opportunity to pose for photographs with soldiers made it an ideal War on Terror junket for many members of Congress. Under these circumstances, for the Supreme Court to consider any case whose outcome might challenge or even appear to challenge the foreign policy powers of the presidency threatened to reveal the inherent weakness of the Supreme Court vis-à-vis the presidency and Congress.

Despite the intense press attention they received after President George W. Bush issued his order authorizing military commissions on November 13, 2001, the criminal trials of captured terrorists before such commissions have advanced at a glacial pace. Where the Roosevelt administration's military commission tried the captured German and German-American saboteurs who were the appellants in *Ex Parte Quirin* only two months after they were taken into custody, it took the Bush administration more than nineteen months from the announcement of the order to name, though not formally charge, the first six of the prisoners to be prosecuted.[28] Neither the White House nor the Pentagon appeared in any haste to prosecute anyone at Guantánamo.

As would be expected, those named as defendants fought their imprisonment and prosecution. The first of the two decisions involving an American citizen, *Hamdi v. Rumsfeld*, began as a petition for a writ of habeas corpus filed by Esam Fouad Hamdi, the father of Yaser Esam Hamdi, in the federal District Court for the Eastern District of Virginia in June 2002.[29] After being taken prisoner in Afghanistan by the Northern Alliance, the younger Hamdi had been delivered to the United States and transferred to Guantánamo in January 2002. His transfer to the naval brig in Norfolk, Virginia, in April 2002 followed recognition that he was a citizen of the United States. Despite that status, he was denied access to legal counsel with the explanation that he was an enemy combatant. When his father filed suit in Virginia as his "next friend," or the representative for a person unable to act on his own behalf, the son was moved again, this time to the naval brig in Charleston, South Carolina. When the District Court for the Eastern District of Virginia ordered that Hamdi be allowed access to legal counsel, the Justice Department appealed, and the U.S. Court of Appeals for the Fourth Circuit reversed that decision, writing that the Authorization for Use of Military Force (AUMF), which was passed by Congress as Senate Joint Resolution 23 and signed by the president,[30] provided all the legal authority necessary to capture and hold enemy combatants. Having established the legal authority to wage war and thus to imprison those captured as a consequence, the Court of Appeals concluded that Hamdi's presence in the war zone in Afghanistan obviated the need for additional fact-finding inquiry for a ruling. A more complete surrender of the judiciary's constitutional authority to order writs of habeas corpus would be difficult to describe.

That constitutional forfeiture and the insufficiency of the factual record prompted the Supreme Court to reverse the Court of Appeals and declare that Hamdi was entitled to a hearing before a neutral decision maker, during which he would be given an opportunity to rebut the government's factual assertions. In writing the plurality opinion, Justice Sandra Day O'Connor, joined by Chief Justice Rehnquist, Justice Anthony Kennedy, and Justice Stephen Breyer, pounced on the argument that respect for the separation of powers requires that the judiciary accept any evidence in the record as conclusive with respect to petitions for writs of habeas corpus from U.S. citizens taken prisoner outside the country. While the Constitution grants primary responsibility for waging war to the executive branch as the best positioned and most politically accountable for successful execution, a state of war is not a blank check to violate the rights of U.S. citizens. As Justice O'Connor wrote,

as critical as the Government's interest may be in detaining those who actually pose an immediate threat to the national security of the United States during ongoing international conflict, history and common sense teach us that an unchecked system of detention carries the potential to become a means for oppression and abuse of others who do not present that sort of threat.

Balancing the competing constitutional interests requires that, in the absence of a military tribunal with responsibility for determining whether a captive is entitled to prisoner-of-war status under the Geneva Conventions of 1949, lower courts petitioned for a writ of habeas corpus must ensure that at least minimum due process has been granted.

Justice O'Connor also used the phrase "most extreme rendition," which may have been a thinly veiled warning to the Bush administration of future constitutional scrutiny of the practice of "extraordinary rendition," or covert action to take terrorism suspects into custody without the formal or even informal approval of the foreign government in whose territory it occurs.

In a concurrence, Justice David Souter, joined by Justice Ruth Bader Ginsburg, disagreed that the Authorization for Use of Military Force provided the requisite authority for imprisoning American citizens without a hearing. They argued that under the Non-Detention Act, which replaced Cold War–era legislation and was adopted after recognition that the internments of Japanese-Americans during the Second World War had been unjust, explicit authority to imprison American citizens was necessary. Moreover, they went on to observe that Hamdi would qualify as a prisoner of war under the Geneva Conventions of 1949 because the government had claimed Hamdi was taken captive while bearing arms as a member of the Taliban.

In his dissent, Justice Antonin Scalia, joined by Justice John Paul Stevens, concluded that Hamdi was entitled to actual release rather than to a mere hearing, because Congress had not passed legislation suspending the writ of habeas corpus, nor had criminal proceedings been filed against him. Predictably, Scalia arrived at his interpretation of the Constitution by divining the "original intent" of the framers by what is known from the historical record, and then lectured on the errors of judicial activism he perceived in the plurality. If the executive and the legislature have failed to do what is necessary and proper, then the judiciary should not step outside its normally modest role to correct their errors.

Justice Clarence Thomas brought up the rear with a dissent that endorsed the administration's position by rejecting any balancing of different constitutional interests. Rather chillingly, Thomas argued for simply allowing the executive to make the conclusive factual findings necessary to imprison those that it considered to be enemy combatants. His privileging of national security over civil liberties stood in direct opposition to the republican tradition of America's original Patriots.

The second of the decisions involving a U.S. citizen, *Rumsfeld v. Padilla*, began with a motion to vacate a material witness warrant under which José Padilla had been arrested by federal agents as he disembarked in Chicago from a flight from Pakistan to the United States via Switzerland on May 8, 2002.[31] Following his custody transfer to New York, Padilla was declared an enemy combatant by presidential order, and custody was transferred from civilian authorities to military authorities, who then moved him to the naval brig at Charleston, South Carolina. Attorney Donna Newman, acting as Padilla's "next friend," filed a petition for a writ of habeas corpus in the federal District Court for the Southern District of New York, rather than filing in the District Court for South Carolina, a discrepancy that permitted the majority on the Supreme Court to slide past the difficult and important constitutional question and decide the case as if it were primarily a question of lower-court jurisdiction. The district court ruled that the president has the authority to imprison American citizens declared to be enemy combatants even when they are arrested within the United States. Padilla appealed, and the Court of Appeals for the Second Circuit then reversed the district court, granting the writ of habeas corpus after concluding that the president lacked the requisite congressional authorization for the military imprisonment of Padilla.

The Supreme Court granted Padilla's petition for a writ of certiorari and in its majority decision in *Rumsfeld v. Padilla* ordered dismissal of the habeas corpus petition without prejudice and held that the New York district court was not the proper forum to consider the petition.[32] In a brilliant dissent, Justice Stevens, joined by Justices Souter, Ginsberg, and Breyer, castigated the government for the cheap trick of secretly moving the prisoner to a different jurisdiction, and then directed the attention of the majority of justices to the primary constitutional and political significance of the case.

Executive detention of subversive citizens, like detention of enemy soldiers to keep them off the battlefield, may sometimes be justified to prevent persons from launching or becoming missiles of destruction. It may not, however, be justified by the naked interest in using unlawful procedures to extract information. Incommunicado detention for months on end is such a procedure. Whether the information so procured is more or less reliable than that acquired by more extreme forms of torture is of no consequence. For if this Nation is to remain true to the ideals symbolized by its flag, it must not wield the tools of tyrants even to resist an assault by the forces of tyranny.

Note that the four justices assumed that the purpose of imprisoning the captured was to isolate them to prevent them from posing any further security threat and that the purpose of torture was to elicit information. Despite being trapped by the assumptions in the official explanation for the Guantánamo decision, however, the minority simultaneously sounded the alarm about the threat to liberal democracy posed by indefinite detention and identified it as a form a torture. Given the near hysteria surrounding Padilla as plotting to construct and detonate a dirty bomb, that was a demonstration of political courage.

When Padilla petitioned the U.S. Supreme Court for the first writ of certiorari, his transfer from military to civilian custody was ordered by President George W. Bush. In the subsequent *Padilla v. Hanft* decision, the Supreme Court denied a second petition for a writ of certiorari and thus refused to hear the case because Padilla had received the relief he sought and the constitutional argument he made was as yet mooted as hypothetical.[33] Justice Ginsberg dissented from the decision to deny the writ, writing that the important constitutional question was left unanswered: whether the president possesses authority to imprison indefinitely a U.S. citizen who is arrested on American soil and distant from a zone of combat, based on a declaration that the citizen was an enemy combatant at the time of arrest.

The Supreme Court ruling of greatest immediate importance for the prisoners at Guantánamo decided two cases: *Rasul v. Bush* and *Al Odah v. United States.*[34] *Rasul v. Bush* began when relatives of the two Australian nationals in Guantánamo, Mamdouh Habib and David Hicks, filed petitions for writs of habeas corpus in the federal District Court for the District of Columbia. Two British nationals in Guantánamo, Shafiq Rasul and Asif Iqbal, were also named in the original filing but were released before the case reached the Supreme Court. *Al Odah v. United States* began as filings that the Supreme Court treated as petitions for writs of habeas corpus by Fawzi Khalid Abdullah Fahad al-Odah and eleven other Kuwaitis. Both of these cases were dismissed by the district court for lack of jurisdiction over aliens imprisoned outside the United States, and the decisions were affirmed by the U.S. Court of Appeals of the District of Columbia Circuit.

Here a different majority on the Supreme Court demonstrated the courage that had been lacking in *Rumsfeld v. Padilla* and reversed the lower courts' decisions. Writing for the majority, Justice Stevens, joined once again by Justices Souter, Ginsberg, and Breyer but also by Justice O'Connor, held that the district court had jurisdiction to hear cases from noncitizens held as prisoners in Guantánamo. They reasoned that if the United States is not formally sovereign over its naval base in Cuba, nonetheless it possesses "complete jurisdiction and control" under the 1903 Lease Agreement between the United States and Cuba. Thus the majority, in the best tradition of *Ex Parte Milligan*, read the absence of any distinction between the treatment of citizens and noncitizens based on geography in the Judiciary Act of 1789, together with the history of the writ in English common law, as indicating that its legislative intent was to give federal courts the authority to issue writs of habeas corpus.

Application of the habeas statute to persons detained at the base is consistent with the historical reach of the writ of habeas corpus. At common law, courts exercised habeas jurisdiction over the claims of aliens detained within sovereign territory of the realm, as well as the claims of persons detained in the so-called "exempt jurisdictions," where ordinary writs did not run, and all other dominions under the sovereign's control. . . . Later cases confirmed that the reach of the writ depended not on formal notions of territorial sovereignty, but rather on the practical question of "the exact extent and nature of the jurisdiction or dominion exercised in fact by the Crown."

In his brief concurrence, Justice Kennedy made essentially the same point by describing Guantánamo as being, from "a practical perspective," a place that "belongs to the United States." Although otherwise unremarkable, Kennedy's concurrence prompted a vociferous denunciation by Speaker of the U.S. House of Representatives Tom DeLay. "We've got Justice Kennedy writing decisions based upon international law, not the Constitution of the United States," said the Texas Republican during an April 19, 2005, interview on a conservative talk radio program. "That's just outrageous. And not only that, but he said in session that he does his own research on the Internet? That's just incredibly outrageous."[35] Bedeviled by what would ultimately prove a politically fatal ethics probe, DeLay may have been criticizing Justice Kennedy out of a desire to deflect public attention from the scandal. Misdirected outrage is what attracts the middle-aged white males who comprise the primary audience for conservative talk radio. DeLay was not trained as an attorney, but unlike the bulk of his listeners he was probably aware that international treaties to which Washington is a signatory are incorporated as part of the law of the land, and that doing research with Internet tools such as Lexis-Nexis was by then common among attorneys. Some or all of the members of DeLay's own congressional staff must have been familiar with such tools.

In an angry dissent, Justice Scalia, joined by Chief Justice Rehnquist and Justice Thomas, complained that the decision of the majority unfairly "springs a trap on the Executive, subjecting Guantánamo Bay to the oversight of the federal courts even though it has never before been thought to be within their jurisdiction—and thus making it a foolish place to have housed alien wartime detainees." His basic complaint was that the decision embarrassed the Bush administration in its attempt to exploit what it believed to be a human rights vacuum. He then argued that the ruling of the majority might extend to requiring federal courts to hear the cases of prisoners in custody in distant theaters of war where the U.S. military exercises authority, such as Afghanistan and Iraq.

The flaw in Scalia's slippery-slope contention had already been exposed during oral argument. Presenting the case for the prisoners, attorney John J. Gibbons pointed out that Guantánamo was unique in that there was no status-of-forces agreement between the United States and Cuba. Bilateral status-of-forces agreements are normally negotiated to govern the legal relationship between U.S. military bases and the host countries. For example, the agreement between the United States and Japan provides that members of the U.S. military stationed at bases in Japan are subject to prosecution in Japanese courts for violations of Japanese criminal law. The authority exercised by the U.S. military in countries with active war zones like Afghanistan and Iraq was, at least in principle, temporary rather than long term. The wars waged there might be the longest in U.S. history, but the assumption of temporariness still obtained. Guantánamo is unique in being an old U.S. military base without such an agreement, and thus there was no slope on which the federal courts might begin to slip. The obvious reason for Justice Scalia's anxiety was that the Bush administration and any similarly inclined administration in the future would be deprived of the opportunity to exploit an effectively lawless zone between the international law of war and U.S. constitutional law. After spending much of his judicial career insisting on the priorities of legal certainty and limited government over other possible values in the interpretation of the law, Scalia had denounced a decision of the majority that brought a greater degree of legal certainty to an isolated location where the raw coercive power of the executive was otherwise unconstrained by the rule of law. For the Supreme Court's most articulate conservative, however, what ultimately mattered was not adherence to abstract principles but protecting the power of other neoconservative decision makers. As was true of many other neoconservatives, his core commitments were to the authority of the state exercised to achieve conservative policies rather than to the law as such.

Although senior Bush administration officials no doubt took considerable solace from Justice Scalia's dissent in *Rasul*, nonetheless they were compelled to respond to the decision of the majority. Nine days after it was handed down, Deputy Secretary of Defense Paul Wolfowitz issued the Order Establishing Combatant Status Review Tribunal. Despite the fact that most of the prisoners captured in the war in Afghanistan already had been held at Guantánamo as enemy combatants for two and a half years, Wolfowitz's order was the first official statement that actually defined the weighty term "enemy combatant."

For purposes of the Order, the term "enemy combatant" shall mean an individual who was part of or supporting Taliban or al Qaeda forces, or associated forces that are engaged in hostilities against the United States or its coalition partners. This includes any person who has committed a belligerent act or has directly supported hostilities in aid of enemy armed forces.

This definition differs somewhat from the "individual subject to this order" in the November 13, 2001, presidential order that established the authority of the secretary of defense to establish military commissions. The earlier order referred directly only to members of al-Qaeda and not to members of the Taliban, though presumably its reference to persons who "harbored" members of al-Qaeda could include Taliban. The Wolfowitz definition is also somewhat broader, including any individual held at Guantánamo who had been captured while fighting or aiding the fight against the U.S. military or the military of an ally of the United States. By implication, this recognized the possibility that some of the prisoners might be non-Afghan Taliban and not members of al-Qaeda. That mattered because the Taliban were the national army of Afghanistan, and its members were thus reasonably entitled to recognition as prisoners of war under even restrictive readings of the Geneva Conventions. Foreign nationals who join the armed forces of another state are normally entitled to the same status in the international law of war as the nationals of that state.

That the Combatant Status Review Tribunals and Administrative Review Panels deviate from the functioning of judicial bodies operating under the rule of law is patent. Even with the best of intentions, the three commissioned officers sitting on each panel could not be entirely impartial in their decision making. Their loyalties are owed not to abstractions like truth, justice, or the law, but instead to the U.S. Constitution and to their military services. Moreover, they owe obedience to superior officers and would be exceedingly peculiar professional soldiers if they lacked interest in furthering their individual careers. Displaying too much independence on a panel could damage one's reputation among fellow officers, and such reputations are crucial to a military career. As is true of even the most rigid bureaucratic organizations, personal relationships influence professional advancement.

The rules articulated in Wolfowitz's order reduced the relative decision-making power of officers on the panels and denied prisoners the basic minimum of due process expected under the rule of law. A majority vote rather than unanimity was all that was required for decisions by the panels, and the standard for the decision making was a mere "preponderance of the evidence." The majority rule in such a tiny pool of voters reduced the incentive for any panel member to vote against the other two. So too did the weaker legal standard. In the English common law tradition, unanimity is required for jury decisions, and criminal convictions require proof "beyond a reasonable doubt." Prisoners were also denied the right to legal counsel of their own choosing, a right guaranteed not only to defendants in criminal trials in the United States but also to participants in federal and state civil administrative hearings. Rather than representation and legal advice from counsel of their own choosing, prisoners were assigned a non-lawyer military officer with an appropriate security clearance to serve as their "personal representative," something that would tend to undermine a vigorous defense and make any prisoner suspicious and reluctant to participate in his own defense.

Prisoners were allowed to testify on their own behalf, and thus, unless they took the risk of objecting, by implication to communicate their endorsement of the legitimacy of the panel proceedings. Many of the prisoners appear to have chosen to remain silent in protest for this reason. Prisoners were also allowed to call witnesses, but the panels had the authority to determine whether requests for witnesses were reasonable. While this is a normal power given to judges in any courtroom, the panel proceedings were anything but normal courtrooms. Prisoners were permitted to be present during the proceedings with the important exception that they could not be present during the introduction of classified material as evidence. The obvious result is that the prisoner would be unable to anticipate which exculpatory evidence to introduce as part of a defense case, to argue for other interpretations of the classified material, or to argue that the classified material had been obtained under conditions that undermine its credibility. These conditions might involve torture or the gray zone between legitimate interrogation and torture that the other military authorities at Guantánamo and in Washington had been so interested in exploiting. Under the rules set out in Wolfowitz's order, the panels were free to consider as evidence any reasonably available information, presumably including that extracted from the prisoner under torture either in U.S. military custody or in the custody of a foreign state, with ever fewer institutional restrictions on the use of torture. Taken together, the composition of the panels and the rules under which they operated suggest a court more like the Papal Inquisition of the Roman Catholic Church or the Star Chamber than with anything accepted as fair in the English common law tradition.

Between August 2004 and January 2005 the Combatant Status Review Tribunals conducted hearings and made decisions for all of the prisoners at Guantánamo. Of the 558 panel hearings that were conducted, 38 resulted in decisions that the prisoner in question was a "non-enemy combatant." Secretary of the Navy Gordon England explained the reasons for these decisions:

I would say what I'll call thin files. That is, the files may say that they were in al Qaeda training camp, they may say they trained with al Qaeda, but the files are thin and not enough data that you would classify them as an enemy combatant. So I would say thin data files.[36]

England offered no admission that the original decisions to ship each of these prisoners to Guantánamo were anything other than reasonable. Nor did he admit that any of the prisoners had been imprisoned for two and a half years because mistakes were made in screening prisoners in Afghanistan, where U.S. military officers and intelligence agents had been tricked by Afghan and Pakistani allies into paying for prisoners on the basis of flimsy accusations. To admit such errors might lead to the recognition that others had been made.

Determining the degree of threat to the United States or its allies posed by each individual prisoner was the responsibility of yet another body composed of three military officers: the Administrative Review Panel. Rather than making final decisions, these bodies were instead charged with making recommendations for continued detention or release to the civilian official named by the secretary of defense. These provided the legal and political cover necessary for releasing prisoners who had been selected by mistake or deception in Afghanistan as well as those who appeared so damaged psychologically by their imprisonment that they were now thought harmless. Because all of those released through this mechanism had been already determined to be enemy combatants by the Combatant Status Review Tribunals, by definition none had been imprisoned through any error of the armed forces or the Bush administration. Releasing prisoners on the basis of recommendations made by the Administrative Review Panels may have also been intended to provide a measure of insulation against criticism from the political right in the United States that the military had released prisoners who might later rejoin their comrades still in arms, by showing that each prisoner had been subjected to an additional level of scrutiny.

Under the order of November 13, 2001, and subsequent rules, the military commissions shared many of the problems that make the Combatant Status Review Tribunals and the Administrative Review Panels controversial. Each military commission is a panel of three to seven current or retired U.S. military officers, which will make its decisions unanimously in cases involving capital punishment and by majority vote in cases involving imprisonment. Retired military officers may not be susceptible to the career pressures of serving military officers, but nonetheless they are subject to the kinds of institutional loyalties that tend to undermine judicial impartiality. Although defendants may hire civilian defense counsel, they are also required to be represented by assigned military counsel, a measure likely to prevent the passing of secrets to or from the defendant but also likely to undermine his confidence in the fairness of the proceedings and thus perhaps undermine his participation in his defense. Contrary to the common law tradition, hearsay evidence is admissible. And the decisions of these military commissions are not subject to appellate review by a federal court. In the tradition of the military commission in *Ex Parte Quirin*, only the secretary of defense or the president can review the decisions.

Administrative problems also undermined the due process rights of the prisoners. Among these were delays in approving security clearances for interpreters to assist defense counsels in communicating with their clients. Well-qualified Arabic-English translators were rare. U.S. Navy Lieutenant Commander Philip Sundel, defense counsel for Yemeni defendant Ali Hamza Ahmad Sulayman al-Bahlul, who was designated as one of the first three Guantánamo prisoners to face a military tribunal, declined his service's recommendation that he employ a former Guantánamo interrogator as an interpreter.[37] Given that the defendants and their attorneys already faced disadvantages in these judicial proceedings far beyond those of ordinary criminal trials, the distrust engendered by the participation of a former interrogator as interpreter would have been an obvious obstacle to communication between attorney and client. That was perhaps the purpose for the proposal. Sundel instead requested a German scholar with experience working in Yemen, but approval of her security clearance was delayed.

British attorney Helena Kennedy described the military commissions, and the tepid reaction of the government of Prime Minister Tony Blair to the trial of British citizens and permanent residents before them, in scathing language.

The judges of these tribunals will be members of the armed forces appointed by an American politician, Paul Wolfowitz, and he will also appoint defense lawyers from a vetted military panel. The procedural rules allow for the admissibility of statements made by prisoners even if they are under physical and mental duress at the time "if the evidence would have value to a reasonable person." . . . There was not a squeak of disapproval by the British government publicly about the nature of the camps and the disregard for international law by the United States, despite there being British citizens detained in them. It was only when it was announced that two of the British men would be put on trial before the military commissions that the Prime Minister was pressed into action by a public outcry. The Attorney-General was sent to Washington to seek the return of British prisoners or if that failed to dicker over how the military commissions might be made to look as if they complied with legal standards. A promise was extracted that the death penalty would not be used against British citizens.[38]

Ironically, failing to follow through with the threat of criminal prosecution against many of the prisoners held at Guantánamo worked against American and British interests. Consider the comment of an Afghan named Abdul Salam Zaeff. Released in 2005 after more than three years of imprisonment, Zaeff demanded trials for those still being held. "I don't want these people to be released without having a fair trial, because only then will the world see that America doesn't have any evidence to justify holding them for four years."[39] His was a legitimate concern. Transcripts from important trials may serve as the master narratives in political conflicts, officially designating those who were and were not morally culpable. The moral ambiguity presented by the missing trial transcripts invites de-legitimation of authority.

On November 8, 2004, four months after the *Rasul* decision was handed down, the U.S. District Court for the District of Columbia granted, in part, the petition for a writ of habeas corpus filed by Hamdan and ordered that, unless a competent tribunal determines he is not entitled to prisoner-of-war status under the Geneva Conventions of 1949, any trial for the offenses charged must be conducted under rules like those for a court-martial in the Uniform Code of Military Justice, which permit the defendant to be present during the trial and permit the defense to have reasonable access to evidence presented by the prosecution.[40] That part of Hamdan's petition that called for release from solitary confinement and return to the normal prisoner population was mooted by the last-minute decision of the prison authorities to return him from Camp Echo to Camp Delta, a transfer that took place "late on the Friday afternoon before the oral argument held on Monday." The single most significant conclusion reached by the district court was that the relevant provisions of the Geneva Conventions were self-enforcing, that they did not require additional implementing legislation by the U.S. Congress to give them effect as domestic law.

On July 15, 2005, the U.S. Court of Appeals for the District of Columbia Circuit reversed that lower court decision, ruling that the trial of Hamdan could proceed before the military commission without the specific protections required for court-martial under the Uniform Code of Military Justice. While the three judges of the D.C. Circuit were forced to admit that the *Rasul* decision meant the federal courts possessed jurisdiction over habeas corpus petitions filed by prisoners in Guantánamo, they concluded that did not make the Geneva Conventions judicially enforceable: "That a court has jurisdiction over a claim does not mean the claim is valid." That thin sliver of *Eisentrager* was still good law as far as they were concerned.

In what is now recognized as a landmark constitutional decision on the power of the president and the enforceability of the Geneva Conventions, the Supreme Court reversed the appeals court in *Hamdan v. Rumsfeld* on June 29, 2006. Writing for a plurality that included Justices Souter, Ginsberg, and Breyer, Justice Stevens abandoned *Eisentrager* and concluded that Common Article 3 of the Geneva Conventions guarantees a minimum of protection to individuals even when they are not associated with either a signatory or nonsignatory power in an armed conflict. "The procedures adopted to try Hamdan," he wrote in unambiguous language, "violate the Geneva Conventions."[41]

Stevens identified obvious problems with the military commissions, among them that the accused and his civilian counsel were excluded from learning what evidence was presented during the closed portions of the hearings, and that both hearsay and coerced confessions could be introduced into evidence. The appeals process from military commission decisions—authority to review decisions given initially to a panel of three military officers, then to the secretary of defense and finally to the president—elicited what appears to be thinly veiled sarcasm. "We have no doubt," wrote Stevens, "that the various individuals assigned review power under Commission Order No. 1 would strive to act impartially and ensure that Hamdan receive all protections to which he is entitled. Nonetheless, these review bodies clearly lack the structural insulation from military influence. . . ."

Justice Kennedy wrote a concurrence focused on the separation-of-powers issue arising because of the conflict between the courts-martial procedures provided in the Uniform Code of Military Justice enacted by the U.S. Congress and the procedures in the military tribunals established for the Guantánamo prisoners. Justice Thomas, joined by Justice Scalia and the new conservative appointee, Justice Samuel Alito, wrote a dissent arguing that the decision to try Hamdan is entitled to deference because what constitutes military necessity is a policy judgment. Then, as in his *Hamdi* dissent, Thomas once again managed to express an idea that should shock the modern conscience. "Traditionally," writes Thomas, "retributive justice for heinous war crimes is as much a 'military necessity' as the 'demands' of 'military efficiency' touted by the plurality, and swift military retribution is precisely what Congress authorized the President to impose on the September 11 attackers in the AUMF." The problem that should occur to anyone is that this reasoning would lead the Supreme Court to defer to the president even if the White House ordered the military to conduct summary executions of prisoners.

During a press conference in Chicago nine days after the decision was handed down, President Bush was unable to hide his irritation at being questioned about his administration's defeat in the highest court, complaining that the question asked by the reporter was "loaded" and then clumsily attempting to narrow its scope in answering.[42] After stating that he was "willing to abide by the ruling of the Supreme Court," surely an unnecessary affirmation from the chief executive in the planet's oldest liberal democracy, Bush then revealed obvious uncertainty about the meaning of the *Hamdan* decision: "They didn't say we couldn't have done—made that decision, see. They were silent on whether or not Guantanamo—whether or not we should have used Guantanamo. In other words, they accepted the use of Guantanamo, the decision I made." He further exposed his failure to read the decision or recall much from his briefing about the case by arguing that the Geneva Conventions do not apply to the Guantánamo prisoners. "They don't wear uniforms and they don't represent a nation-state," he said, and, "The Geneva Conventions were set up to deal with armies of nation-states." Beyond his ignorance of the content of the decision, his response suggests that he believed the decision could be recast in the same manner that his administration had attempted to recast acts of Congress through signing statements. There was no escaping the impression that Bush was less than fully cognizant that his authority was limited by the U.S. Constitution.

On July 7, 2006, Deputy Defense Secretary Gordon England responded to the *Hamdan* decision by issuing a memo acknowledging that Common Article 3 of the Geneva Conventions was applicable.[43] The tone of the memo was grudging at best, claiming as it did that all existing procedures and policies save those involving the military commissions were already consistent with that part of the Geneva Conventions.

Congressional response to the *Hamdan* decision reflected its partisan divisions. Republican committee chairs scrambled to schedule hearings on the decision in the Senate Judiciary Committee and Senate and House Armed Services Committees to defend their president and themselves against possible political damage. Individual Senate and House Democrats held up the ruling as vindicating their criticisms of the administration's foreign policies. One of the most scathing assessments was offered by Democratic senator Patrick J. Leahy of Vermont:

For five years, the Bush-Cheney Administration has violated fundamental American values, damaged our international reputation, and delayed and weakened prosecution of the war on terror—not because of any coherent strategic view that it had, but because of its stubborn unilateralism and dangerous theory of unfettered Executive power augmented by self-serving legal reasoning. Guantánamo Bay has been such a debacle that even the President now says it should be shut down. But the damage keeps accumulating under this President. . . .

Military justice is swift and effective. Courts-martial have been used to bring some members of our own Armed Forces, who violated the law, to justice. Others are being investigated.

Meanwhile, not one of the prisoners at Guantánamo Bay, who the President has called the worst-of-the-worst, has been brought to justice. Iraq may well complete its trial of Saddam Hussein before a single Guantánamo detainee is tried. The system the Administration created was fatally flawed, and it has created perverse results.[44]

Leahy's speculation proved correct. Saddam Hussein was tried and executed before any of the Guantánamo prisoners faced trial. With the *Hamdan* judgment it was clear that the narrative supporting the administration's Guantánamo decision was unraveling. Rather than concede, however, the administration and supporters continued to repeat the three rationales—threat, intelligence, and prosecution—comprising the official explanation for the decision while they went looking for new prisoners to better play the assigned roles. In mid-2006, prisoners who had been held in CIA black sites or secret prisons in Poland, Romania, and elsewhere were transferred to the Cuban base, a move that served both to defuse criticism by human rights activists and elected officials in the European Union about the CIA's extraordinary renditions and secret prisons in the territory of EU member states and to salvage the reputations of the Bush administration officials responsible for the Guantánamo decision. Among this new group of fourteen prisoners were individuals alleged to have committed acts genuinely worthy of prosecution, such as Khalid Sheikh Mohammed, whom the press invariably described as the "September 11 mastermind." The false note in this development was that neither this nor the previous Guantánamo decision was necessary to conduct such judicial proceedings. The fourteen men in question had already been held and interrogated elsewhere for years and could have been tried in either civil courts or military commissions in the United States.

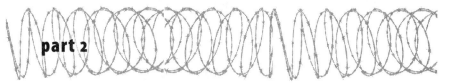

part 2

THE ALTERNATIVE EXPLANATION

7 Spectacle of Victory

Exposing the triple rationale of threat, intelligence, and prosecution as hollow raises the obvious question: What really explains the Guantánamo decision? The answer lies in the calculations of political advantage made by senior Bush administration officials and in the neoconservative ideology of many of these officials and their intellectual supporters outside the administration.

Although almost certainly unwilling to admit it publicly, some in Washington might have conceived of the Guantánamo prisoners as effective hostages, captives whose lives might be threatened to elicit restraint by the leaderships of al-Qaeda and its various regional and national affiliate groups. Threats against their lives could be made even without the intention to follow through.

That some of the prisoners were nationals of allied countries in Western Europe and the Middle East made them hostages of a different sort. Publicity about the small number of prisoners with Australian, British, Canadian, French, German, or Swedish passports could be used to highlight the multinational nature of the enemy and to prod allied governments into greater surveillance of their immigrant Muslim communities. Indeed, that may be why some of them were selected for transfer to Guantánamo. Anxiety about Muslim immigration was increasing on both sides of the Atlantic, with conservatives voicing complaints about London becoming Londonistan. Some in the Bush administration may have believed that the attention of the governments of Saudi Arabia and Yemen—two countries that were hotbeds of Salafism—might be focused on American concerns if hundreds of their citizens were in custody. Public and diplomatic interest in these and other countries about the legal status and physical treatment of fellow citizens or permanent residents held in legal limbo made prisoner release a potentially useful bargaining chip in other international negotiations. That hundreds of the Afghans and Pakistanis held at Guantánamo were released and repatriated before many of the Arabs was no accident. At best, however, these were secondary considerations.

Other motivations for the decision could also be cited. While traditional conservatives in the United States might be quietly uncomfortable with such an abrupt expansion of the power of the executive branch, they would endorse using the Cuban base as a prison camp because it provided another justification for the continued, provocative U.S. military occupation of this little corner of eastern Cuba. Although the Soviet Union no longer existed, conservatives had not lost the urge to wage a Cold War or even hot war against its former allies and clients. As a symbol of successful communist revolution and pan–Latin American nationalism, the government of Fidel Castro was a continuing irritation to American Cold Warriors. Guantánamo had been a source of friction between Havana and Washington since Castro took power. Using it once again as a location to hold a special class of prisoners served to remind Cubans and everyone else in Latin America of the reach of the United States.

Still, this is clearly a post hoc justification, a story told to assuage the sense of unease felt by many in the seemingly unfamiliar national security environment after 9/11. The primary focus of investigation in this book, however, is on the Guantánamo decision when it was made.

There are three actual reasons for the Guantánamo decision. The first is that the decision offered a timely spectacle. Rather than being compelled by the necessity to deal with especially dangerous prisoners, Americans were presented with an image of captives as evidence of quick military victory in one war so that another war could be launched. The second is that the decision satisfied the popular desire for vengeance. Rather than an invaluable opportunity for intelligence collection, it offered punishment of those who bore a passing resemblance to the al-Qaeda and Taliban leaders responsible for the September 11,

2001, terrorist attacks. The third and perhaps most complex reason is that the decision announced the intention to establish a new international order. Rather than a mechanism or venue for prosecuting war criminals, the decision offered a message that a new power relationship existed with respect to enemies, allies, and neutral states. A common thread in arguments offered in defense of the Guantánamo decision in international law and in U.S. constitutional law by neoconservatives inside and outside the administration can be detected: weakening the constraints of international law on the exercise of American military power in the world and weakening the constitutional limits on presidential power vis-à-vis the other branches of government and individual liberty. In the moral universe of neoconservatism, constructed on the work of University of Chicago political philosopher Leo Strauss, no shame attaches to the dominion that the powerful exercise over the weak. Indeed, failing to dominate is shameful because it exposes the weak to disorder. Hegemonic superpowers, with the United States as their only contemporary example, require powerful executives if they are to dominate their international environment effectively, and executives may become more powerful only at the expense of legislative and judicial decision makers and nongovernmental elites. Presidential power ought to be unrestrained, they believe, because the United States must defend and propagate the cultural values of the West. Precisely where the West begins and ends is never specified, but it is assumed crucial for preserving the intellectual legacy of the ancient eastern Mediterranean. Had it been widely known, the elaborating of foreign policy and constitutional principles from the ramblings of a mousy classics professor would have seemed peculiar or even risible to most Americans. The neoconservatives, however, were careful to downplay or even disown the source of their inspiration.

Thus the decision was made to provide a spectacle of victory, indulge the popular desire for vengeance, and announce the creation of a new international order.

What is the evidence for the spectacle, punishment, and announcement rationales? Although official secrecy and the disciplined repetition of the official explanation render their specific thought processes opaque, context and conviction offer crucial windows onto their thinking. Political decision making is a function of policy goals and of assessments of the opportunities and risks inherent in the choices presented by events. Choices are made from among possible courses of action based on whether they reach some near-term objective and are rational, at least in the narrowest sense of the concept. Policy goals are a function of political ideological indoctrination. Therefore the places to look for evidence probative of the spectacle, punishment, and announcement rationales are the domestic and international opportunities and risks of the Guantánamo decision, decisions made by the same decision makers in related contexts, decisions made by other decision makers in similar contexts, and the foreign and domestic policy goals together with the political ideology that produced them.

✳   ✳   ✳

When American and international publics have forgotten everything else from the television and newspaper coverage of Guantánamo, they are likely to recall images of the prisoners themselves. Video and still photographs of heavily shackled prisoners in prison-orange jumpsuits hobbling along or crouching behind chain link fencing and barbed wire have left enduring impressions of a defeated and captive yet dangerous enemy. Less powerful but perhaps more enduring are the map images of the location of their naval base prison on the island of Cuba. After the first flurry of reports, news coverage of the story would tend to elide the rest of Cuba, leaving the base floating almost like a separate island in the Caribbean. To the mass audiences for broadcast and print news who could not be physically present in the war zone or outside the prison camps, these images offered the spectacle of military victory at the apparent end of the war in Afghanistan.

Proving military victory to the satisfaction of domestic public opinion is one of the recurring political problems of war. Failing to do so would mean failing to justify the sacrifice of lives and wealth in waging war. Credible evidence of victory in some form is necessary when geographic distance prevents independent, firsthand confirmation. Before film and electronic news coverage, that usually required parades of prisoners of war through villages and city streets. Such demonstrations appear to be most important as propaganda for captor states when enemy soldiers are believed to be superior warriors. Following the Continental Army's stunning victory over the much feared Hessian mercenaries fighting for the British at the Battle of Trenton in 1776, the American captors marched their 1,000 Hessian prisoners through the streets of Philadelphia before sending them to detention in Virginia. With the development of film and electronic news media, the display of captive prisoners of war could be used as a propaganda device to reach larger audiences. Following the Red Army's victory over the German Wehrmacht in the encirclement of Minsk and Bobruisk in 1944, a column of 50,000 German prisoners was paraded past the Kremlin before reporters who captured the event in newspaper stories, radio broadcasts, and motion picture newsreels. Following the Viet Minh victory over the French at the Battle of Dien Bien Phu in 1954, the Vietnamese captors exploited both traditional and modern forms of prisoner parade propaganda when they marched their 7,000 prisoners five hundred miles north through the Vietnamese countryside to internment camps, and at one point past Soviet-supplied motion picture cameras. The unambiguous message in each spectacle was that a terrifying enemy had been bested in battle.

American news audiences are more familiar with a smaller-scale but equally compelling form of prisoner parade: the so-called perp walk. Criminal suspects are briefly exposed to waiting photo and television journalists either when they are first arrested or while they are being transferred in custody. "Perp," a shortening of "perpetrator," resonates with the moral condemnation, punitive efficiency, and hardened sensibilities portrayed in popular culture as hallmarks of successful criminal enforcement. Together with mug shots—official jail photographs used to record identity—the images of prisoners taken during perp walks provide the authorities with compelling evidence of success against wrongdoing even as they punish the arrested by public humiliation.

The difficulty of demonstrating victory is magnified when the defeated enemy is fierce but comparatively small in number. Displaying too few of the captured risks arousing public suspicion that the security threat has been exaggerated or that the military was incompetent. That was the problem faced repeatedly by the U.S. Army in fighting the Indian wars in the latter half of the nineteenth century. One response was to increase the numbers of captured displayed by including non-combatants among them. Following the U.S Army's victory over the Santee Sioux in the 1862 Dakota War, the Americans marched a column of 1,658 captive Santee through New Ulm, Minnesota, for internment at Fort Snelling.[1] The town had been raided during the short war, and the parade gave its residents the chance to exact a measure of cowardly revenge by menacing the cowed and bedraggled Santee captives, a majority of whom were women, children, or the elderly, with jeering and acts of petty violence. The temptation to inflate the numbers by including noncombatants was reflected in the decision to imprison all of the Chiricahua Apache rather than just Geronimo and his sixteen warriors in Florida from 1885 to 1887 and then to hold them in exile for years afterward. Larger numbers better justify the remembered insecurity and the satisfaction derived from the triumph.

Today, U.S. military personnel assigned to tours of duty at Guantánamo aptly describe it as being stationed "on Island."[2] The military base is much like an island in its physical isolation from the rest of Cuba. The decision to establish a prison there for a special category of prisoners has numerous historical precedents in the United States and abroad. That examples of infamous island prisons such as Alcatraz or Devil's Island are easily named may make island prisons seem more exceptional than they actually are. In fact, governments have frequently held special categories of prisoners in island prisons. Their use by foreign governments is detailed in appendix 2. Here, however, it is their use by the U.S. government that deserves attention.

During the American Civil War the Union imprisoned Copperheads and Confederate prisoners of war in island fortresses including Fort Lafayette, Governor's Island, and Bedloe's Island in New York Harbor, Fort Warren in Boston Harbor, Alcatraz Island in San Francisco Bay, and Johnson's Island in Lake Erie.[3] Alcatraz was later used to imprison rebel Hopis in the 1870s, Filipino prisoners of war during the 1899–1902 Philippine-American War, and American conscientious objectors during the First World War. Conscientious objectors, whether motivated by religious or political conviction, were threatening symbols of popular resistance because many Americans opposed U.S. entry into the First World War. The use of Fort Pickens on Santa Rosa Island to imprison Geronimo and his Chiricahua Apache warriors has already been discussed. Fifty prominent Filipino nationalists were exiled to Guam to suppress resistance to the American occupation of the Philippines.[4] Massachusetts used Castle Island in Boston Harbor to imprison criminal convicts in the early nineteenth century. German and Austrian enemy aliens were interned on Ellis Island in New York Harbor during the First World War, a period during which immigration effectively halted.[5] Among them was the conductor of the Boston Symphony Orchestra, Karl Muck. Although a Swiss national and thus a citizen of a neutral country, Muck was deemed insufficiently loyal because he had refused a request to play "The Star-Spangled Banner." During the Second World War and for three years thereafter, Ellis Island was again used to intern enemy aliens.[6] The Cold War began before the release of the last remaining enemy aliens from the Second World War in June 1948. Foreign nationals denounced as communists and awaiting deportation soon replaced them. North Brother Island in the East River in New York was used to isolate smallpox victims from the mid-nineteenth to the early twentieth century and as a prison for juvenile drug offenders in the 1950s and 1960s. Deer Island in Boston Harbor was used to imprison political prisoners deported during the 1919–20 Palmer Raids.[7] McNeil Island Federal Prison in Puget Sound was used to imprison conscientious objectors during the Second World War.

What made islands attractive to political decision makers as locations for prisons? The puzzle is that while building, staffing, and provisioning modern prisons on islands normally costs more than doing so on the mainland, they offer little if any additional security. The probable solution to the puzzle is that governments imprison special categories of prisoners on islands because the image of physical isolation across a body of water symbolizes captivity and exclusion from society more compellingly than isolation behind ordinary prison walls. The message communicated to citizens and enemies alike is the same: here is a demonstration of the coercive capacity of the state to protect society by simultaneously imprisoning and expelling a threatening enemy.

Guantánamo Bay Naval Base is not a prison island per se. It is a military base with a military prison on an island. For official Washington, however, it has functioned as an island prison. Decades of Cold War tension between the United States and Cuba manifested in trade sanctions, travel restrictions, and guards, barbed wire, and minefields surrounding the base, combined with its anomalous status in constitutional law, have transformed it into a supremely isolated location. Decision makers anxious to emphasize the simultaneous expulsion and isolation of specific prisoners could not hope for better imagery.

What makes some prisoners so threatening to the state that they require both expulsion and imprisonment? Typically they are neither ordinary criminals nor ordinary war captives. Instead they are more often rebels who occupy the liminal zone between crime and war. Thus in the examples offered from American history, those imprisoned were soldiers in a secessionist rebellion, rebellious aborigines and colonial nationalists, enemy aliens associated with a threatening immigrant population, ideological dissidents, pacifist rebels against war itself, incorrigible youth, and bearers of infectious disease. Some are rebels against modern society itself. Ordinary criminals and prisoners of war are absent from the list because neither their acts nor their identities are threatening to the political, social, and economic order.

Despite Rumsfeld's description of the Guantánamo prisoners as extraordinarily dangerous criminals, they could more accurately be described as representatives of the rebellious former clients who dared to attack their powerful and generous former patron. The latter-day Afghan mujahidin who had once been such effective junior partners in the Cold War had betrayed their benefactors with a perfidious surprise attack that revealed the Bush administration as less than competent to fully protect the security of the United States. The same popular outrage might have been felt if the perpetrators of 9/11 had been members of the Cuban or Hmong refugee communities. What must have made the feelings of betrayal among the neoconservatives more intense was that al-Qaeda and the Taliban were in a sense theirs, the unwanted progeny of the Reagan Doctrine. Although the Carter administration actually began giving covert military aid to the Afghan Islamists, the Reagan administration handed out weaponry in much greater quantity and sophistication as part of its policy of rolling back Soviet influence in the Third World. Ordinary Americans might ignore the connection, but the neoconservatives could not. Disloyalty was not among the many sins they could condone.

Captive al-Qaeda and Taliban could not be paraded through the streets of American cities like captured Hessians during the Revolutionary War or captured Santee during the Dakota War without causing unacceptable levels of civil disorder. The major al-Qaeda and Taliban leaders were not even in American custody. However, prisoners could be displayed for the press in a spectacle of military victory in an effective island prison as were the Chiricahua Apache, the British fascists, and the Haitian refugees. As is true of other spectacles, this too was conducted with the understanding that it was being presented for multiple audiences.[8]

For the American news audience, the execution of the Guantánamo decision was a spectacle of both righteous retribution and military victory, one that also hinted at the possibility that information extracted during interrogation might succeed in linking Baghdad to September 11, 2001. That linkage, now thoroughly discredited, was one of the pretexts developed by Washington and London for the 2003 invasion of Iraq. Almost any evidence to support it would have been greeted with jubilation by Republicans and New Labour.

Senior officials of the Bush administration must have weighed the political advantages and disadvantages in selecting from among the different possible courses of action following the September 11, 2001, attacks on the World Trade Center and the Pentagon. Once the immediate panic abated, and perhaps before that, the inner circle would have begun to assess the attendant risks and opportunities. The determination to appear decisive would have been foremost in their minds not only because that is what is expected of leaders during a crisis but also because exaggerated posturing might deflect public attention from questioning the administration's competence after it failed to prevent the attacks and from recalling the origins of al-Qaeda in the blowback from the Reagan administration's foreign policy on Afghanistan. The latter was crucial for the future of the not yet eight-month-old

Bush administration because so much of its foreign policy, rhetoric, and personnel had been drawn from the Reagan administration. The measured language, cautious policies, and moderate personnel of the administration of George H. W. Bush were conspicuous by their absence in the current administration. That the record of the Reagan presidency was one of unparalleled success is an article of faith among Republicans. Had the public fully grasped the connection between the genesis of al-Qaeda and the Taliban as blowback from the Reagan Doctrine and the presence of so many of that policy's personnel in the George W. Bush administration, Republicans might have been punished in opinion polls, lost the 2002 and 2004 congressional elections, and lost the presidency in 2004. Reelection is always on the minds of senior officials in first-term presidential administrations. Dissociation of the current administration from the consequences of actions taken by the Reagan administration was essential.

Fortunately for the Bush White House, rather than making causal connections, ordinary Americans were seized with bellicose patriotic fury. They were transfixed by horrific video images of American Airlines Flight 11 and United Airlines Flight 175 flying into and collapsing the twin towers of the World Trade Center, broadcast in agonizing repetition for days following the event. Encouraged by elected officials and popular news media in the United States, and largely supported by international sentiment outside the Middle East, American public opinion swung in favor of military action to avenge the thousands of deaths and the outraged national honor. Many Americans viewed the attacks as the most horrendous public event in their lifetimes. An overwhelming proportion of Americans believed the only proper historical analogy was to the December 7, 1941, Japanese surprise attack on Pearl Harbor,[9] a product not only of the emotional power of the televised images but also of deliberate framing by the major news sources. So intense was the emotional response that any effort to explain the origins of al-Qaeda ran the risk of being mistaken for support for the enemy.

The Authorization for Use of Military Force (AUMF), a joint resolution passed by the U.S. Congress on September 14, 2001, gave the president the legal authority to use all necessary and appropriate force against those nations, organizations, or persons he determines planned, authorized, committed, or aided the terrorist attacks that occurred on September 11, 2001, or harbored such organizations or persons, in order to prevent any future acts of international terrorism against the United States by such nations, organizations or persons.[10]

That legislative language was carefully selected by Congress to grant a narrower scope of discretionary authority than the Bush administration had sought in a proposed draft of the joint resolution that would have permitted it to "deter and pre-empt any future acts of terrorism or aggression against the United States."[11] It was hardly a secret on Capitol Hill that some in the administration had a longer wish list of targets for military action in the Middle East. Although lacking the force of law, the language that Bush used in his signing statement for the Congressional joint resolution asserted an expansive authority to use military force. Since the Reagan administration, presidents have employed signing statements as opportunities to contribute additional legislative history, or perhaps more accurately executive intent, to bills passed by Congress in a gamble that courts will give such intent weight when interpreting the meaning of a piece of legislation. The signing statement for the AUMF indicates that from the beginning the administration intended to wage war against more than the authors of the September 11, 2001, attacks.

Once senior Bush administration officials had fully, and in some cases reluctantly, accepted that primary or sole responsibility for the attacks lay with al-Qaeda rather than the government of Saddam Hussein in Iraq, the decision was made for war against Afghanistan. That did not preclude a war against Iraq, and the administration's plans for this second war were developed simultaneously and covertly. President Bush and his advisors knew that his extraordinarily high approval ratings in the aftermath of 9/11 would inevitably decline, and so too might willingness to believe that Baghdad was somehow linked to al-Qaeda or was developing weapons of mass destruction.[12]

Waging war against the Islamic Emirate of Afghanistan, the Taliban government led by Mullah Mohammed Omar, Amir al-Mu'muinin or

Commander of the Faithful, made sense because the regime had permitted al-Qaeda to operate within its territory. This permission was a consequence of the shared origins of the Taliban and al-Qaeda in the Soviet-Afghan War of 1979–89 and the decade or more of civil war that followed. *Taliban* (singular, *talib*) is the Arabic word for "students." In the context of recent political history, reference to the Taliban indicates the legions of militant young cadres who served as the ideological movement and coercive apparatus of the fundamentalist Salafi regime in Kabul before being toppled by the United States and its Afghan warlord allies in early 2002. In newly established regimes with extreme political projects, it is often true that those who enforce its dictates are also among its most fervent adherents. The Taliban, almost all ethnic Pashtuns, were recruited from the thousands of young men and boys living and studying in madrassas or religious schools located in southeastern Afghanistan and in the impoverished, lawless backcountry of Pakistan's North-West Frontier Province, the federally administered tribal areas, and Balochistan Province. Although comprising only one-fifth of the total population of Pakistan, ethnic Pashtuns and their close ethnic cousins the Balochis are majorities in their respective Pakistani provinces.[13] Nearly three-fourths of the population of the North-West Frontier Province and nearly all of the population of the federally administered tribal areas is Pashtun. The population of Balochistan is 55 percent Balochi, while another 30 percent is Pashtun.

Across the border in Afghanistan, Pashtuns comprise a plurality of the population at approximately 40 percent. The other principal nationalities in the country are the Tajiks, Uzbeks, and Hazaras, who are thought to constitute, respectively, 20, 10, and 15 percent of the population. The absence of recent national censuses means that the ethno-national composition of Afghanistan could only be approximated. Ethnic identities constructed on language are reinforced by a population distribution within Afghanistan that culturally and politically connects the various Afghan ethnic groups to the neighboring states in which their ethnic groups are dominant or powerful: Pashtuns to Pakistan, Uzbeks to Uzbekistan, Tajiks to Tajikistan, and Hazaras to Iran.

When Pashtuns from Afghanistan fled in their millions east and south into Pakistan during the ten-year Soviet-Afghan War, they were sometimes "herded" across the border by Soviet air strikes. The Soviet Union had intervened militarily in Afghanistan on December 27, 1979, to save the new government of Prime Minister Hafizullah Amin from an Islamist rebellion. Leader of the Khalq (Popular) faction of the People's Democratic Party of Afghanistan and a Pashtun like most of the members of his party faction, the mercurial Amin had taken power beginning in July 1979 by purging members of the Parcham (Flag) faction of the party from leadership positions and then in September assassinating their leader, President Nur Muhammad Taraki, an ethnic Tajik like most of the members of his party faction.[14]

The factional struggle for control of the ruling party took place at the same time that conservative opposition in the countryside was erupting in response to land reform and social reforms intended to improve the status of women. The economic dependence of tenant farmers on landlords was undermined by new legislation limiting the amount of farmland that could be owned and canceling the debts of tenants. Patriarchy was challenged by legislation making education compulsory, setting a minimum marriage age for women, and banning arranged marriages and dowries.[15] Provincial rebellion against whichever regime controlled Kabul is a recurring theme in Afghan history, so it is unsurprising that the combination of the reaction against land reform and social reform and the factional infighting in the PDPA leadership served as invitations to rebellion. Although intervention by the Red Army helped the Soviet Union's client regime survive that rebellion in the near term and brought internal order to the PDPA, over the long term it alienated much of the population. Where Afghan patriotism was weak in Afghanistan, Pashtun national cohesion was strong. Pashtun identity is woven largely from stories of feuding between clans and resistance to foreign invasions. Among the Afghans most alienated by the intervention of the Red Army were the hundreds of thousands of ethnic Pashtuns who had fled to Pakistan.

Refugee youth are always ripe for recruitment to militant causes. Their insecurity and alienation give them little to lose and much to gain by joining extremist causes, and in Pakistan the recruiters were waiting in the madrassas. Staffed by preachers affiliated with the Deobandi movement, the South Asian counterpart to the Salafiyya movement of the Arab countries, funded by monies raised from among the faithful by Salafiyya clergy and influential laity in Saudi Arabia and the neighboring Gulf states, and protected by Pakistan's Inter-Service Intelligence or ISI, the country's virtually autonomous secret police organization, the madrassas were the venues for first indoctrinating and then recruiting an army of angry young fanatics. The result was a militant movement fired by unquestioned belief that marched from victory to victory in Afghanistan.

Prominent among the wealthy and well-connected Saudis who supported the religious militants was multimillionaire construction heir and militant anticommunist Osama bin Laden.[16] Whether the man who would become the world's most wanted fugitive was recruited or trained for his role as an anti-Soviet guerrilla leader by the American CIA is disputed, but it is far from improbable. In any event, the then unknown and now infamous Osama bin Laden played a major role in organizing the Maktab al-Khidimat, the Afghan Services Bureau, which purchased arms and recruited guerrillas from outside Southwest Asia. Perhaps as many as one hundred thousand young men from across the Middle East, North Africa, Central Asia, Southeast Asia, and the growing Muslim communities of Western Europe and North America received military training either in guerrilla camps in Pakistan or later in Afghanistan. Most of the recruits would see only limited military action in Afghanistan, but they returned to their countries as highly politicized jihadis. More significant than their immediate contribution to combating the Red Army in Afghanistan, these veterans returned to their home countries ready to continue the Islamist struggle either there or anywhere else where Muslims might do battle with non-Muslims. An armed religious pan-nationalism had emerged to challenge the weaker, sometimes secular and sometimes tepidly Islamic nationalisms across the Middle East. As many as twenty thousand veterans returned to Saudi Arabia, where their status as fighters in a holy cause gave them political influence among that country's new middle classes. Thousands more returned to Egypt to provide cadres for the broad

Islamist movement in that country's teeming urban slums and impoverished villages. One thousand may have returned to Algeria to fight in the Front Islamique du Salut (Islamic Salvation Front) or FIS and in the Group Islamique Armé (Armed Islamic Group) or GIA. In each of these countries, religious radicals would challenge largely secular regimes using both the gun and the ballot.

The extraordinary blowback—the long-term political consequences of encouraging an Islamist insurgency as an ideological and military counter to the influence of the Soviet Union in the 1980s—was foreseeable.[17] Social scientists have long known that military veterans are an easily mobilized, often radical political constituency. Indoctrination in military discipline, pleasurable memories of comradeship and perhaps guilty memories of the intense excitement of the violence of combat, resentment of the comfort and safety of civilian life, and desire for recognition and material benefits rewarding their military service—all tend to make them vulnerable to recruitment into authoritarian political movements. Restless and dissatisfied First World War veterans were recruited into the paramilitary corps that helped to bring fascist movements to power in Italy and Germany in the interwar period. Although the "Islamofascist" label promoted by some conservative pundits seemed an all too obvious effort at name-calling, the Islamist veterans of Afghanistan scattered across the Middle East in the beginning of the twenty-first century nonetheless resembled sociologically their fascist counterparts in Europe and elsewhere in the mid-twentieth century. Both populations were composed of angry young men determined to find meaning in their own lives by violently imposing their often newly acquired authoritarian beliefs on others.

Tellingly, the master narrative imposed on the events of September 11, 2001, contains only the briefest of references to blowback. The *9/11 Commission Report* notes that the United States played a role in helping to create al-Qaeda,[18] yet fails to describe the attacks as wounds that were self-inflicted, if indirectly. Nor has Washington made much progress in admitting that what appeared such brilliant strategy at the time has come back to haunt those who unleashed the menace.

There are two reasons why the bipartisan political leaders on the 9/11 Commission obeyed what was for all intents and purposes a taboo against discussion of the important role of the U.S. government in the birth of al-Qaeda. The first is that the presentation of the United States as blameless victim in the aftermath of September 11, 2001, would have been undermined by a detailed admission of Washington's role in creating the monster that attacked it. Admitting even indirect responsibility for creating al-Qaeda reduces the scope for the expression of rhetoric of patriotic renewal through redemptive, purifying violence like that following the 1898 sinking of the USS *Maine* or the 1941 attack on Pearl Harbor. Historical facts can be an obstacle to telling an emotionally persuasive story. The second reason is that the Bush administration had resurrected the language of the Reagan administration to explain its foreign policy. Consider this passage from President Reagan's declaration of March 10, 1982, as Afghanistan Day:

The Afghan people have paid a terrible price in their fight for freedom . . . Every country and every people has a stake in the Afghan resistance, for the freedom fighters of Afghanistan are defending principles of independence and freedom that form the basis of global security and stability.[19]

Then compare it with a statement by President George W. Bush in 2002:

We've seen in Afghanistan that the road to freedom can be hard; it's a hard struggle. We've also seen in Afghanistan that the road to freedom is the only one worth traveling. Any nation that sacrifices to build a future of liberty will have the respect, the support, and the friendship of the United States of America.[20]

What connects the foreign policy rhetoric of the two presidents is exploitation of the theme of heroic international struggle, which the United States assumes responsibility to support, and repetition of the word "freedom." The latter became such a cliché during the Bush administration that comics joined political commentators in offering informal word counts following each of the president's speeches. Deploying rhetoric from the Reagan years offered the Bush administration a way to rally support from part of the public. The presence of many high-ranking former Reagan appointees and the instinctive partisan defense of a previous Republican administration would account for the willingness of the Bush White House to use similar rhetoric to justify its foreign policy. Particularly remarkable is the rhetoric's plasticity. The same evocations of values used to justify arming Islamists during the Reagan administration could be used to justify driving Islamists from power during the Bush administration two decades later.

The blowback from the Reagan administration's determination to use the Islamists in the proxy war with the Soviet Union had another, less obvious cost. Not only did it sow the seeds of what would grow into a truly global terrorist network, but it once again tied Washington to Islamabad and its insurmountable political, economic, and social problems. In the two and a half years that separated the July 5, 1977, military coup that brought General Zia ul-Haq to power and the December 17, 1979, invasion of Afghanistan by the Red Army, the relationship between the United States and Pakistan had become progressively chillier. Every decision by the very pious General Zia seemed to alienate the comparably pious President Jimmy Carter. After declaring martial law, General Zia launched a Sunni Islamist culture war, introducing puritanical censorship of print and electronic media, decreeing a variety of medieval punishments for ordinary and moral crime, establishing a federal Sharia court, and on April 4, 1979, executing the elected civilian prime minister that he had overthrown: Zulfikar Ali Bhutto.[21] The Carter administration responded by publicly criticizing the Pakistani human rights record and its nuclear weapons program. The overthrow of Shah Muhammad Reza Pahlavi of Iran in 1979 by a Shi'a Islamist movement deprived the United States of its most important Islamic client state in the Middle East and Southwest Asia, and also strengthened the bargaining position of General Zia in negotiating any renewal of the old patron state–client state relationship between Islamabad and Washington. Whether the ruthless Islamist strongman in Army House actually believed that his prayers had been answered is unknown, but Zia must have been delighted when Carter lost his bid for reelection. In this the general was surely joined by the leaders of other military governments who had felt the sting of criticism by Washington for their human rights records.

With the election of Ronald Reagan in 1980, all of Islamabad's unconfessed sins were forgiven. In return for serving as the cross-border safe haven for the Islamist insurgency inside Afghanistan, Pakistan received a five-year $3.2 billion aid package, permission to buy the latest model F-16 fighters available to foreign states, control over distribution of the river of weapons and money flowing from the United States, Saudi Arabia, and other Gulf states to the insurgent groups in Afghanistan, and the shelving of sanctions for human rights violations and nuclear proliferation.[22]

The renewed Pakistani-American alliance meant that Washington would pull its punches whenever questions were raised about violations of human rights in Pakistan, support for terrorism in the Indian-controlled half of Kashmir, and nuclear weapons proliferation in South Asia. No doubt that was possible because American journalists and decision makers were not much interested in the people most likely to be adversely affected. They were numerous, often poor, Muslim or Sikh or Hindu, and lacked strong ethnic lobbies in Washington. They could not even claim to be victims of communist aggression. If they fell victim to torture, terror, or nuclear bombardment, that would be unfortunate, but their lives clearly mattered less than whatever contribution that risk would make to the geopolitical struggle between Washington and Moscow.

In the three decades since their simultaneous independence in 1949, Pakistan and India had already gone to war three times. Once both had constructed and deployed nuclear weapons, the proximity, and thus vulnerability, of every major city in Pakistan and northern India meant that millions of noncombatants might die in the event of war. However, what mattered to the officials of the Reagan administration in 1980 was not the possibility of some future strategic nuclear exchange killing millions of relatively impoverished nonwhites but the chance to bleed the Red Army, to weaken the Soviet Union in Afghanistan as the United States had been weakened by the war in Vietnam. Afghanistan would cost the Soviets 15,000 dead, or less than one-third of the number of Americans who died in Vietnam, but the social and political effects of the war for the Soviet Union were as just as profound as Vietnam had been for the United States. The price for weakening the Soviet Union and saving the people of Afghanistan from land reform and female liberation is estimated at 1.3 million dead and another 5 million made refugees. Washington's interest in Afghanistan and Pakistan quickly waned after the Soviet military withdrawal in 1989, but across the Middle East the Islamists were intoxicated by what they interpreted to be their triumph against the atheist superpower.

To the surprise of many observers, the Democratic Republic of Afghanistan in Kabul did not collapse immediately after the Soviet military withdrawal. Instead, President Muhammad Najibullah and his predominantly ethnic Pashtun comrades in the People's Democratic Party of Afghanistan continued fighting against the inevitable for another three years. In the last obscene political victory of the Reagan administration's Cold War, on September 27, 1996, former president Najibullah, who had taken refuge in the United Nations compound in Kabul after been deposed in 1992, was seized by the Taliban, beaten, castrated, and then shot to death. His body hung from a goalpost at the soccer stadium in Kabul.

The Islamist insurgency in Afghanistan was never unified as a political movement or even under a single military command, a reflection of the country's ethno-national diversity and the movement's multiple state sponsors. As victory over Najibullah's government became more certain, the movement fragmented even further. When victory finally came, Afghanistan became an instant failed state. Warlords ruled provinces or regions, governing by levying punitive taxes and taking a percentage of the profits from opium growing and smuggling. The best historical parallel to Afghanistan between 1989 and 1992 is China in the 1920s and 1930s, two decades of fragmentation when warlords also ruled by levying punitive taxes and taking a percentage of the profits from opium growing and smuggling. Government authority in Afghanistan descended to its nadir when warlords divided Kabul with forty-two checkpoints where their thugs extracted bribes or simply robbed and raped their victims at gunpoint.[23]

During the interregnum, Osama bin Laden and his foreign followers in the Afghan Bureau continued to support favored Afghan Islamist militias with money, weapons, and fresh foreign jihadis. Even before Kabul fell to the Islamist militias in 1992, however, they were conceiving a new struggle against different enemies, principally their former ally: Washington. Osama bin Laden and his lieutenants, guerrillas, and financial supporters explained their new war as motivated by religiously inspired outrage at the presence of U.S. military bases in territory sacred to Muslims and at U.S. political and military support for Israel, an explanation widely accepted across the Muslim world. Sounding both medieval and modern, bin Laden styled his new struggle after the Soviet-Afghan War as an Islamic jihad against "Crusaders and Zionists."

The grievances that al-Qaeda's leaders sought to alleviate had a basis in fact. Beginning with the Reagan administration, the United States established a series of permanent military bases in Saudi Arabia and elsewhere around the Persian Gulf. Mecca and Medina in Saudi Arabia are the two holiest cities in Sunni Islam, while Jerusalem is the third. The presence of armed unbelievers either in proximity to holy sites, as in the case of the U.S. military bases in Saudi Arabia (though they were hundreds of miles from Mecca and Medina), or in actual control of holy sites, as with the Israelis in Jerusalem, carried the threat of desecration. Their presence in Saudi Arabia was also a standing affront to the assumption that lands under Islamic rule should remain forever under Islamic rule, an idea captured in the distinction between the Dar al-Islam or "land of submission" and the Dar al-Harb or "land of war." Where the former is conceived as a territorial realm of peace and moral order only realizable under an Islamic government, the latter is conceived as a territorial realm of conflict and moral disorder awaiting eventual transformation through conquest and conversion. The occupation of Muslim lands by non-Muslim armies thus threatens the continuity of Saudi Arabia as the territorial core of the Islamic world.

While U.S. military bases in Saudi Arabia and U.S. support for Israel no doubt outrage many Muslims, something less tangible may also motivate the antipathy. Modern religious fundamentalism everywhere draws strength from anxieties produced by social change to mobilize mass support in the name of restoring the real or more probably imagined moral certainties of the past. Specific theological content appears to be irrelevant. Islamic, Christian, Jewish, and Hindu fundamentalisms are all driven by the same desire for moral certainty in an uncertain world.

The United States and Western Europe represent forms of modernity that many people living in Islamic countries find simultaneously highly attractive and morally repugnant. Modernity necessitates both continuous adaptation to social and economic change and sufficient individual liberty to adapt to change successfully. If the economic prosperity, technological prowess, and military might of the liberal democracies are attractive features, the seeming moral chaos of their secular institutions dismays many in other societies.

For many Islamists, the United States represents more than just the most recent non-Muslim imperial power to dominate the region and station military forces on the Arabian peninsula, although it is surely that as well. For decades the United States was the non-Muslim society most likely to seduce Muslims into abandoning the familiar security of unexamined religious belief and practice. The portrayals of wealth, sexual promiscuity, and violence without consequence that comprise so much of America's cultural exports inevitably and simultaneously offended and tempted the pious in poorer societies. Yet behind the curtain of crass mass culture they could also see a relatively open and inclusive society, notwithstanding its recent angry xenophobia, with the largest national economy on the planet, governed by the oldest liberal democracy, and capable of projecting military force anywhere because its military budget almost equals the combined military spending of all other countries. Success like that is attractive. If no U.S. military units were stationed in Arab countries and if there were no U.S. support for Israel, Islamists still might perceive the United States as a threatening alternative model to the kind of social order they seek to establish. That the United States has military bases in Saudi Arabia and offers virtually unqualified political and military support to Israel simply makes the distress of that recognition unavoidable and acute.

Irregular forces created by foreign powers to solve problems often develop into problems in their own right. Historical examples are common. The *illaloes*, a paramilitary force originally recruited by the British to patrol the border between Ethiopia and Somalia in the 1940s, became *shifta* or bandits in the 1960s. The Abu Sayyaf Group, which became an al-Qaeda affiliate, was reportedly one of several "intelligence projects" of the Philippine military that were recruited to combat terrorism but themselves turned to terrorism and crime.[24]

The transformation of Al-Qaeda, however, represented something far more dangerous for its creators than the criminalization of irregular forces. In 1992 the foreign, largely Arab, Islamist leadership in Afghanistan who would organize al-Qaeda would have understood that the looming military and political victory presented them with the sort of crisis that faces every organization when it actually completes the organizational mission: what to do then with the organization. The British Royal Air Force (RAF) and the March of Dimes offer classic cases in which organizational leaderships responded successfully to the crises caused by unambiguous success. They merit examination because the former was a combat organization and the latter a fundraising organization. Al-Qaeda is both.

With the end of the First World War, a number of British politicians argued that maintaining the RAF as an independent military service would no longer be necessary because another major war in Europe was at least a decade in the future and maintaining a third military service would intensify interservice rivalry. Saving the RAF required deft political maneuvering by its supporters, and a plausible argument. The winning argument was that in a period when Britain desperately needed to reduce expenditures, the RAF squadrons could help to garrison the empire less expensively than stationing traditional British colonial army units.[25] Over the next three years, the RAF was deployed against colonial rebels in Afghanistan, Somalia, and Mesopotamia. (That all three countries would become home to al-Qaeda or its affiliates in the twenty-first century may be nothing more than coincidence, but the tragic irony is plain.) The RAF's new mission was a successful temporary patch until the next interstate war. Until then garrisoning the empire from the air was a mission that could last for decades. The Second World War forced the technical development of different forms of aerial warfare, something that guaranteed that the RAF would have no shortage of military missions to fulfill in the postwar period.

When confronted in 1955 with the ineluctable fact that Jonas Salk's polio vaccine was accepted as effective and safe, the professional staff of the National Foundation for Infantile Paralysis, an organization considerably less well known than its March of Dimes fund-raising campaign, decided to change its mission from combating polio to preventing birth defects.[26] Launched in 1938, the March of Dimes was simply too effective as a fund-raising brand name to abandon. Unlike polio, birth defects have the virtue of being a collection of maladies, which could not be stopped with the discovery of a magic bullet. Where polio had but one cause, birth defects have multiple causes and thus multiple public health and medical treatment responses. The mission transplant proved successful, and the charity survived to raise money for a worthy cause to this day.

RAF and March of Dimes leaders responded to their respective crises of victory by articulating new missions, which were sufficiently similar to their previous missions that they could plausibly claim special expertise, yet were also rather more open-ended. Here were new raisons d'être that might keep the organizations and their personnel in business for the long haul.

Rather than disband the apparatus in the face of success, Osama bin Laden and his fellow Islamist guerrillas reorganized themselves as al-Qaeda or "the Base" and articulated their institutional mission as defeating the enemies of Islam: the United States, its allies, especially Israel, and its client states across the Muslim world. Their hatred for the United States was certainly no less intense than their hatred for the Soviet Union, just as the determination of the March of Dimes leadership to battle birth defects was no less steadfast than their determination to defeat polio. Given all the effort that had gone into building such an effective organization, it was too good to disband, and there was important work yet to do. That al-Qaeda emerged primarily as a response to the organizational crisis brought on by completing the original mission lacks the kind of drama normally desired by participants who perceive themselves to be involved in a great struggle. But what is true is no less so for being prosaic.

When the anti-Soviet Islamist guerrilla armies of the warlords proved unable to establish public order and security in Afghanistan in the period between 1992 and 1996, the Taliban launched a war to displace or absorb them. Never united during their long guerrilla war against the Soviets and their Afghan allies, the warlords fell out over the limited spoils of victory. The economy and infrastructure of Afghanistan were in ruins, but there was money to be made from the opium trade. Osama bin Laden and al-Qaeda were invited back to Afghanistan by Taliban leader Mullah Mohammed Omar to help the movement consolidate political power. The al-Qaeda leadership needed a new home base after being expelled by the Islamist government of Sudan, and Afghanistan was familiar. Al-Qaeda offered the Taliban not only the foreign jihadis who lent an appearance of support from around the Muslim world, but also much needed money to buy weapons, food, and Afghan allies.

So close was the resulting relationship between the Taliban and al-Qaeda that distinguishing the national government from the international organization was difficult. Although history is replete with examples of new revolutionary regimes giving support to expatriate revolutionary organizations, the relationship in Afghanistan was so close that the Taliban seemed an al-Qaeda affiliate. Individuals appear to have moved fluidly between the two entities, because religion meant more than nationality to their leaders. This extended even to family relations: Osama bin Laden married one of Mullah Mohammed Omar's nieces.

Obsessive concerns with religious purity and political secrecy isolated the leaders of both from information and opinion outside the narrow realm of Sunni Islam, distorting their perceptions of events and preventing them from making anything like objectively rational calculations about the consequences of their actions. To find an adequate parallel for the isolation from the international community and resulting miscalculation one would have to look to the 1975–79 Khmer Rouge regime in Cambodia. However unevenly, the writ of the Taliban regime ran across most of Afghanistan. Subsequent descriptions of the country as a failed state comparable to contemporaneous Somalia appear to be patent post hoc efforts to justify the denial of prisoner-of-war status under the Geneva Conventions to the captured.

If the Taliban government of Afghanistan and its al-Qaeda guests were largely irrelevant to the Bush administration prior to September 11, 2001, they were profound embarrassments afterward. As blowback from the Reagan administration's foreign policy of supporting Islamist guerrillas during the 1979–89 Soviet-Afghan War, the Taliban and al-Qaeda were ugly reminders that the foreign policy "successes" of the Reagan administration planted the seeds of future problems. Moreover, the Taliban and al-Qaeda were obstacles to achieving the administration's other foreign policy goals. They needed to be defeated and defeated quickly, so that the administration could focus on replacing the Baathist regime of Saddam Hussein in Iraq with a U.S. client regime while American public opinion was still bellicose.

The 2001–2 war in Afghanistan appeared to most observers to be both brief and successful, and that assessment survived largely unchallenged until the resurgence of the Taliban in southern and eastern Afghanistan in early 2006. When the United States sought to make use of Pakistan once again in late 2001, this time as a staging area for its invasion of Afghanistan, the relationship between the two governments was strikingly similar to what it had been in 1980. Pakistan was by then ruled by yet another military strongman, General Pervez Musharraf, who had seized control in a coup from an elected civilian government two years previously. Repeating the historical cycle begun by Carter and Zia, the next Democratic president, Bill Clinton, first subjected Islamabad to public criticism for its human rights abuses and nuclear weapons program. The administration banned all U.S. arms sales to Pakistan after the latter's first nuclear weapons test in 1998. Relations between Washington and Islamabad grew so chilly that when Clinton traveled to South Asia in March 2000, he spent five days in India and a mere five hours in Pakistan. Then, just as after the 1979 Soviet invasion of Afghanistan, following 9/11 all of the Pakistani government's sins were forgiven by a brand-new Republican administration. No doubt aware the Bush administration was hurrying to punish the Taliban in response to perceptions that it had been caught napping on September 11, 2001, and perhaps also aware that it was intent on launching a war against Saddam Hussein's Iraq, General Musharraf followed the example of Zia in extracting as much as possible from the United States as a quid pro quo for cooperation in the American plan for Afghanistan. Although Musharraf failed to win cancellation of all of Pakistan's international debt, he did receive a five-year, $3 billion aid package, permission to buy the much-sought-after latest model of the F-16 fighters available to foreign states, and the designation of Pakistan as a Major Non-NATO Ally or MNNA under U.S. law. That prized status meant that Pakistan joined a short list of countries like Australia, Egypt, Israel, New Zealand, the Philippines, South Korea, and Thailand, which have preferential access to U.S. weapons and other military assistance.

Successful, brief, and bloodless, or so it appeared to the American news audiences for broadcast and print news, the war in Afghanistan seemed a model post-Vietnam use of armed force by the United States. Operation Enduring Freedom, the heroic-sounding appellation adopted to replace the equally heroic-sounding but religiously incorrect Operation Infinite Justice, drove the Taliban from power in four months of fighting from October 2001 to February 2002. Small units of the U.S. Army Special Forces and CIA together with Britain's Special Air Service coordinated ground assaults by the ethnic Uzbek and Tajik warlord militias of the Northern Alliance with air strikes by the U.S. Air Force, U.S. Navy, and RAF.

The fall of Kabul on November 13, 2001, signaled defeat for the Taliban, but two subsequent battles in 2001 were of note. The first was the battle to recapture Qala-i-Jangi, a desperate and losing revolt by captured Taliban and al-Qaeda prisoners. The second was the Tora Bora Breakout, a successful fighting retreat across the border to safety in Pakistan by Taliban and al-Qaeda leaders.

On November 25, between 500 and 700 recently captured Taliban and al-Qaeda prisoners revolted and seized control of their ancient mud-walled Qala-i-Jangi fortress prison near Mazar-i-Sharif, close to the border with Uzbekistan. Most were killed in three days of fighting that included air strikes. Among the surviving recaptured prisoners was a twenty-year-old U.S. national named John Walker Lindh, a Muslim convert who had taken the name Suleyman al-Faris. Although Lindh would never be transferred to Guantánamo Bay, his capture and trial would be successfully exploited for propaganda purposes in the United States in a manner that speaks to the utility of military captives for their captors.

Between September 11, 2001, and the capture of Iraqi president Saddam Hussein on December 13, 2003, no individual prisoner attracted more public interest in the United States than the "American Taliban," as Lindh was soon tagged by the press. Lindh was one of only two U.S. nationals known to have been captured in the war in Afghanistan while fighting with the enemy, but that doesn't account for his celebrity.[27] The other American was Yaser Hamdi, a Saudi-American who received far less attention from the press because he appeared far less "American" than Lindh. The soon infamous American Taliban was a former Roman Catholic from an affluent California family who had converted to Islam at the tender age of sixteen and then spent years living in Yemen and Pakistan before journeying to Afghanistan in 2001.

While in Yemen, Lindh reportedly studied at two Salafi institutions: the Dar al-Hadith madrassa and Iman University. Dar al-Hadith was established by the Yemeni Salafi cleric Sheikh Muqbil bin Hadi al-Wadi'i. Deported to Yemen from Saudi Arabia for extremism, al-Wadi'i neither publicly endorsed violence nor denied his connections to al-Qaeda. Iman University was established by Sheikh Abdulmajeed al-Zindani, another Yemeni Salafi cleric, and one who had been named by the U.S. government in 2004 as a Specially Designated Global Terrorist, as close to a shoot-on-sight order as can be imagined.

Following Lindh's capture, conservative news commentators in the United States sneered that his conversion to fundamentalist Islam and his willingness to join the Taliban were only what could be expected after an upbringing in the supposed moral vacuum of affluent, ideologically liberal Marin County, California. Their strident "culture war" criticism of the Lindh family, and of Lindh's father for his willingness to defend his son, directed public attention away from the disturbing details of Lindh's mistreatment after capture. Patriarchal authority might be deemed a conservative "family value," but standing by a family member in the face of fierce public criticism was not. Nor did their condemnation extend to comparisons between the younger Lindh's willingness to take up the gun for his Islamist convictions and the kind of evangelical Christianity that motivated Eric Rudolph to conduct terrorist bombings in the United States. Drawing such a parallel would not serve the interests of an ideological movement that depended so heavily for its success at the polls on an evangelical Christian voting bloc.

Lindh was one of hundreds of recently captured Taliban and al-Qaeda fighters herded into Qala-i-Jangi fortress near Mazar-i-Sharif by the Uzbek militiamen of warlord general Abdul Rashid Dostum. Lindh was fortunate that he was not one of the hundreds of Taliban fighters captured at the same time and forced into sealed containers for the nightmarish ride to Sheberghan prison. Many died of untreated battlefield wounds, wounds suffered when guards fired into the sealed containers, dehydration, and asphyxiation.

Lindh survived the battle for control of Qala-i-Jangi, was taken into custody by the U.S. Marine Corps after days in hiding, and was then imprisoned aboard the USS *Peleliu*,[28] where he signed a confession under conditions that undermined his subsequent criminal prosecution in the U.S. federal district court. Physically weakened by his wounds, hypothermia, hunger, and sleeplessness, humiliated by being strapped naked to a stretcher and exhibited as a prize to the press, Lindh was denied the opportunity to speak to his attorney and told that he would be denied medical treatment for his wounds unless he signed the confession. He signed. Convicted and sentenced to twenty years' imprisonment for serving in the Taliban and carrying weapons, he was not punished for the other charges in the grand jury indictment relating to terrorism because his confession was made under duress.

On November 30, 2001, two days after the suppression of the prison revolt at Qala-i-Jangi, air strikes announced the beginning of the three-week-long assault on the Tora Bora mountain redoubt of the remaining Taliban and al-Qaeda. Located south of Kabul and very close to the rugged border with Pakistan, the complex of two hundred caves or cave entrances at Tora Bora had been fortified during the Soviet-Afghan War and later expanded under al-Qaeda direction. The air attack was followed by ground assaults by three Afghan militias commanded by three competing warlords. During the sporadic cave-by-cave combat, the loose perimeter established by the three militia armies allowed more than 1,000 al-Qaeda fighters, many with their dependents, to slip across the border to safety in Pakistan. A wounded al-Qaeda sympathizer interviewed by reporter Philip Smucker at the battle claimed that approximately 250 Yemenis, 180 Algerians, between 350 and 400 Chechens, and an unknown number of Saudis and Egyptians were among the al-Qaeda fighters in Tora Bora as late as December 11.[29]

Lying in wait across the border in Pakistan, at least in principle, were units of the Pakistani Army. Despite their familiarity with the terrain, the Pakistani units captured only about 300 Taliban soldiers and al-Qaeda fighters, who were then transferred to the custody of the United States and transported first to Bagram Air Base and from there to Guantánamo.[30] In his 2006 autobiography, Pakistani dictator Musharraf described the military operation as a smashing success, but stated that the number of captured was 240 and described them only as "al-Qaeda operatives."[31]

Those captured turned out to be mostly small fry, numerous enough to permit the Pentagon to claim a military victory that otherwise was clearly rather hollow. The majority of the Taliban and al-Qaeda at Tora Bora escaped across the border by evading Afghan militia and Pakistani Army patrols, bribing Afghan militia leaders and Pakistani officials to look the other way, or simply being allowed to enter by sympathizers among officers of the Pakistani Army and ISI. Given the close ties between the Pakistani government and their Taliban clients prior to September 11, 2001, such complicity was almost predictable. The Pakistanis viewed Taliban-controlled Afghanistan as providing strategic depth in the event of a total war against much larger India. Pakistan was believed less vulnerable because Afghanistan offered territory into which the Pakistani Army might retreat in the event of a successful Indian invasion as well as potential manpower in any protracted war fought along the Indo-Pakistani border. The Pakistani ISI also used al-Qaeda camps in Afghanistan for training the Kashmiri Muslim separatists that it armed and financed.

Among those who escaped across the border into Pakistan during the Tora Bora breakout were the most important prizes for the U.S. military: Osama bin Laden and Mullah Mohammed Omar.[32] Whether Osama bin Laden had in fact escaped during the battle emerged as a point of contention during the 2004 U.S. presidential campaign. Both President Bush and Vice President Cheney insisted that the U.S. government did not know whether the al-Qaeda leader had escaped from Tora Bora and dismissed the charge made by Massachusetts senator and Democratic Party presidential nominee John Kerry that the U.S. military could have captured him then.[33] The Democratic challenger blasted the incumbent president for having "outsourced" the task of capturing the al-Qaeda leader to tribal warlords, rhetoric combining a straightforward attack on Secretary of Defense Donald Rumsfeld's military reforms at the Pentagon and a thinly veiled reference to the Bush administration's international trade policy.

Ironically, one of the few important pieces of military intelligence to emerge from the interrogations conducted at Guantánamo Bay shows that Kerry was correct and Bush and Cheney either lied outright or were badly misinformed by their military commanders. The provenance of the intelligence supports the conclusion that it was Bush and Cheney who lied. The information that Osama bin Laden escaped from Tora Bora appeared in a document originally submitted by the military during a hearing to determine the factual status of a prisoner being held at Guantánamo and was then revealed through a Freedom of Information Act request by Associated Press reporter Robert Burns.[34]

Given the political context of early 2002, one of the principal reasons for making the Guantánamo decision becomes clear: senior Bush administration officials needed compelling evidence of a military victory in Afghanistan to show to the American people, and they needed it immediately. Described as veritable terrorist supermen, several hundred of the ordinary soldiers taken prisoner in Afghanistan were hauled to Guantánamo to serve as substitutes for the senior leaders of the Taliban and al-Qaeda that officials had wanted to capture and parade before the cameras. Moreover, they were made to serve as substitutes because the senior officials of the administration were intent upon waging a different, and in their estimation much more important, war against Iraq. Displaying the prisoners and the subsequent political furor surrounding military tribunals diverted attention from the difficult task of winning the peace in Afghanistan, something that the administration would fail to accomplish before the end of its second term in office.

Why was so much of the American public willing to accept a spectacle of victory as a substitute for the real thing? The answer may lie in the second Bush administration's medicalization of the response to the collective trauma of September 11, 2001. According to Columbia University anthropologist Karen M. Seeley, the government sought to manipulate the public mood by urging Americans to focus on their emotions and seek therapy rather than to analyze the government's motives or version of events. The result was a willingness to believe those in authority and the concomitant willingness to obey without challenge.[35] Thus the acceptance of evidence of military victory in the form of emotionally charged video and print images rather than sober assessments by reputable figures outside the administration.

8 Punishment

Human rights activists have long claimed that U.S. military and intelligence agencies practice torture and, more often, teach and supervise the practice of torture by the military and intelligence services of U.S. client states. Such claims received little news coverage in the United States, in all probability because the idea that their government both practiced and taught torture was too morally repellant for a majority of American journalists or ordinary Americans to credit. The operating assumption was that respect for the rule of law and the rights of individuals guaranteed that the United States behaved differently from the sorts of authoritarian states that practiced torture. Among the minority of Americans who suspected their government of complicity in torture, the practice might still be dismissed as rare and perhaps justifiable, or wearily accepted as one more moral outrage among many. Even after the revelations of what mainstream U.S. news media euphemistically termed "prisoner abuse" during the Abu Ghraib prison scandal, most Americans could continue to conceive of torture as rare or necessary. Many concluded that Abu Ghraib's horrors were an aberration—the work of rogue figures in the enlisted ranks—rather than evidence of a larger phenomenon.

Even after September 11, 2001, a majority of Americans still found the idea that their government systematically practiced torture unacceptable, but a disturbingly large minority were willing to believe and endorse it as necessary under some circumstances. The findings from a cross-national public opinion poll conducted in May–June 2006 in twenty-five countries revealed that American respondents were markedly more likely to approve the use of torture to interrogate suspected terrorists than were respondents from other advanced industrial democracies.[1] Among the Americans polled, 36 percent agreed with the statement "Terrorists pose such an extreme threat that governments should now be allowed to use some degree of torture if it may gain information that saves innocent lives." Only 24 percent of British respondents agreed, as did 22 percent of the Canadians and Australians polled, 19 percent of the French, 21 percent of the Germans, 14 percent of the Italians, and 16 percent of the Spaniards. The story was similar in many of the other countries, both democratic and authoritarian. Only 24 percent of Mexican and Turkish respondents agreed, as did 25 percent of respondents in Egypt, 27 percent in Poland, 29 percent in Ukraine, 31 percent in South Korea, and 32 percent in Brazil and in India. Note the statement's assumption about the instrumental purpose of torture. The wording makes explicit what is more often implicit in most contemporary discussions about torture: that it is intended to extract important information from prisoners. Almost entirely missing from the contemporary discussion about torture is its only other instrumental purpose: punishment.

Government officials obey two strictures with respect to the subject of torture. First, they refuse to admit that their governments ever practice torture as a policy even when it is common knowledge and is spoken about euphemistically in comments by other government officials in phrases such as "harsh interrogation methods." Concern about adverse public opinion and prosecution under international law no doubt motivates their discretion. Second, they refuse to admit that torture is ever practiced to punish prisoners rather than to collect information.

The truth is that torture is always punishment. Torture constitutes punishment whether or not its purpose is also to extract information from the victim. The intention to torture is the intention to punish. In earlier periods of U.S. history, police officers routinely subjected criminal arrestees from the working class and racial or ethnic minorities to the "third degree," which meant interrogation using lies, threats, isolation, deprivation of food and water and sleep, and beatings. Especially beatings. In addition to extracting confessions from the arrested, police violence was commonly used to exact retribution. Minor criminal arrestees might be beaten and then released without being charged to save the expense of a trial. Or criminal arrestees connected to an urban political machine might be beaten and then released without charge in the belief that they were immune from conviction by corrupt courts. Deniable informal police violence thus served as a substitute for the orderly formal process of prosecution, trial, and sentencing, and was commonly excused by politicians and the public as necessary to solve crimes.

The torture of prisoners captured in war, in the guise of interrogation, demonstrates the power of the state over its enemies through the torturer's infliction of suffering on the victim with impunity. By tradition, victory in modern interstate wars is demonstrated by the ritual subordination of the enemy state through the signing of surrender papers by senior political leaders and military officers and by the ritualized penetration of the territory of enemy states via military marches through its major cities. The objective is to publicize and thus eliminate any doubts in the minds of the enemy about the power of the victors. The problem for states waging wars of counterinsurgency is that comparable opportunities to stage convincing ritual demonstrations of military victory are limited or unavailable. Displaying the bodies of dead insurgents is typically too ghoulish to make good wartime propaganda. Simply killing elusive enemy insurgent leaders risks transforming them into martyrs for the cause, and new insurgent leaders may quickly take their place. The humiliation of capture and public trial offers captors the opportunity to avoid creation of rebel martyrs and instead reduce insurgent leaders to mere criminals brought to justice. The difference between the contemporary public perceptions of Che Guevara and Abimael Guzmán offers a telling case in point. Where the cowardly assassination of a wounded Guevara following his capture by the Bolivian army and the photograph of his bullet-riddled corpse provided the material for transformation of a summary execution into a virtual crucifixion, the arrest of Guzmán without a shootout and his subsequent pusillanimity during trial are repellant. Where Guevara is revered in death by much of the Latin American left—and his likeness remains a powerful image of rebellion, though increasingly detached from the historical context of his glory days with Fidel and Raúl Castro—Guzmán retains none of the luster he enjoyed as Shining Path leader, but is merely an ignored and pathetic figure languishing in a Peruvian prison cell.

The difficulty of performing convincing ritual demonstrations of victory in wars of counterinsurgency is compounded when insurgencies present low-profile or even anonymous leaderships. That was the situation faced by the United States in its struggle against al-Qaeda and its affiliates. Most of the insurgencies linked to al-Qaeda differ significantly from revolutionary insurgencies in Latin America, Africa, and Asia in the relative absence of public veneration of and dependence on the charismatic authority of individual leaders. According to political psychologist Marc Sageman,

> Unlike many political organizations, Salafi groups are careful to avoid a cult of personality, for they believe that everything belongs to God. Indeed, they take seriously the notion of Islam as submission, and this is not compatible with a narcissistic cult of personality, which often degenerates into a pyramidal organization, with all the controls lying with the leader. Al Qaeda's structure is quite opposite, with a large degree of local autonomy and initiative.[2]

Some popular veneration of al-Qaeda leaders is inevitable, but that need not reflect the sort of dependence on individual leaders that makes insurgencies vulnerable. Decentralization makes organizations like al-Qaeda difficult to defeat because they cannot be easily "beheaded" by capturing or killing their senior leadership. Even when attrition of their ordinary combatants reduces their size and effectiveness such that continued struggle is pointless, there may be no leadership left with whom authorities may negotiate surrender. Victory parades are useful in interstate wars or civil wars but ring hollow in prolonged wars of counterinsurgency. In fact they may do nothing more than present insurgents with new targets.

Under such frustrating circumstances, occupying armies faced with insurgencies appear to employ torture during interrogation less to extract information than to demonstrate the power of the state. The knowledge that the state is humiliating captured enemies by interrogating them under torture may work as a substitute for the military victory parade. Conducted in occupied countries, victory parades are intended to make entire populations aware of their unambiguous defeat and render them less capable of further resistance. Torture achieves the same purpose on an individual level by rendering prisoners psychologically and physically incapable of military or political opposition. Britta Jenkins of the Behandlungszentrum für Folteropfer (Treatment Center for Torture Victims) in Berlin states:

The brutal torturer and the "friendly" torturer—the one who feigns intervening in order to help the person under torture, who shows understanding, whether in word or deed—both have the same goal: to destroy the integrity of the human being in front of them, to isolate him from society, by using different methods of torture that deprive him of his fundamental trust in society and make him look crazy in the eyes of society.[3]

Although more sophisticated forms of torture are less likely to result in lasting physiological injury, subjects may present any combination of the range of psychological and psychosomatic symptoms comprising post-traumatic stress disorder, including insomnia, nightmares, flashbacks, chronic anxiety, inability to trust others, deliberate self-injury, violence, substance abuse, sexual dysfunction, inability to concentrate, depression, guilt, memory loss, and paranoia.[4] Based on experience with victims of torture in Germany and Brazil, Dr. Mechthild Wenk-Ansohn states:

Traumatizing events linger like fresh wounds in the memory, where they are constantly reproduced. They surface as nightmares after dark and as thoughts and images during the day. They are sometimes triggered spontaneously or may arise in the train of some everyday event that recalls the trauma: the sound of heavy footsteps on the floor of the asylum hostel, a special smell, an appointment with the public authorities or at the doctor's that brings the interrogation back to mind. Traumatized persons . . . linger in a state of inner tension and excitation, or in a state of paralysis; both are an expression of the basic mood of anxiety. Anxiety is often coupled with the feeling that there is no way out, that all is hopeless.[5]

Releasing debilitated prisoners also serves as a demonstration of the power of the state to punish family members and communities for associating with individuals suspected of supporting rebellion and insurgency.[6] Thus what might be presented by the captor state as an act of mercy also works as a form of collective punishment directed against those who must thereafter provide support for the physically and psychologically debilitated released captive. That emotional cost includes what some psychotherapists have called vicarious or secondary trauma, in which the emotional wounds to the victim extend horizontally through close relationships. The economic and emotional burden of supporting a victim of torture would be especially difficult for families and communities in poor societies and in societies traditionally resistant to psychotherapy. That describes the situation of most of the prisoners released from Guantánamo.

The Guantánamo camps were the termini for prisoners transferred from other prisons and jails, primarily in Afghanistan. The overwhelming majority were initially captured in Afghanistan and first confined in prisons there. Some of those prisons were operated by Northern Alliance warlords who were later appointed as officials of the Transitional Islamic State of Afghanistan. The two most infamous of these prisons were controlled by warlord and 2003 Afghan presidential candidate Abdul Rashid Dostum: Sheberghan and the Qala-i-Jangi fortress near Mazar-i-Sharif. The former may have held as many as 3,500 prisoners at one point.

The captured were typically transferred first from the warlord-controlled prisons in the provinces to two large prison camp complexes operated jointly by the U.S. Army, Marine Corps, and CIA outside the city of Kandahar and at Bagram Air Base thirty miles north of Kabul.

The 840 acres of Bagram Air Base allowed for multiple autonomously functioning prison camps and interrogation centers, including one operated by the British Army and MI6, while serving as an important military air base. A runway 10,000 feet long could be used by large cargo and bomber aircraft. Smaller, temporary prisons in Kabul and elsewhere in the country were also established by the CIA. Some of the prisoners in the custody of the U.S. Marine Corps were also held in the brigs aboard ships in the Arabian Sea, including the USS *Bataan* and USS *Peleliu*.

Although the total number of prisoners who have been held in prisons in Afghanistan operated by the United States has not been announced, a report by the U.S. Army's inspector general to the powerful Senate Armed Services Committee said that approximately 50,000 prisoners had been moved through prisons in Afghanistan and Iraq since September 11, 2001. Other estimates put the figure closer to 65,000. That report, prompted by public outrage about the revelations of abuse at Abu Ghraib prison in Iraq, was the product of an investigation of sixteen military prisons outside the United States.[7] Perhaps one-third or more of those 50,000–65,000 prisoners passed through prisons controlled by the United States in Afghanistan.

As if the Afghan nightmare were somehow incomplete, there was an unauthorized private-sector lockup operated by three entrepreneurial Americans in the country to collect the sizable bounties being paid by Washington for captured wanted guerrillas.[8] The $50 million price on the head of Osama bin Laden and smaller yet hefty amounts offered for other Taliban and al-Qaeda figures led them to kidnap and torture victims in their search for information and perhaps sadistic gratification. After their operation was discovered, the Afghan police liberated eight Afghans who were found hanging upside down in the jail. During the September 2004 trial of the three Americans, the former captives testified that they had been waterboarded. Led by onetime U.S. Army Special Forces noncom Jack Idema, identified as having fought with the Northern Alliance as a mercenary, the bounty hunters asserted that they had been "operating a counter-terrorism operation under deep cover" with the full knowledge and cooperation at the highest levels of the Department of Defense.[9] The three received sentences of eight to ten years for their multiple kidnap-tortures, but all were released after serving three years or less.[10]

The increasing dependence of the U.S. military services on civilian contractors in a wide variety of roles, including security officers and interrogators, lends plausibility to their assertions of official knowledge and cooperation. Shedding what were described as peripheral functions to concentrate on the "core competencies" of the military services was central to the military reforms pressed by Secretary of Defense Donald Rumsfeld. That the U.S. Army operating in an occupied country would have transferred custody of a terror suspect to a group of fast-talking American bounty hunters speaks volumes about its organizational competence in fulfilling the responsibilities of military captors to manage the movement of captives and gather intelligence from them while respecting their human rights to the extent possible. Outsourcing in this case has made the U.S. military incompetent in at least one area traditionally understood to be a core competency of occupying armies.

Evidence of military incompetence and contempt for human rights comes from reports of mistaken mass arrests. In one incident in January 24, 2002, twenty-one villagers from Uruzgan Province were killed in an assault and another twenty-seven villagers captured and airlifted, shackled and hooded, to the U.S. Army base outside Kandahar after they were incorrectly identified as members of the Taliban and al-Qaeda. Confined in what they described as wooden cages, the unfortunates were "beaten, kicked and punched with the soldiers' fists, feet and in some cases, gunstocks."[11] So-called "beat and greet" intimidation rituals during which new prisoners are subjected to unprovoked physical brutality to convince them of their powerlessness against prison authorities have long been commonplace in American jails and prisons. The treatment recounted by the detainees of the Immigration and Naturalization Service held at Union County Jail in New Jersey is similar to that described by former prisoners who were held at Guantánamo Bay and at Abu Ghraib prison in Iraq.[12] Prisoners released almost exactly three years after the reported assaults on the villagers from

Uruzgan Province described similar kinds of mistreatment, but occurring between their arrest and their arrival at Bagram Air Base.[13] At the very least, tactics like this do little to endear the United States or NATO to the Afghans. Popular resentment at the presence of foreign military bases and anxiety about the treatment of family and friends held as prisoners boiled over into rioting on July 26, 2005, when more than a thousand people demonstrated against the detention of eight of their fellow villagers at the main entrance to the base by throwing stones and chanting, "Die, America."[14] Afghan resentment of the American occupation has only deepened over time.

Physical brutality permits a degree of control over prisoners, although intimidation by itself may be insufficient to induce many prisoners to provide the kind of information that would be useful as military and political intelligence, the ostensible purpose for their imprisonment and interrogation. Manipulating the emotional state of these prisoners is required for that. Interrogations included reasonably plausible and frightening threats to turn prisoners over to one or another of the Afghan warlords who were then part of the Northern Alliance and later part of the Transitional Islamic State of Afghanistan for execution, threats to turn them over to governments in the Middle East to be tortured, threats to shoot them as spies, threats to send them to Guantánamo indefinitely, and promises that they would be allowed to enter the Federal Witness Protection Program in the United States or be freed to serve as agents of the United States in Afghanistan.[15] Other than transfer to Guantánamo for indefinite detention, the extent to which these threats or promises were carried out is unknown and may never be known.

In his nightmarish prison memoir, Murat Kurnaz describes being held in an open pen with other prisoners in Kandahar before being transferred to Guantánamo. There he was threatened with execution by shooting, waterboarded or subjected to partial drowning, given electric shocks to the soles of his feet, hung by his wrists for hours, constantly beaten by guards and interrogators, denied adequate water, food, clothing, blankets, exercise, cleanliness, and minimal information about his geographic location, observed by female military personnel while he bathed and defecated, given food containing pork in violation of Islamic dietary rules, denied contact with his family, German diplomatic officials, or legal counsel, and denied the practice of his religion by praying.[16] He also describes watching as his guards beat and kicked a fellow prisoner to death.

In two well-documented cases U.S. Army interrogators tortured prisoners to death at Bagram Collection Point.[17] One of the prisoners, Mullah Habibullah, died on December 4, 2002, after six days of being kicked and beaten while he was shackled and hooded. Lying on the floor of his cell unable to stand, and choking on phlegm he was coughing up while being taunted by his interrogators, Habibullah died from a pulmonary embolism caused by blood clots from having had his legs beaten. Another prisoner, an illiterate peasant named Dilawar who suffered from preexisting coronary heart disease, died on June 6, 2004, after his interrogators shackled him, threatened him with rape, placed him in painful stress positions, held his head under water to induce fear of drowning, slammed his head into tables and walls, and kicked and beat his legs and groin. Army medical personnel determined that his legs had been essentially "pulpified" as if he had been run over by a bus. Publicly, however, the U.S. Army claimed that the deaths of Habibullah and Dilawar were due to natural causes. U.S. Army medical personnel were thus made complicit in the attempt to cover up the actual causes of death, misrepresentations that clearly violate accepted standards of medical ethics.[18]

U.S. Army investigators found ample evidence of frenzied sadism at Bagram.[19] Military policeman Specialist Willie V. Brand told investigators that he had subjected Dilawar to some thirty knee strikes because he was annoyed with the victim, and that other guards also struck Dilawar simply because they were amused to hear him scream out, "Allah."[20] Sexual sadism was also part of the abuse of prisoners held at Bagram. One interrogator allegedly placed his penis on the face of a prisoner and later mounted the clothed prisoner in a mock sodomization. Other prisoners released from Bagram report being purposefully humiliated by being stripped naked in front of female soldiers and subjected to repeated painful anal examinations. Stripping in front of members of the opposite sex emphasizes their physical vulnerability, deprives them of the modest clothing required by Islam, and reduces them to an animal state. Repetition of sanctioned cavity searches provides uniformed sexual predators with opportunities for what becomes, in effect, homosexual rape.

Deaths of prisoners in government custody are anything but rare. In every society ordinary prisoners die in the custody of the state, usually because of preexisting medical problems, behaviors caused by social and psychological problems that led to their original incarceration, and violent acts committed by other prisoners. Prisoners die for some of these same reasons in every war. The fact that some prisoners die from these ordinary causes while in U.S. military custody is unfortunate but unsurprising. However, when they die during or as a consequence of interrogation, something exceptional has occurred. The response of the military's investigators and lawyers at Bagram was to conceal what had happened to Habibullah and Dilawar by first muddying and then creating an incomplete factual record.[21] The response of their superiors at the Pentagon was to delay any review of their criminal investigations. That changed only when it became the focus of press coverage. Uniformed bureaucratic organizations that depend on a measure of esprit de corps for their effectiveness but are answerable to higher authority in a liberal democracy often respond initially to the discovery of wrongdoing with concealment or obstruction. When that fails, some lower-level members of the organization are then offered up as scapegoats to protect both the organization and individuals higher in the chain of command. Even then the pace of prosecution is likely to be dilatory and the punishments light. That is what happened in the Habibullah and Dilawar cases.

By 2005, the Army Criminal Investigation Command had been compelled to undertake sixty-eight investigations into the deaths of seventy-nine prisoners in the custody of the U.S. Army in Iraq and Afghanistan.[22] The Naval Criminal Investigative Service has undertaken investigation of eight deaths of prisoners in the custody of the U.S. Navy and U.S. Marine Corps. More than twenty-five of those were described as suspected or confirmed criminal homicides.

Only one of the [new] deaths occurred at the Abu Ghraib prison in Iraq, officials said, showing how broadly the most violent abuses extended beyond those prison walls and contradicting early impressions that the wrongdoing was confined to a handful of members of the military police on the prison's night shift.[23]

Conduct morally repugnant and criminal under international and domestic law had become commonplace in U.S. military prisons. The boundary that ought to separate legitimate warfare from state terror was systematically trespassed.

What is clear, then, is that many of the prisoners who were transferred to Guantánamo from other prisons had experienced physical brutality and psycho-physiological manipulation long before they arrived. The effects of that treatment were then compounded by transfers of custody made without warning or explanation, an effective method of further disempowering and disorienting prisoners. Being shackled, hooded, in some cases drugged—presumably sedated to make physical control easier but also possibly injected with drugs intended to heighten disorientation or anxiety—and loaded on U.S. Air Force C-130 and C-141 aircraft for a twenty-hour flight would have added to the strangeness of the experience. Some of the Afghan and Pakistani prisoners would have never flown before. Some of them suspected they would be thrown into the ocean to drown in a gruesome execution and body disposal protocol akin to similar executions during the Dirty War in Argentina. The flight crews and guards did nothing to disabuse them of the idea.[24] The Argentine navy had "disappeared" some 2,000 leftists in "death flights" by throwing them, drugged and naked, from aircraft to drown in the waters of the South Atlantic.[25] Their disappearance was intended to increase anxiety and uncertainty among colleagues and family members of the victims. Credible accusations that captured combatants of the North Vietnamese army and National Liberation Front or Viet Cong were executed in the same manner and for same the purposes by the U.S. military during the Vietnam War have also been made.[26] For captives hauled from lockups in Afghanistan already weakened by war wounds, suffering from other war zone illnesses such as malaria, or otherwise psychologically traumatized by their experience at Bagram or in Kandahar, the additional physical stress and psychological terror of the flight to Guantánamo would have been profound.[27]

What began with primitive wire mesh cages in an enclosure topped by razor wire when the first prisoners began arriving in Cuba eventually developed into an elaborate prison camp. Mahvish Rukhsana Khan, the Afghan-American attorney for several of the prisoners, offered the following description of the mature camp circa 2007:

> There are nine camps (of which we are presently aware) named 1, 2, 3, 4, 5, 6, 7, Echo, and Iguana. Each numbered camp is subdivided into several blocks with alphabetical names: Alpha, Bravo, Charley, Delta, Echo. There's also India, Tango, Romeo, Whiskey, Foxtrot and Zulu.
>
> Camps 1, 2, and 3 consist of rows of adjacent steel-mesh cages with one man per cage. Camp 4 is a medium-security prison for "compliant" detainees and houses up to ten men per room. They are allowed to watch nature films, sports, or prescreened movies once a week. Camp 4 prisoners are also allowed to pray and eat communally, and they have greater access to reading material, an exercise bike, and a soccer ball. . . .
>
> Once Camps 5 and 6 were built—these contain solitary-confinement cells—many prisoners were transferred there from Camps 1, 2, and 3. Camp 7 holds the fifteen high-value detainees and is run by a special military unit, code-named Task Force Platinum.[28]

Camp Iguana was constructed for the handful of juvenile prisoners, including Omar Khadr.

Feelings of isolation and uncertainty after arrival were heightened by denying prisoners the right to speak to other prisoners and by informing them that they were being held indefinitely and incommunicado. That sense of isolation was maintained by regularly transferring prisoners held in solitary confinement to new blocks to prevent or disrupt friendships that might develop through whispered conversations under the cell doors between prisoners in neighboring cells. Prisoners who feel isolated and uncertain are susceptible to more profound emotional distress—as the multiple suicides and attempted suicides reported at Guantánamo attest—which would make them even more vulnerable to interrogation. After being beaten by guards and being held in solitary confinement for as long as eight months, Yemeni national Salim Ahmed Hamdan experienced sudden mood swings and suicidal urges.[29] One recurring observation in the memoirs of prisoners is the debilitating depression that accompanies feelings of being abandoned and forgotten by friends and family. That psychosis can be induced by prolonged solitary confinement has been understood for a century.[30]

Although those who spoke for the U.S. military euphemistically described the treatment of prisoners as "incentive based," meaning that their behavior was controlled through a regimen of small material rewards and punishments, it would be more accurate to describe the treatment of prisoners in terms of modulated physical and mental stress, unpredictable violence, and humiliation, all of which was intended to disorient the victim.

Beyond punishment for its own sake, the prison regimen may also be intended to induce a level of psychological regression in the subjects sufficient to break their will to resist, both during and after imprisonment. In a sworn statement made after his release in late March 2007, David Hicks described being beaten for hours after his capture and fearing he would be shot unless he cooperated with interrogators. He also observed another prisoner being attacked with dogs and yet another having his head slammed into concrete until unconscious.[31] Murat Kurnaz reports that he was subjected to months of solitary confinement and suffocated in a closed solitary confinement cell filled with tear gas.[32] This is not a regimen constructed from incentives, unless the incentive is conceived in terms of avoiding punishment. Released prisoners reported "short shackling" or being handcuffed to the floor and subjection to rock music played at painfully high volumes. The interrogation described by former French prisoners Mourad Benchallali and Nizar Sassi resembles that experienced by some prisoners in Northern Ireland in the 1970s and by prisoners in occupied Iraq at the now infamous Abu Ghraib prison: continuous shackling, prolonged isolation, sleep deprivation, light deprivation, denial of bathroom breaks, strapping to intravenous drips, threats with firearms and attack dogs during interrogation, displays of disrespect toward the Koran, questioning by provocatively dressed, partially nude, or nude women, smearing of prisoners' faces with what they were told was menstrual blood, and demeaning them by compelling them to bark and perform dog tricks, wear a woman's bra, dance with a male guard, and watch pornographic films.[33]

Although the probable effects of subjecting prisoners to physical distress and physical threat are universally understood, the efforts to outrage the religious and sexual sensibilities of prisoners appear unintimidating or even puerile to persons who have not been indoctrinated in the anxious religious pieties and sexual repression characteristic of the Islamists. In fact, such outrages might have had real value for interrogators by contributing to the stress that breaks the will of some prisoners. Resistance to questioning may collapse in response to the appropriate combination of physical and emotional stresses. Attacking a prisoner's religious or other cultural sensibilities is a classic method of increasing stress. Any doubts that showing disrespect for the Koran could elicit strong emotional responses from Muslims were dispelled by the violent demonstrations and official condemnations across the Islamic world when *Newsweek* reported that a copy had been flushed down the toilet at Guantánamo.[34] This and similar reports of disrespect shown to the Koran were strongly and consistently denied by spokespersons for the U.S. Department of Defense, but they bear an unmistakable resemblance to the actions of mock interrogators that are reported by a participant in the U.S. Navy's Survival, Evasion, Resistance and Escape or SERE training conducted at Warner Springs Training Area, Naval Air Station North Island, California. In that case, devout Christians were forced to watch as a copy of the Christian Bible was verbally disparaged and kicked about in the dirt.[35]

British-Zambian convert to Sunni Islam Martin Mubanga was subjected to such treatment while imprisoned at Guantánamo. In several letters to his family in Britain, written in an artful combination of

Cockney, street slang, rap lyrics, and Jamaican patois opaque to military censors, Mubanga disclosed that his guards and interrogators attempted to elicit cooperation with threats of beatings and sodomitical rape and promises of better food and prostitutes.[36]

Saudi citizen Mohammed al-Qahtani, who was captured near Tora Bora in December 2001, was reduced to pleading that he be allowed to commit suicide. His treatment included being forcibly shaved, deprived of sleep, kept in a painfully cold room, force-fed intravenously, ordered to bark like a dog, forced to listen to rock music at ear-splitting volumes, and having his hands shackled to his sides so that he could not pray.[37]

According to attorney Joshua Colangelo-Bryan, his Saudi-Bahraini client Jumah al-Doussari was wrapped in Israeli and American flags during one interrogation, and an interrogator urinated on his copy of the Koran.[38] Claims made by released prisoners that interrogators and guards demonstrated purposeful disrespect for the Koran in this and similar ways have been repeatedly, consistently, and forcefully denied by the Pentagon. Whatever value such action might have for undermining the will of the prisoner, the admission that such tactics were used would further inflame opinion in Islamic countries against the United States.

Whether motivated by inhumane treatment or by the utter hopelessness of being imprisoned indefinitely, or perhaps by both, al-Doussari attempted suicide on twelve occasions. Speaking for the Pentagon, Navy commander Jeffrey Gordon dismissed the twelve suicide attempts as a tactic "to gain public sympathy."[39] Following the coordinated suicides of a Yemeni and two Saudi nationals, Guantánamo base commander Rear Admiral Harry Harris Jr. characterized their suicides as acts of propaganda: "They have no regard for life, neither ours nor their own. I believe this was not an act of desperation, but an act of asymmetrical warfare waged against us."[40] Perhaps this statement reflected his thinking or the opinion of officers charged with responsibility for executing the Guantánamo decision. Perhaps Harris simply succumbed to the temptations of rhetorical escalation out of frustration. Conceiving a more profound failure to understand the prisoners would be difficult.

Numerous accounts by prisoners released from Guantánamo describe having been questioned after being stripped, a method used by interrogators to heighten the sense of physical and psychological vulnerability.[41] This is consistent with the technique employed at Abu Ghraib prison in Iraq, where nudity and sexual humiliation were used routinely to soften up prisoners prior to their being questioned and simply for the sadistic entertainment of the soldiers responsible for guarding them. None of the reports of former prisoners released from Guantánamo suggests the out-of-control nightmare of Abu Ghraib. Instead they report indignities and brutalities selected less to entertain the pathologically sadistic than to punish prisoners in the guise of increasing their stress to enhance vulnerability to interrogation.

Advised by Behavioral Science Consultation Team physicians and psychologists, the Guantánamo interrogators also exploited the physical and emotional weaknesses of individual prisoners discovered through physical examinations and the examination of confidential medical records, which include psychological diagnoses and treatment. Investigative research by Steven H. Miles published in the British medical journal *Lancet* even revealed that U.S. military doctors collaborated in designing techniques to exploit the weaknesses of specific prisoners.[42] In effect, the medical and psychological sciences were deployed to develop a more sophisticated, more individualized repertoire of abuse than was possible in the past.[43] The result of such medicalized torture was that some prisoners experienced misery tailored to their individual physical and mental weaknesses. With this the U.S. military descended to another level in moral depravity. Here was something more than the misery of an incarceration that could not be shared in solidarity with other prisoners because of isolation, and something more than the misery of an incommunicado and indefinite incarceration. To resist would require immense reserves of personal discipline or ideological commitment.

Complaints about the participation of medical personnel in interrogation and the exploitation of medical records finally led the Pentagon to issue Instruction 2310.08E, "Medical Program Support for Detainee Operations," on June 6, 2006.[44] The new policy forbade medical personnel from supervising, directing, or conducting interrogations of prisoners. While stating that medical records were not absolutely confidential and that prisoners should be disabused of expecting absolute confidentiality, it also required that all requests for medical records other than for medical treatment must be recorded and must include the name of the person requesting the information, the stated purpose for the information disclosure, and the name of the medical unit officer authorizing the disclosure. The obvious purpose of this latter requirement was to deter such participation by creating a paper trail permitting the identification and by implication possible subsequent prosecution of individuals who would exploit medical records for torture. Such methods in future would be the province of the CIA and not the Pentagon.

9 Announcement

Politics stops at the water's edge. National interest supersedes any political advantage in domestic politics that might be gained in conducting international affairs. In the century before America abandoned its Western Hemisphere–centered geopolitical strategy for a globalist foreign policy, the adage was more than patriotic piety. For the last century, however, international and domestic politics have been inextricably linked. The foreign policy decisions made by the Bush administration after September 11, 2001, including the Guantánamo decision, reflect recognition of danger in the near term and opportunity over the long term. Behind the façade of conservative consensus projected by members of the administration were deep ideological disagreements. As was true of all other modern presidential administrations, its appointees brought policy-making priorities and ideological commitments. Disagreements over domestic policy distinguished the "country club" Republicans for whom reducing taxes was the primary domestic priority from the populist social conservatives for whom protecting traditional sources of moral authority was the primary domestic priority. Should the administration assign precedence to legislating new tax breaks or further restricting access to abortion? Where domestic policy conflicts among conservatives were easy to recognize, disagreements over foreign policy that divided the traditional conservatives from the neoconservatives were largely obscured from view. What traditional conservatives and neoconservatives shared was contempt for the liberal internationalism that had motivated much of the international law produced in the last half of the twentieth century.

Concealed by their shared hostility toward international organizations, the United Nations in particular, and toward international legal regimes like the Rome Statute for the International Criminal Court, was a more fundamental disagreement. Where the traditional conservatives embraced the formal equality between sovereign states that was the basis for international law, instinctively opposing the signing of new treaties limiting Washington's freedom of action in pursuit of the national interest, the neoconservatives rejected them as logically inconsistent with the demands of acting as a hegemonic power. From the perspective of the traditional conservatives, international organizations and legal regimes were suspect because they threatened to reduce U.S. national sovereignty, conceived as the legal, military, and economic capacity to govern independently of other national governments. They rejected responsibility for or responsibility to other states in the international system. From the perspective of the neoconservatives, however, formal legal equality granted to all sovereign states under international law was a problem because it threatened to limit American power *as* the new global hegemon. Sovereignty was at best an exercise in hypocrisy and at worst positively detrimental if taken literally as law. Nothing should be accepted that hobbled the imposition of a new order in the international system of states in the name of a universally desired and applicable liberal democratic political ideal.[1]

Broadly defined, "liberal democracy" describes a government that protects individual liberty and permits citizens to participate meaningfully in their own governance. While American conservatives of all stripes endorse the desirability of such a regime in the United States, and in all probability the other Western powers, neoconservatives would go further and insist upon its desirability for all countries.

Where the first impulse among traditional conservatives was to advocate rather modest foreign policy goals consistent with skepticism about what is possible in politics, the first impulse among neoconservatives is to endorse aggressive action to achieve ambitious foreign policy goals. Neoconservatism was born out of the collapse of the Cold War ideological consensus during the Vietnam War, the historical moment when anticommunist liberal intellectuals realized both the depth of their disagreement with the New Left about goals and the extent of their agreement with traditional conservatives about means.[2] The archetypical Cold War liberal convert to neoconservatism in the 1970s and 1980s was an overachieving member of a white ethnic minority sufficiently satisfied with the degree to which the New Deal had opened doors to social advancement and resentful of the power of nonwhite ethnic minority leaders in the Democratic Party. Acutely conscious of having been recently admitted into the halls of power and privilege, such converts to neoconservatism were more interested in defending American power in the world than in further egalitarian domestic social change. Most of them eventually changed their party affiliation from Democrat to Republican, but many of the younger cohort of neoconservatives never experienced the separation trauma of abandoning ideological liberalism or the Democratic Party.

Cold War anticommunism and Zionism comprised the foreign policy agenda of the neoconservatives in the beginning. They played prominent roles in the Committee on the Present Danger's opposition to the SALT II treaty with the Soviet Union and warned of the Soviet Union's growing influence with insurgent leftists and nationalists in the Middle East, Latin America, and Africa. When the Cold War tensions gradually eased, neoconservatives shifted the focus of their rhetoric not to the four remaining communist states in East and Southeast Asia but instead to the threat posed by terrorism, a reflection of their intellectual Eurocentrism and Zionism. Communism in Asia might be denounced, but it was the political and cultural fate of Europe and the Middle East, and to a lesser extent of Latin America and southern Africa, that mattered more to the neoconservatives.

Neoconservative geocultural myopia is attributable generally to the Atlanticism of the American foreign policy establishment and specifically to the influence of University of Chicago political philosopher Leo Strauss, a Jewish refugee from Weimar Germany whose dense and elliptical commentaries on the classics became a secretive call to arms for conservative intellectuals to defend what he and they perceived as mortal threats to Western civilization emerging in the modern world: secularism, internationalism, scientism, legalism, moral relativism, and the mediocrity produced by liberal democracy. Nicholas Xenos, a political theorist at the University of Massachusetts at Amherst, locates Strauss squarely on the far right of the political ideological spectrum, citing writings in which he is critical not of the fascism of the Nazi regime in the Germany from which he had fled but merely of its anti-Semitism.[3]

For Strauss and his followers, the source material for Western civilization was located in the Greek and Roman classics and in medieval Jewish and Christian theology rather than in the Enlightenment and the modern world to which it gave birth. Claims for truth made by the law, natural sciences, and social sciences are necessarily subordinate, from their perspective, to claims for truth offered by political philosophy and in particular those articulated by none other than Leo Strauss and company. Among the several disturbing sentiments expressed by Strauss, one relevant to discussions of the controversial decisions of the Bush administration was the notion that the limits of constitutionalism could be dispensed with to defend the liberal state from its "unscrupulous and savage enemies."[4] Whether Strauss was recommending policies such as incommunicado detention without trial, torture, or extralegal killing to the defenders of the liberal state is not clear—so much that Strauss wrote is oblique—but it could be taken as license for precisely those sorts of state crimes. The problem inherent in dispensing with constitutional legal limits is that it is likely to produce a descent into normless savagery. Contradictory, to be sure, yet entirely in keeping with the "do as I say, not as I do" elitism practiced without apology by neoconservatives. Like other conservatives, they place a very high value on order and believe that it is best maintained by ideas that reinforce traditional authority. That explains why the Straussians, as his followers are called, propound moral absolutes and defend natural law theory and established religious authority. They understand the rules to be there for the governed and not necessarily for those who govern. Indeed, license to change or break the rules is understood to be inherent in the exercise of political power.

Consistent with the *quod licet Jovi, non licet bovi* conviction that elites must make rather than obey the rules they articulate, neoconservatives embrace an expansive view of presidential power, which in turn serves their goal of establishing the United States as long-term global hegemon.[5] If American presidents are to fulfill their role as leaders in the defense of Western civilization, they require the power to act in foreign affairs independently of decision makers in the other branches of government and elsewhere in American society. In this the neoconservatives endorse what has been the general trend in the development of American politics since the New Deal and the Second World War. The presidency emerged from the crises of the mid-twentieth century more powerful than in previous periods.

From the neoconservative perspective, effective defense of Western civilization requires that the United States, as the preeminent liberal democratic state, impose order on the planet with military force or the threat of military force. Their assumption is that the American economy is fully capable of sustaining global military dominance and that Americans should accept that obligation unflinchingly. Rather than world government constructed from international institutions such as the United Nations, the goal is international order maintained by the military and economic dominance of the United States. In this conception of international politics, Washington must act less like an honest policeman than like a mafia boss, in the manner described by the character Henry Hill in the 1990 Martin Scorsese film *Goodfellas*: "All they got from Paulie was protection from other guys looking to rip them off. That's what it's all about. That's what the FBI can never understand—that what Paulie and the organization offer is protection for the kinds of guys who can't go to the cops. They're like the police department for wiseguys."[6] If every power in the international system is a "wiseguy" and the international hegemon is a mafia boss, then international law is nothing more than what the hegemon dictates.

In the heady days after the collapse of the Soviet Union and the fall of communism in Eastern Europe, neoconservatives could dream big. In their risk acceptance in initiating war and in their territorial ambition, they occupied a place on the spectrum between the leaders of mid-twentieth-century fascist powers and the Soviet Union. Where the fascists accepted greater risks in initiating war than the Soviets, their territorial ambitions were less global. The leaders of Nazi

Germany envisioned a Greater Germany north of the Alps and across Eastern Europe. Their counterparts in fascist Italy envisioned a new Roman Empire ruling the Mediterranean, the Middle East, and the Horn of Africa. The military regime in Japan planned to rule the entire Pacific Rim. By contrast, the leaders of the Soviet Union envisioned a world where the Leninist party-state was the universal political regime and the centrally planned socialist economy the universal economic model. By the 1980s, communist true believers might still perceive the Soviet Union's control not only of its own vast territory but also of client states in Eastern Europe and scattered across the Third World as the partial realization of the millennial hope. Ultimately, they felt, history could be relied upon to generate economic crises that would complete the transformation.

Neoconservatives were similarly inclined to conceive of history as an ally in the march toward their preferred universal end states—liberal democracy as political regime and American-style capitalism as economic model—but they were also willing to use military aggression to nudge it along. Where that would be deployed was a function of the Eurocentrism that led them to devalue Asia and Africa vis-à-vis Europe and the region geographically proximate to Europe, the Middle East. The initially successful invasion of Iraq seemed to many neoconservatives the best evidence of the power of the hegemon to force the pace of historical progress. After sorting out the Middle East, perhaps Asia and Africa would beckon.[7]

The geopolitical project of the neoconservatives was given detailed expression by a group of defense intellectuals, Paul Wolfowitz, Lewis "Scooter" Libby, and Zalmay Khalilzad, in the 1992 draft document that was part of the Department of Defense's annual review, the Defense Planning Guidance.[8] Its central recommendation was that the United States should use the opportunity presented by the end of the Cold War to ensure perpetuation of its preeminence by discouraging the emergence of rival powers and eliminating rogue states that posed threats to the new international order. This same sweeping agenda was further promoted by the Project for a New American Century, which was established in 1997 by Robert Kagan and William Kristol. What would justify assertion of global hegemony by the United States? In contrast to the Soviet Union, it would impose a liberal democratic international order.

In a lengthy expression of neoconservative foreign policy goals in the movement's chief organ, the *Weekly Standard*, Max Boot defended the unilateralism at the heart of U.S. dominance of the international system in a 2003 essay that fuses Hobbesian assumptions about international relations with the American mission to spread its universal values:

> Important as allies are, they matter less in a world in which America wields unrivaled power. Our primary goal should be to preserve and extend what Charles Krauthammer called the "unipolar moment." That moment has now stretched into a decade and shows no sign of waning. This confounds the confident prediction of academic theorists that any hegemon will call into being an opposing coalition. It happened to Napoleonic France and Nazi Germany. It hasn't happened to America. Why not? The reason should be obvious to anyone without a Ph.D.: America isn't like the empires of old. It does not seek to enslave other peoples and steal their lands. It spreads freedom and opportunity.[9]

Where neoconservatives and traditional conservatives agree on the importance of military power in international affairs and hold in contempt international law and international organizations, they differ about Israel and democracy promotion as goals of U.S. foreign policy. Traditional conservatives have been guided by the logic of Realpolitik. They have also treated Israel as simply another state in the international system rather than one to which Washington owes a special responsibility. Unlike the neoconservatives, traditional conservatives have been suspicious of expanding the powers of the presidency. The problem for the traditional conservatives is that they have found it easier to describe what they oppose than what they propose, and as a consequence they have been on the defensive in articulating the foreign policy agenda for conservatism.

If neoconservatives and traditional conservatives differ about foreign policy goals and presidential power, they typically agree about the choice of means. Throughout the Cold War, both supported high levels of U.S. military spending and the deployment of additional and new nuclear weapons systems that threatened the strategic nuclear balance with the Soviet Union. Both opposed the efforts by the Carter administration to discourage human rights abuses committed by authoritarian anticommunist client states of the United States. The revived isolationist impulse among traditional conservatives in the period following the collapse of communism in Eastern Europe evaporated with the attacks on September 11, 2001.

No objection was made in either of the conservative camps to using Guantánamo to imprison hundreds of those captured in the war in Afghanistan, a decision providing further justification for the continued, provocative military occupation of that corner of eastern Cuba. Long before the neoconservatives aspired to global American hegemony, the United States had achieved hegemony in the Western Hemisphere. For most Americans, that dominance was normalized in vaguely recalled history lessons about the Monroe Doctrine, gunboat diplomacy, and banana republics. For decades only Cuba represented a consistent challenge to American hegemony.

That the U.S. military has occupied the entrance of a strategically important port in the sovereign territory of Cuba against the wishes of its government for more than half a century fails to register in the awareness of most Americans as particularly anomalous. Before 2002, few would have even remembered that there was a U.S. naval base located on Cuban soil. If most Americans know that Cuba is close to southern Florida, few could locate Guantánamo on the other end of the island in Oriente Province. That geographic ignorance was not alleviated by news coverage of the Guantánamo decision. After the initial flurry of reports about the decision to use the base once again as a prison, references either to Cuba or to Cuban reactions became scarce. Television news coverage in particular seemed to lift the base entirely out of Cuba and thus made it even more of an island prison.

In contrast, for most Cubans continued U.S. military occupation of Guantánamo represents a standing affront to national pride that dates from the traumatic struggle for independence against first Spain and then the United States. Although Spain lost its continental possessions in the Americas in a series of independence wars between 1807 and 1827, it held on to its insular Caribbean and Pacific possessions until they were seized by the United States in the Spanish-American War of 1898. That brief interstate war and the protracted Philippine-American War that followed had their origins in Cuban nationalism and Gilded Age American imperialism. In 1895, Cuban revolutionaries José Martí and Máximo Gómez Báez returned from exile in the United States to launch an insurrection against Spanish colonial rule. To deprive the Cuban guerrillas of their base of popular support, General Valeriano Weyler y Nicolau adopted a policy of *reconcentración*, of interning the rural population behind barbed wire in the first modern concentration camps. Mass internment of the civilian population to isolate it from guerrillas and deprive the latter of support is a classic counterinsurgency strategy. It is also an instrument for holding the civilian population hostage so that they may be punished for the behavior of the guerrillas that they support. As many as 200,000 Cubans died of hunger and disease in the camps. American press coverage highlighting Spanish colonial brutality helped to mobilize public opinion in favor of war against Spain, the pretext for which was found in the February 15, 1898, accident that destroyed the USS *Maine* in Havana Harbor. As was true after September 11, 2001, sensational news coverage could arouse an intense and uncritical military patriotism.

Victory in the Spanish-American War of 1898 gave the United States an instant empire: Cuba, Puerto Rico, the Philippines, and Guam. Domestic political struggle between the proponents and opponents of territorial expansion predating the American Civil War meant that some of the new possessions became colonies and others quasi-colonies.[10]

Their value as new territories—sources of minerals and tropical cash crops, markets for American manufactured goods, strategic locations for military bases, and indicia of success in the competition for international prestige among the great powers—was deployed by the imperialist lobby to persuade Congress to accept the new conquests. The anti-imperialist lobby countered by deploying Anglo-Saxon chauvinism and the "scientific" racism of the period to prevent incorporation of the new possessions as states in the Union. Political resolution meant compromise to reflect the relative influence of the imperialist and anti-imperialist lobbies by devising distinct legal-juridical statuses for each of the new possessions in accordance with their differing levels of political and economic subordination to the United States. After three years of American military occupation, Cuba was granted formal sovereignty at the price of accepting the terms of the humiliating Platt Amendment in the Cuban constitution—the formal authority of the U.S. government to intervene in Cuban foreign and domestic affairs—and indefinitely relinquishing possession of Guantánamo Bay as a naval base to its liberator. In effect, Cuban nationalists were forced to accept the status of citizens in what was effectively a protectorate of the United States.

Puerto Rican nationalists received even less than their Cuban counterparts; their island was designated a commonwealth of the United States.[11] When their nation was annexed by the United States, Philippine nationalists launched a war of independence in 1899. Today few Americans are aware of the Philippine-American War, which cost the lives of some 220,000 Filipinos and 4,000 Americans. Guam, one of the Marianas, was designated an unincorporated territory of the United States, while the other, smaller Marianas and the Caroline Islands would pass along a daisy chain of great power sovereignties. Sold to Germany for $4.5 million, the Marianas were given to Japan after the First World War as a League of Nations trust territory as a reward for its military alliance with Britain, then given to the United States as a United Nations trust territory after the Second World War before becoming a commonwealth territory of the United States three decades later.

The specific form of legal-juridical subordination varied, but the common marker of that subordination was the establishment of a permanent U.S. naval base: Guantánamo Bay Naval Base in Cuba, Naval Station Roosevelt Roads in Puerto Rico, Subic Bay Naval Base in the Philippines, and Naval Base Guam on Guam. As a major maritime power whose geopolitical attention was focused on the Western Hemisphere and insular Pacific, the United States gave priority to acquiring naval bases over the other possible benefits of owning a colonial empire. Before the Panama Canal was constructed, American naval strategist Alfred Thayer Mahan described Cuba and Hawaii as crucial territorial acquisitions necessary to protect what would become the path between the seas that would allow the easy movement of American naval forces between the Atlantic and Pacific Oceans. Hawaii became an American territory in 1898. Mahan and the other imperialists conceived a naval base at Guantánamo Bay as a veritable American Gibraltar situated strategically astride the Windward Passage between Cuba and Hispaniola and thus permitting U.S. military dominance of the Caribbean.

The authority by which the United States exercises control over the 45 square miles of outer Guantánamo Bay is based on a 1903 treaty signed with its new Cuban protectorate. Termed a lease agreement, it recognized Cuban "ultimate sovereignty" yet gave "complete jurisdiction and control" to the United States for an annual payment of $2,000 a year in gold coins. Because the treaty specified no termination date, the leasehold was perpetual. After the 1959 Cuban Revolution, Guantánamo Bay Naval Base became a more anomalous possession as the sole U.S. military base on the soil of a communist state. Two decades after the end of the Cold War, U.S. Marines and the Cuban Frontier Brigade still confront one another along the 17.4 miles of fence and landmines that separate the military base from the rest of Cuba's Oriente province.

Older Cubans and Cuban-Americans would be reminded of the bitterest years of Cold War confrontation by the 2002 announcement that the United States intended to convene tribunals at Guantánamo. Following the defeat of the United States–supported invasion on April 15–19, 1960, at the Bay of Pigs or Playa Girón, 1,209 captured anticommunist Cuban exiles were tried for treason before Cuban revolutionary tribunals. Several of the convicted were executed and the remainder sentenced to thirty years in prison. Before they would be released one year and eight months later for $53 million in food and medicine, Washington orchestrated a sophisticated public relations campaign in the United States to win their freedom and justify the policy toward Cuba that would include appearances by anticommunist Cuban leaders on popular television programs.[12] Upon arrival in the United States the freed prisoners were feted as heroes. For that brief moment in the Cold War, nothing was too good for this population of repatriated former insurgents. Although the Bush administration's 2002 Guantánamo decision drew only restrained criticism from Havana, it must have struck Cubans as yet another example of imperialist hypocrisy. If imprisonment and trials were unfair for anticommunist Cuban insurgents, why were they not also for (presumably) Islamist Afghan insurgents?

Before September 11, 2001, the population of the military base was only 2,500 sailors, Coast Guard personnel, marines, their dependents, and civilian contractors. Following the Guantánamo decision their numbers swelled to nearly 10,000, an additional 7,500 non-prisoners at the base who were there to deal with a maximum of only approximately 700 prisoners. Some Americans might also have recalled that the base was the location where tens of thousands of Haitian and Cuban boat people had been interned in the 1980s.

If the Cuban base no longer possessed the same strategic value that it held before airpower rendered it militarily nearly obsolete, and if it was no longer useful as a symbol of American hostility to communist Cuba after the collapse of the Soviet Union, prior to the 2004 decision of the U.S. Supreme Court in *Hamdan v. Rumsfeld* it still had no equal as a legal purgatory. Here Washington could still hold in custody those it was reluctant to allow on American soil for fear they would then acquire the legal rights of "persons" under the Fourteenth Amendment to the U.S. Constitution. Geographic proximity to Haiti and Cuba made the earlier decisions to intern Haitian and Cuban refugees there plausible as exigent. The same cannot be said about the serious consideration that was given to interning Kosovar refugees there in the 1990s and the 2002 decision to transfer some of those captured in the war in Afghanistan. These latter two decisions belie any claim that detention at Guantánamo Bay Naval Base was somehow valuable for practical reasons rather than for its presumed peculiar legal status.

Although the Soviet Union no longer existed and an isolated Cuba was an improbable national security threat to the United States, old political habits are hard to break. Even with the Soviet Union a memory and the successor Russian Federation reduced to a regional power, neoconservatives and traditional conservatives alike agreed on the need to continue the Cold War against Havana. For four decades the government of Cuba led by Fidel Castro had symbolized opposition to American hegemony over Latin America. The privations of life in Cuba notwithstanding, pan–Latin American nationalism nonetheless won Havana a measure of respect across the region. Using the base as a location to deposit a population in custody served to remind all of Latin America of the reach of U.S. power in the region and around the world. Whether intentional or inadvertent, the Guantánamo decision was a provocation.

The way in which the Bush administration executed its decision could also be read as a provocation to American peace activists. The first prisoners transferred to Guantánamo were herded into Camp X-Ray for temporary confinement in 320 rudimentary cells designed for individual prisoners, each one a wire mesh cage eight feet on a side. Separate groups of twelve cells were surrounded by razor wire. Prisoners transferred from the U.S. military prisons at Bagram or Kandahar would already have experienced life in wire mesh cages. The prisoners in Camp X-Ray were later either repatriated to Afghanistan or transferred laterally to Camp Delta, the first of the five new prisons constructed at Guantánamo by Kellogg, Brown and Root or KBR, then a subsidiary of the Halliburton Company. Built on the site of the old cinder block internment camp for Haitian refugees, Camp Delta's 612 individual eight-by-six-foot cells were provided with a tiny sink, squat flush toilet, and metal frame bed bolted to the wall.[13]

Awarding the $500 million Contingency Construction Capabilities Contract II to KBR was no ordinary exercise in military pork barreling. At a stroke, the responsible Pentagon procurement officers managed to punish contemporary opponents of the administration's foreign policies and strike a retrospective blow against critics of the Vietnam War. Kellogg, Brown and Root was one of a number of firms denounced for war profiteering by peace activists during that earlier war. Perhaps senior procurement officers convinced themselves that awarding the contract to KBR would be cathartic, a means of exorcising the political ghosts of the 1960s by conjuring them again in a new popular war. Or perhaps they were simply confident that after September 11, 2001, any public criticism could be faced down. Whatever their reasoning, their decision reminded many of a scandal that had helped transform American public opinion about the Vietnam War.

To be sure, there was a superficially plausible official explanation for the decision. Kellogg, Brown and Root was one of only a handful of large military construction firms with experience in building secure facilities in geographically distant locations very quickly. As is true of so much of its procurement decision making, the Department of Defense appeared "boxed in" by an oligopoly of large military construction firms. Unsurprisingly, the management in those firms preferred to keep it that way. The only serious alternatives to selecting from among the possible three large military construction contractors would be to resurrect the military service's once astonishing capacity for military construction and to open contract bidding to other firms, including domestic construction firms, which would have to be assured they would not face political reprisal when bidding for other federal government construction contracts, and foreign construction firms. Undertaking either of these alternatives would damage the interests of the two most senior neoconservatives in the Bush administration. Rebuilding the construction capacities of the military services would be contrary to the most important component of the military reforms of Secretary Rumsfeld: eliminating anything other than the "core capabilities" of the military services. Opening competition to other domestic construction firms or foreign construction firms might reduce the profits of KBR and its two sister firms. Kellogg, Brown and Root was of course blessed with what can only be described as extraordinary political connections. Vice President Cheney had been the CEO of the Halliburton Company between 1995 and 2000. Kellogg, Brown and Root was the best-known subsidiary of Halliburton, a corporation whose "core capability" business was oil drilling, which made it vitally interested in American foreign policy and domestic energy policy.

Memories of the war in Vietnam elicited visceral reactions from many Americans when it was revealed that KBR would be constructing the new prisons at Guantánamo. After hearing claims about the conditions in South Vietnamese political prisons in 1970, two members of the U.S. House of Representatives, Augustus F. "Gus" Hawkins from California and William R. Anderson from Tennessee, investigated Con Son Island.[14] Hawkins was the first African American elected to the California State Assembly and would serve in the U.S. House from 1963 to 1991. Anderson was famous as the captain of the nuclear submarine USS *Nautilus* when it was the first ship to sail under the North Pole, and would serve in the U.S. House from 1965 to 1973. Another member of their small group, congressional staffer Tom Harkin, who would go on to be elected first to the U.S. House and later to the U.S. Senate, played a key role in publicizing their shocking discovery. Harkin withstood withering criticism and political pressure from supporters of the war to publish his photographs and a brief account of the conditions in *Life* magazine.[15] Three other members of the U.S. House who were also in South Vietnam with Hawkins and Anderson to tour the prison system were disinclined to believe reports of bad conditions and skipped the opportunity to investigate conditions on Con Son Island. The three were Donald Clancy, an Ohio Republican who served in the House from 1961 to 1977, Robert Mollohan, a West Virginia Democrat who served from 1953 to 1957 and from 1969 to 1983, and Albert Watson, a South Carolina Democrat who served from 1963 to 1971.

That Hawkins, Anderson, and Harkin gained access to Con Son Island was a function of congressional authority over appropriations; Saigon was utterly dependent on the military and financial support voted by the U.S. Congress, and that gave the three the political clout they needed to compel inspection of the island's facilities. That they gained access to the tiger cages was a function of assertiveness.

What Hawkins, Anderson, and Harkin discovered when they departed from the itinerary of the official tour was horrific. First constructed as a French colonial prison, the facility held thousands of prisoners in "tiger cages," four-by-nine-foot stone pits covered by iron grates, each holding three to five prisoners. Chained to the floors, miserable prisoners were periodically covered in clouds of dry lime thrown by guards or trustees from a catwalk in what could be described as "sanitary torture." Food was inadequate. The captives were tortured to extract confessions. Malnutrition, dysentery, tuberculosis, and permanent paralysis of the limbs attributable to the continuous shackling were the common result of the mistreatment. Soon after the revelations about Con Son Island erupted as a public scandal, the U.S. Navy quickly awarded a $400,000 contract to the construction consortium of Raymond, Morrison, Knudson–Brown, Root and Jones, or RMK-BRJ, to construct 384 new isolation cells.[16] Despite the announcement, the initial news report of abuses on Con Son Island further eroded American public support for the war effort, and as was clear from the public discussion of conditions at the prison at Guantánamo, use of the term "tiger cages" and its misunderstood but still emotionally resonant connection to KBR lost little of their emotional punch with time.

Beyond presenting the American public with visual evidence of military and political victory in the war in Afghanistan, punishing several hundred examples of the Islamists who dared to betray their onetime patrons with a surprise attack, and reminding Latin American leftists and pan-nationalists of unrivaled American mastery over the region, what could the neoconservatives have believed they were gaining from the Guantánamo decision? Recall that the decision was not only about the place of imprisonment but also the political-legal identity of the prisoners themselves. The Bush administration officially designated them as "unlawful combatants" and explicitly denied them the status and protections of prisoners of war under the Geneva Conventions. Nothing would have prevented the Bush administration from recognizing them as prisoners of war under the Geneva Conventions and imprisoning some of them at Guantánamo. Why would the neoconservatives want to challenge international law on the treatment of prisoners of war? Just as changes in domestic political regimes require dramatic demonstrations of new authority, imposition of a new international order requires convincing demonstrations of power.

Neoconservatives were nothing if not bold in taking American foreign policy in a new direction in the first term of the Bush administration. Manifestations of the new direction included the "un-signing" of the Kyoto Protocol and attempts to undermine subsequent negotiations on climate change, the "un-signing" of the Rome Statute creating the International Court of Justice, and the negotiation of bilateral agreements with vulnerable allies that insured immunity from prosecution before the court for U.S. nationals. To drive home the point, states other than NATO members, major non-NATO allies, and Taiwan that refused to negotiate such bilateral agreements were subject to denial of International Military Education and Training (IMET) funds under the 2002 American Servicemen's Protection Act. The IMET program is one of the largest mechanisms for disbursing U.S. military aid. Less well known were the refusal to enforce orders issued by the International Court of Justice with respect to the death penalty and the assertion of a national exclusion from a proposed global ban on the illicit transfer of small arms and light weapons, justified on the basis of an interpretation of the Second Amendment to the U.S. Constitution preferred by firearms manufacturers and the gun rights lobby.[17] Announcing that those captured in the war in Afghanistan would be denied prisoner-of-war status under the Geneva Conventions and perhaps tried before military tribunals was entirely in keeping with the neoconservative determination to undermine existing international law and institutions of international governance. Neoconservatives sought to declare them irrelevant in as dramatic a fashion as possible. The unmistakable message was that the rules did not apply to the global hegemon.

International relations theorist Jeffrey Legro identifies a two-stage process by which the foreign policy ideas of great powers change.[18] First, the foreign policy consensus is subjected to some shock, typically taking the form of military defeat, which induces a collapse of support for the ideas that comprised that consensus. Second, either a new foreign policy consensus emerges from the collapse as support for new ideas is consolidated or there is a return to old foreign policy consensus. Legro describes 9/11 as such a shock and the acceptance of ideas comprising a still unconsolidated new foreign policy consensus, which he calls American Supremacy.

This new "American Supremacy" view is distinct from the post–World War II Atlantic Pact orthodoxy in its three-part structure emphasizing unilateral action (as a rule, not as an exception), the preventive use of force (vs. reactive containment), and in the geographical reach of its efforts to intervene overtly (not covertly) in the domestic affairs of other countries including forcible democratization. None of the legs of this stool are new; it is their combination, intensity, and the ways in which they are presented that creates a qualitative difference. . . . the new thinking minimizes the multilateralism ethic that has been a foundation of the postwar order. The United States has of course always acted unilaterally at times; the difference is that it was justified as an exception, not as a norm. The United States now identifies great power cooperation as one of the pillars of its national security strategy. Yet this view of cooperation is not one of institutionalized multilateralism but of "coalitions of the willing," where states are brought together to deal with issues of the moment—usually in cases where the United States cannot do it alone and/or multilateralism is easy.[19]

Although administration officials began communicating their new foreign policy ideas soon after taking office, the political environment created by domestic public opinion and international support following September 11, 2001, gave them much greater scope to act on those ideas.

Washington under the Bush administration was hardly the first government to allow the dangerous combination of ideological conviction and personal ambition to produce an extreme foreign policy environment. The People's Republic of China experienced a comparably wrenching rupture in its foreign policy making during the Great Proletarian Cultural Revolution of 1966–69. Before and after that high noon of ideological extremism, Chinese foreign policy sought a world order "with no military alliances, no great power domination of international forums, no lingering traces of imperialism, and no obstacles to economic development," in response to the bipolar world order defined by the Cold War between the United States and the Soviet Union.[20] During that tumultuous period, Chinese foreign policy was captive to a Manichean worldview in which states in ideological agreement with Beijing's Marxist-Leninist Mao Zedong Thought were deemed friends of China and all other states were its enemies. At one point in this terrifying period, young Red Guards actually occupied the Chinese Foreign Ministry and issued policy directives while senior diplomats were forced to write self-criticisms. Beijing escaped a major international crisis in these years, but it would have been hard pressed to respond effectively if it had been challenged militarily by either of the superpowers.

Nor was Washington under the Bush administration the first government to use the treatment of prisoners of war in violation of international law to signal its new status. During the Second World War, the militarist leaders of the Japanese Empire abandoned their previous scrupulous adherence to international law by treating prisoners of war with shocking brutality. Russian prisoners of war captured in the Russo-Japanese War and German prisoners of war captured in the First World War were well treated by their Japanese captors. During the Second World War, however, the Japanese military ignored international legal norms in its treatment of Chinese, American, British and British Commonwealth, French, and Filipino soldier captives. Those who survived the moment of capture might later die of inadequate nutrition while working at forced labor. What this and the harsh treatment of the subject civilian populations in its East and South Asian possessions signaled was that Japan intended to impose a new order across its new empire. In the aftermath of the Second World War, thousands of Japanese decision makers were tried and executed for their cruelties toward their captives. If the neoconservatives in the Bush administration failed to demonstrate brutality comparable to the Japanese militarists, they nonetheless shared an understanding of international affairs as the struggle by great powers to impose order that is effectively unrestrained by international law, and an appreciation of the power that states exercise over the disposition of prisoners to signal their status as a hegemon.

With the Guantánamo decision the Bush administration was signaling that under the new order it possessed the power to deny captives the protections of international humanitarian law and U.S. constitutional law. Washington could transfer those captured in a war zone on one side of the planet to a prison on the other side of the planet, where they would be paraded before cameras, imprisoned indefinitely, and tortured. Short of televising their summary execution, the kind of punishment meted out in Afghanistan under the Taliban, what greater expression of a captor state's power over prisoners taken in war is possible?

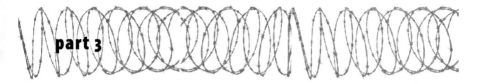

part 3

REPERCUSSIONS

10 Closing Guantánamo

Closing Guantánamo was one of the least ambiguous of the campaign promises made by candidate Barack Obama during his 2008 run for the White House. Of all the reasons for his failure to fulfill, the most important is that it was handicapped, from the moment it was announced, by the adoption of two of the original rationales for the Guantánamo decision. Included under the subhead "4. Restoring Our Values" of the campaign document detailing "Obama's Plan to Defeat Terrorism Worldwide" were the following:

Close the Guantanamo Bay Detention Center. Guantanamo has become a recruiting tool for our enemies. The legal framework behind Guantanamo has failed completely, resulting in only one conviction. President Bush's own Secretary of Defense, Robert Gates, wants to close it. Former Secretary of State Colin Powell wants to close it. The first step to reclaiming America's standing in the world has to be closing this facility. As president, Barack Obama will close the detention facility at Guantanamo. He will reject the Military Commissions Act, which allowed the U.S. to circumvent Geneva Conventions in the handling of detainees. He will develop a fair and thorough process based on the Uniform Code of Military Justice to distinguish between those prisoners who should be prosecuted for their crimes, those who can't be prosecuted but who can be held in a manner consistent with the laws of war, and those who should be released or transferred to their home countries.

Restore Habeas Corpus. The right of habeas corpus allows prisoners to ask a court to determine whether they are being lawfully imprisoned. Recently, this right has been denied to those deemed enemy combatants. Barack Obama strongly supports bipartisan efforts to restore habeas rights. He firmly believes that those who pose a danger to this country should be swiftly tried and brought to justice, but those who do not should have sufficient due process to ensure that we are not wrongfully denying them their liberty.[1]

Although markedly at odds with the emotionally charged rhetoric deployed by both the Bush administration and the rival McCain campaign, the two pledges reveal that the rhetoric of the Obama campaign was anchored by the threat rationale even without endorsing the idea that the original Guantánamo decision was necessary to contain especially dangerous prisoners.

That anchoring was evident again in his January 11, 2009, interview with George Stephanopoulos on ABC's *This Week*. When asked whether he still intended to close the camp, Obama fell back on the threat rationale, albeit in language more qualified than Bush would have used, to explain why that was a challenge. He described the prisoners as "a bunch of folks that have been detained, many of whom may be very dangerous," and described the process he wanted to conduct as one that would not "result in releasing people who are intent on blowing us up."[2]

Obama continued that meeting the challenge was important for the perception of American foreign policy by foreign news audiences as part of a national security strategy as much as for the value of adhering to the rule of law as found in international and constitutional law: "But I don't want to be ambiguous about this," he said. "We are going to close Guantanamo and we are going to make sure that the procedures we set up are ones that abide by our Constitution. That is not only the right thing to do but it actually has to be part of our broader national security strategy, because we will send a message to the world that we are serious about our values." Of course, this begged the question whether a different policy calculation would have been made if foreign news audiences had not been paying close attention to the treatment of prisoners held at Guantánamo.

When Obama addressed Guantánamo again on May 21, 2009, it was to announce that he had ordered it closed. In explaining this decision, Obama characterized Bush's decision to establish the prison camp as "hasty" and "motivated by a sincere desire to protect the American people."[3] Moreover, it had failed to result in successful prosecutions and instead undermined the moral authority of the United States. Thus the original Guantánamo decision was just an unfortunate but well-intentioned mistake.

Whether Obama believed either the threat rationale or that his predecessor had made an honest mistake is less important than that he was convinced that segments of American public opinion accepted both as true. Then, as with so many other decisions made by the administration, the path of least resistance was to accept them as premises and make policy accordingly. There is more to the story than the willingness of the Obama White House to follow the grooves carved out by the Bush administration. The unwillingness to challenge the official explanation was matched by the pusillanimity of nearly every other elected official and many of the journalists and scholars who addressed the question. Obama's failure of political courage, moreover, was a gift to opponents of closing the prison camp.

The other obstacles to fulfilling the campaign pledge were more obvious. Former Bush administration officials anxious to protect their historical legacy or nervous about being indicted for having approved acts of torture continued to repeat the three rationales for the original decision with little or no challenge. Current and former Bush administration officials had been publicly discussing closing Guantánamo since 2007. That ended with the election of Obama. Congressional Republicans thereafter sought to prevent the new administration from claiming the achievement of a campaign pledge by evoking the image of the prisoners as terrorist supermen constructed over the previous eight years by the Bush administration and by deploying the sunk-costs argument. They could do that because the Obama administration had endorsed most of the original explanation for the Guantánamo decision and the congressional Democrats were anything but disciplined in their support of their president. Pentagon foot-dragging about transferring any of the prisoners to the reconstructed modern prison at Bagram and the difficulty of persuading third countries to accept prisoners who could not be repatriated represented further obstacles. Each of these obstacles merits further examination.

Republican Opposition

Opposition to closing the prison at Guantánamo by congressional Republicans grew out of their disciplined partisan defense of the original Guantánamo decision. Before 2008, Republicans demonstrated impressive party discipline across the branches of government and houses of Congress. Congressional Republicans joined officials of the Department of Defense and conservative commentators in defending the decision of their president vigorously against international and domestic critics. The effort was devoted as much to blunting the criticism as to refuting it. The Pentagon issued a stream of press releases claiming that intelligence collected through interrogations was helping to win the War on Terror, sent senior officers to testify before congressional committees to repeat that message and to elicit positive assessments from Republican committee members, and flew junketing Republican members of Congress to tour the prison who would then make favorable remarks about the conditions they observed.

In addition to claiming that intelligence useful for operations in the War on Terror had been collected, senior military officers testifying before congressional committees about the treatment of prisoners typically included a mixture of simple denial that any misconduct on the part of military personnel had occurred, exculpatory contextualization of any misconduct, and assertions that prior misconduct had been punished and future misconduct prevented. For example, Air Force lieutenant general Richard Schmidt testified before the Senate Armed Services Committee about his investigation of the abuse of prisoners, stating that he had found only a small number of instances in which interrogators had violated Department of Defense guidelines and that the misconduct was not severe enough to constitute "inhumane" treatment.[4] Although short shackling had been used in 2002 and 2003, Schmidt insisted the practice had been thereafter forbidden. The intelligence officer who had authorized the duct taping of a prisoner's mouth to prevent him from chanting in an effort to resist interrogation had been informally reprimanded and the general had recommended that the officer be formally reprimanded or admonished.

Schmidt also addressed a "non-approved event" in which a female interrogator told a prisoner that the red ink she was smearing on his face was her menstrual blood, explaining that it was merely "a spontaneous act of revenge" after she had been "spit on." Thus this humiliating transgressive act was understandable, though still disapproved, as an emotional response by an individual, albeit a trained military interrogator. The general noted that the interrogator had been verbally reprimanded and removed for thirty days from responsibility for conducting interrogations.

The examples of abuses were thus reduced to nothing more than minor departures from approved and humane interrogation procedures rather than programmed assaults on the psyches of the prisoners. Playing his supportive role in the same hearings, Republican senator John Warner noted that these few cases of misconduct should be viewed against 24,000 interrogations conducted at the prison, a comment suggesting that the cases of misconduct mentioned in the hearing constituted the entirety of the prisoner abuse. Speaking for the Pentagon was only natural for the senior senator from Virginia. Warner represented a state that consistently ranked as one of the two leading recipients of spending by the Department of Defense.

Republican Joel Hefley of Colorado, a member of the House Armed Services Committee and one of seventy-seven members of the House to have taken the military junket to Guantánamo, praised the conditions he found there: "Nobody wants to be in prison, but if you're going to be in prison, this is the one to be in."[5] Although the willingness to picture oneself in the place of another is typically an important part of serious reflection about justice, the facts contradict the congressman. If Hefley had been convicted of a white collar crime—and politicians are rarely convicted of anything else—he would probably have served any prison sentence in a minimum security federal facility and perhaps in its adjacent camp. That is where America's white collar criminals were typically incarcerated. There the prison regimen would not have included being held incommunicado, "beat and greet" intimidation rituals, interrogation for hours on end, short shackling, stripping naked in front of female officers, or otherwise being subjected to inhumane treatment. American political and economic elites like Hefley are not asked to serve time with ordinary criminal convicts, let alone accused terrorists.

The endorsement made by Georgia Republican congressman Phil Gingrey after his tour of the military prison is particularly interesting. During a 2003 interview he asserted, "It's no country club down there, but it's no worse than what I've seen in the county jail in Cobb County."[6] Cobb County is a predominantly white suburban county in the Greater Atlanta metropolitan area, part of which was in his congressional district, Georgia's 11th. That the Cobb County lockup would permit the sort of official misconduct that was taking place at Guantánamo would be a shocking discovery, but then Gingrey was speaking before the revelations about the brutality in the military prisons. That the Marietta OB-GYN-turned-ultraconservative-politician might simply be credulous is suggested by his description of a translated interrogation he observed through a one-way mirror:

"It was very respectful," Gingrey said. "This happened to be a lady who was interrogating. She was very respectful and encouraged the detainee to be forthright. She knew or suspected that he wanted to get back to his homeland and that his cooperation could expedite that process."

We cannot know whether the congressman suspected that what he was shown was selected by his military handlers to be innocuous, or whether he cared that something more sinister might take place when he and other outside observers were not there. What is clear is that as a licensed physician, Gingrey ought to have focused on the serious medical ethics issues raised by the treatment of the prisoners. The medical records of Guantánamo prisoners were used by military medical personnel to design individual interrogation protocols to exploit their personal medical and psychiatric weaknesses. That was an unmistakable violation of medical ethics. The World Medical Association's 1975 Declaration of Tokyo states unequivocally that a doctor shall not "countenance," "condone," or "participate in" the practice of torture.[7] Even more serious accusations of complicity by military medical personnel were leveled in June 2010 when Physicians for Human Rights issued a white paper, *Experiments in Torture: Evidence of Human Subject Research and Experimentation in the "Enhanced" Interrogation Program*.[8] The authors of that report noted that the systematic collection of personal information from human subjects, including prisoners, for any purpose other than direct medical benefit to the patient required informed consent under the Geneva Conventions, the Nuremberg Code, and federal statutes. Federal regulations govern research on human subjects, and the Department of Defense and CIA are subject to them. Among the morally repugnant behaviors by medical personnel at issue were the design of equipment for waterboarding, supervision of waterboarding of prisoners, and calibration of the pain experienced by prisoners to ensure that it fell within the guidelines for a legal defense that the specific interrogation techniques did not constitute torture. Did Gingrey as a physician countenance or condone torture when he unequivocally endorsed the prison regimen at Guantánamo? Was he absolved of having violated his medical ethical duties because he did not witness these practices or was not aware of them? Or, since he was a member of the U.S. House of Representatives and thus possessed of the sort of authority to investigate official wrongdoing necessary for government oversight, did his willingness to be deceived by his military handlers implicate him?

After Obama won the White House, Representative Gingrey was in the forefront of congressional Republicans warning against the transfer of any Guantánamo prisoners to prisons within the United States, going so far as to propose national legislation entitled the No Gitmo in Georgia Act and encouraging representatives from other states to propose comparable Not in My Back Yard (NIMBY) national legislation.

The proposal to transfer the remaining Guantánamo prisoners to the underutilized maximum security Thomson Correctional Center in northwestern Illinois appealed to most local residents and local elected officials of both political parties because of the increased employment and business income it would bring to the area. One estimate was that it would generate 3,000 additional jobs in a relatively economically depressed area. The president of Thomson Village, the Mississippi River town of 500 residents located closest to the prison, commented not only on the economic advantage but on the obvious waste in leaving a prison with 1,600 cells largely empty: "It's been sitting there for eight to nine years and our town is like a ghost town."[9] The facility was one of several constructed to incarcerate a predicted tsunami of young criminal "superpredators," a species of folk devil that had been conjured in conservative law-and-order rhetoric during the 1980s but then failed to materialize. If the prisoners held at Guantánamo were terrorist supermen, then there could hardly be a more secure location to contain them.

Illinois's congressional and state-level elected officials and candidates responded to the proposal by dividing along predictable partisan lines. Where Democrats generally supported it with arguments emphasizing its advantage for the local economy, Republicans opposed it with arguments repeating the threat rationale in the justification for the Guantánamo decision. The senior senator, Democrat Richard Durbin, expressed support with the promise that transferring the prisoners would "bring thousands of good-paying jobs to Illinois when we need them most."[10] Republican gubernatorial candidate Andy McKenna warned hyperbolically against the threat of transferring "Gitmo detainees to our neighborhoods."

Opposition nationwide has been reinforced by news coverage that fails to distinguish the original population of Guantánamo prisoners from the second, much smaller contingent brought in to backstop the original decision. Even the *New York Times* is culpable. In its January 26, 2011, story on the sentencing of Ahmed Khalfan Ghailani after his trial in federal district court in Manhattan, reporter Benjamin Weiser is content to identify him as "the first former detainee at Guantánamo Bay, Cuba, to be tried in the civilian court system."[11] No mention is made that Ghailani was transferred to Guantánamo, from CIA custody, much later than the original population.

Sunk Costs, Bureaucratic Momentum, and Military Opposition

Although they are irrational, sunk-costs arguments for continuing to execute previously adopted policy choices can make for persuasive political appeals. Sunk-costs arguments are irrational because they promise rewards by continuing to act in a manner that was a poor decision initially. They are deployed most often in iterated investment scams where the victim is asked to invest more money in an enterprise for fear of losing the initial investment. Republican congressman Don Manzullo, whose district includes Thomson Village and who is a member of the House Foreign Affairs Committee, coupled the threat rationale of the original justification with the sunk-costs argument in expressing his opposition to transferring prisoners from Guantánamo to the United States by stating that the Guantánamo camps were "set up to house these dangerous terrorists, and they should stay there." One flaw in this reasoning is that few of the prisoners were in fact dangerous terrorists. Instead they appear to have been the difficult-to-repatriate residue.

Bureaucratic momentum complements the sunk-costs argument as an obstacle to closing Guantánamo. The Bush administration spent approximately $2 billion to construct state-of-the-art prison facilities and upgrade other facilities at what was once a run-down backwater base.[12] Included in the expenditures were $18.2 million for a prison hospital, $2.9 million for its separate psychiatric ward, $13 million for a courthouse, and $2.2 million for a barracks building for attorneys and journalists. Then there were the baseball and football fields that cost $7.3 million, the $296,000 go-kart track, the $60,000 batting cage, and twenty-seven playgrounds for the fewer than 400 children resident at the base. These are examples of spectacular waste in government spending, to be sure, but they are also concrete facts that may be deployed by elected officials and military officers alike in making sunk-cost arguments.

The proposal to transfer the remaining Guantánamo prisoners to the new military prison at Bagram, which replaced the facility that had been the scene of brutal abuse, was successfully resisted by the U.S. and NATO commander in Afghanistan, General Stanley McCrystal, who would later lose his command after his subordinates publicly criticized the Obama White House.[13] This opposition, combined with the civilian deference to the military that has characterized American politics since September 11, 2001, deprived the Obama administration of an important option in disposing of the prisoners.

Third-Country Reluctance

Two problems from the Guantánamo decision appear to have been unanticipated. The first problem was the creation of a cohort of celebrity prisoners, who inadvertently functioned as effective political prisoners. Publicity about indefinite imprisonment, probable torture, and threatened prosecution transformed a collection of ordinary men, notably the Australian national David Hicks, the British national Moazzam Begg, and the German national Murat Kurnaz, into martyrs of the Bush administration's foreign policy. Symbols of a new hybrid cultural and national identity, they provided living reminders of everything that seemed to be wrong about the foreign policy of the United States under the Bush administration.

The second problem was the creation of a cohort of noncelebrity "orphan" prisoners: the handful of ethnic Uighur Chinese nationals that both the Bush and Obama administrations declined to repatriate to China in the belief that they would suffer persecution for their beliefs or their potential actions. Uighurs are a Muslim ethnic minority living in Xinjiang, China's restive western province. From the perspective of Chinese foreign policy makers, they are potential terrorists fighting in the cause of Islamist Uighur separatism. From the perspective of American foreign policy makers, they are potential victims of Chinese human rights violations. In the minds of Americans indoctrinated in the Cold War categories, the same human rights violations that are unfortunate when committed by the coercive apparatus of a noncommunist government become horrific when committed by a communist government. Since September 11, 2001, the United States had turned over prisoners to be tortured by the Moroccan, Jordanian, and Syrian secret police and had repatriated prisoners from Guantánamo to states with grim human rights records like Saudi Arabia and Algeria.

The Obama administration, for example, forcibly repatriated Aziz Abdul Naji, a thirty-five-year-old Algerian national who spent eight years of his life in the camp, to Algeria.[14] Naji expressed fear that he would be tortured or killed after repatriation. That would seem an acceptable risk, but forcibly repatriating the Uighurs to China was too much to countenance. Although Washington and Beijing were both at war with a common enemy in Islamist terrorism, the Cold War is still part of the hardwiring of American officials.

Foreign governments willing to accept prisoners who were ready for release but poor candidates for repatriation have been few, and insistent upon generous remuneration. Albania was the first third-party country to accept released prisoners, taking several of the orphaned Uighurs, in large part because of the positive image of the United States for doing battle with Serbia over the majority ethnic Albanian province of Kosovo. Bermuda and Palau subsequently accepted other Uighurs. Cape Verde, Germany, Ireland, Latvia, and Spain agreed to accept small numbers of the other prisoners with which they have no connection such as previous residency.[15] For example, the United States and Germany negotiated at length over the transfer of several non-German prisoners, including Palestinian national Mohammed Tahamuttan.[16] Accepting him was intended to symbolize the improvement in relations between the two NATO allies that had soured during the Bush administration but improved with the Obama presidency.

Human Rights Watch attorney Andrea Prasow points up the reason that releasing the bulk of the remaining prisoners to third countries is likely to fail:

> The Obama administration missed a critical moment when it could have released the Uighurs into the U.S. and demonstrated to the world that it was truly committed to closing Guantánamo. Instead, with a congressionally-enacted ban on any releases into the U.S., the U.S. government finds itself begging other countries to help resettle detainees who can't be returned to their home countries while refusing to take any itself.[17]

The stench of hypocrisy puts off decision makers and publics in third countries that might otherwise accept released prisoners.

Message Effectiveness

The repetition of the official explanation for the Guantánamo decision long after exposure of its illogic and factual inaccuracies deserves explanation. Political messages are most persuasive with news audiences when they are plausible, repeated consistently, and able to evoke fear. Contrary political messages relying on logic and evidence hardly stand a chance in the competition for public opinion. That inequality characterizes the initial reception of the official explanation for the Guantánamo decision. Superficial plausibility, consistent repetition by the Bush White House and the Pentagon, and public anxiety about international terrorism produced by news coverage of the September 11, 2001, terrorist attacks on the World Trade Center and the Pentagon made it initially compelling for most Americans. What gave the official explanation a much longer run is that, while some responsible elites outside the administration criticized the execution of the decision, they did not criticize its claimed purposes. Indeed, they usually endorsed one or more of its three rationales.

Given such dereliction, it is unsurprising that most Americans accepted the Guantánamo decision. Although disillusionment with the administration's other foreign policies grew over time, the percentage of respondents in TNS/Washington Post/ABC News surveys saying that they supported the policy of "holding suspected terrorists without trial" at Guantánamo declined by only 8 percent from September 2003, when it was 65 percent, to June 2006, when it was 57 percent.[18] When asked whether the military prison should be closed, fully 68 percent of the respondents in a subsequent August 2006 Bloomberg/Los Angeles Times survey responded that it should remain open. The reasons are easy to discern. The terror of September 11, 2001, had been cultivated for five years by the Bush administration, and the public had heard few if any dissenting voices in the mainstream news sources about Guantánamo. Unsurprisingly, then, most Americans believed what they were told.

11 After Guantánamo

What became of the Guantánamo decision a full decade after it was officially announced and explained? Although the explanation survived only in bogeyman portrayals of the remaining prisoners conjured by Republican elected officials and pundits, the decision itself survived as a barbed-wire fait accompli. Despite promising to close the prison while campaigning for the White House, President Barack Obama did not order it closed. As with most of the national security policies he inherited from the previous administration, Obama recast rather than repudiated Guantánamo. Unlike his predecessor, he would accept that his authority in the struggle against al-Qaeda (the phrase "War on Terror" having been dropped) was constrained by the U.S. Constitution, legislation passed by the U.S. Congress, the rule of law, international humanitarian law, and perhaps international public opinion. The prison nonetheless would remain open for two purposes.

First, Guantánamo would be the location for trials under the Military Commissions Act of 2009, legislation that Obama supported. Defendants in those trials would be accorded more due process rights than under the rules originally conceived by the Bush administration but still fewer than in trials before a U.S. civilian court. Coerced confessions would be excluded as evidence, but statements made during ordinary interrogations without warning about self-incrimination could be used in prosecutions. Rules regarding the admission of hearsay evidence would be much more permissive than in a trial before a civilian court. Evidence withheld from the defense during discovery could also be introduced; the defense would instead be provided with documents with redacted material or summaries of depositions from witnesses. Each of these represents a significant departure from the conception of the rule of law expressed in the Sixth Amendment.

Among the rules governing contact with clients and the use of evidence under which attorneys for prisoners at Guantánamo with habeas corpus petitions must work, at least one appears to have been issued simply to daunt defense counsel and to engage in political posturing rather than to protect national security. An instruction issued by Christine E. Gunning, a D.C. District Court security officer, and the Clarification and Additional Guidance on Use of WikiLeaks Information prohibited these attorneys from downloading, saving, printing, or disseminating material revealed through WikiLeaks.[1] The counsel for prisoner Abdullah Faraj responded that the rule represented an unwarranted bid by the government to expand the scope of the Nondisclosure Agreement and the Protective Order that the attorneys signed, as well as an impermissible prior restraint on First Amendment liberties. The Nondisclosure Agreement is reasonably understood as setting the terms by which counsels with security clearances receive access to classified information provided by the government.

Second, Guantánamo would be for the location for indefinite "preventive" detention without trial of captured enemies (or those captives mistakenly identified as enemy) for whom there is no other location for disposal outside the territory of the United States. There would be more exacting review of the basis for detention. Torture like waterboarding would be banned. So too would abusive treatment of prisoners other than the indefinite detention itself.

Guantánamo formed part of the larger approach to national security premised on looking forward rather than backward, and perforce ignoring the excesses of the Bush administration. Most notably, on April 21, 2009, Obama declined to name a truth commission, the sort of blue ribbon panel of respected political and legal elites able to offer a definitive assessment, to investigate his predecessor's policy and practice of torture and other violations of international law. Although such a commission was supported by important Democratic congressional leaders, including Senate Judiciary Committee chair Patrick J. Leahy and House speaker Nancy Pelosi, Obama ultimately rejected the call for the truth commission, saying that it would "open the door to a protracted, backward looking discussion."[2] The obvious contradiction was that prosecuting terrorists, whether in civilian courts or before military commissions, would necessitate such a "protracted, backward looking discussion." Obama's statement was followed on April 24, 2009, by an announcement from Attorney General Eric Holder that the deaths of only two prisoners in CIA custody would be investigated but not the torture or the mistreatment of another ninety-nine prisoners who may or may not have been in custody.[3] Nor would the Justice Department prosecute "anyone who acted in good faith and within the scope of the legal guidance given by the Office of Legal Counsel regarding the interrogation of detainees."[4] In effect, then-president George W. Bush, the officials of his administration who adopted and executed the torture policy, and the government lawyers who prepared the legal arguments to justify torture, as well as the torturers who put the policy into practice, would be legally immunized against criminal investigation and prosecution for their actions, which in the view of prominent commentators might include war crimes. None of the principals responsible for the Guantánamo decision and torture policy would be brought to book in a U.S. court. That they might face justice in a foreign court was unlikely but could not be totally discounted.

Although the Obama administration succeeded in recovering much of the lost international reputation of the United States as a government committed to adhering to the spirit of international law, failure to conduct an investigation meant that the domestic accountability deficit would be a continuing burden. The suspicion of many Americans that lawlessness by officials of the executive branch would not be exposed, let alone punished, was palpable. Without the potent threats of public shaming through exposure and of potential prosecution, the constraints on the power of the presidency accepted by the Obama administration might be rejected by a future administration.

In other respects Obama would deploy the same authority and the same weapons of counterterrorism that had been deployed under Bush. A broad interpretation of the state secrets privilege would continue to immunize the national government against lawsuits brought by individuals like Maher Arar who had been subjected to extraordinary rendition and torture. As a consequence, the public scrutiny of government action that violated individual statutory and constitutional rights would be reduced. Although extraordinary rendition would be officially ended and "black sites" or secret prisons operated by the CIA in third countries would be closed, captives might still be held in temporary custody in third countries with cooperative governments when necessary. More important, there would be strenuous effort to avoid alerting and upsetting public opinion in friendly European democracies about these or other covert operations.

There would, however, be rather fewer such captives, because of a shift in policy toward killing them with missile attacks by drone aircraft. Under Obama the focus of the attacks moved from "signature strikes" against suspected terrorist camps to more precise strikes targeting specific individuals believed to occupy leadership positions or to possess special skills such as bomb making. After the number of attacks in Pakistan reached a peak in 2010, the focus shifted to Yemen and Somalia.[5] Public outrage in Pakistan over the killing of noncombatants at events unrelated to terrorism and of family members of suspected terrorists was one likely reason for the transition in policy. Technological advances in drone aircraft and precision weapons was another.

However, something else seems to have driven the transition. On May 29, 2012, *New York Times* reporters Jo Becker and Scott Shane published a story based on White House sources saying that Obama had made himself the last word in a "delegations process" that designated individual terrorists for death or capture.[6] In regularly scheduled Tuesday meetings, the president and his counterterrorism advisors evaluated the intelligence about individual terrorist suspects before deciding their fate. Death rather than captivity was by far the more frequent decision. Although the story portrayed Obama as engaged in a sophisticated analysis based on Just War theory, it appeared on the day of the Texas Republican Party presidential primary, the moment that Mitt Romney collected enough convention delegates to win the GOP nomination.

If the killing of Osama bin Laden in a raid on May 2, 2011, had not already secured Obama's reputation as a war leader, his portrayal as the decision maker responsible for killing each major terrorist figure would be more than enough to refute Republican criticism of Obama as soft on terrorism. The reelection strategy in the Obama White House was not difficult to discern. The president would outflank the Republican nominee on counterterrorism policy. With little need to respond to the war weariness among Democratic voters, who lacked realistic alternatives, Obama could appeal to the bellicosity of Republican-leaning independent voters by appearing tough on terrorism. What could Mitt Romney promise to do that could top personally deciding to kill individual terrorists?

That calculation would also explain the extraordinarily aggressive prosecutions of whistle-blowers under the Obama administration. When Private Bradley Manning of the U.S. Army released a massive quantity of material to the whistle-blowing website WikiLeaks, he was arrested and subjected to what United Nations special rapporteur for human rights Juan Mendez characterized as cruel and inhuman treatment in military custody, including eleven months of solitary confinement for twenty-three hours a day.[7]

The attempt to shut down the WikiLeaks sites where Manning's material was made available, together with urgent formal requests for the extradition of WikiLeaks founder Julian Assange, represent a frenzied effort to punish the two for exposure of embarrassing official secrets and to intimidate others who might follow their example. Among the most damning of the leaks was the release of a video and audio recording of an attack by an Apache helicopter on a minivan in Baghdad on July 12, 2007, that killed Reuters photographer Namir Noor-Eldeen and his driver, Saeed Chmagh.[8] The gun camera video shows the killings, while the audio is of the crew communicating with their superiors and expressing contempt for their targets. International public opinion was shocked by the horrific violence of the images and sounds, and by the realization that the victims were innocent. Bodies were shredded, but so too was public belief in the accuracy of the targeting in U.S. airstrikes.

WikiLeaks also released an enormous number of diplomatic cables that originated in U.S. embassies. Rather than surprising most observers, the cables tended to confirm what they suspected about the opinions held by American diplomats and about their relationships with officials of other governments. Instead, observers were taken aback by the undiplomatic bluntness of the language used. A July 9, 2008, cable summarizing the exchange in Ottawa between U.S. State Department counselor Eliot Cohen and Canadian Security Intelligence Service director Jim Judd about Islamist terror groups in Canada is an example. Judd's comments criticizing the Canadian judiciary for an "Alice in Wonderland" perspective that legally hobbled counterterrorism operations and lamenting a Canadian "knee-jerk anti-Americanism" and "paroxysms of moral outrage" are repeated.[9] If the release of the cables did little or nothing to harm national security, it deeply embarrassed the U.S. State Department.

Although Obama was elected president with the promise of more open government, it soon became clear that his administration would maintain the post-9/11 atmosphere of excessive secrecy established under Bush. Several whistle-blowers who had worked for government agencies responsible for national security became high-profile targets for prosecution: former CIA officers Jeffrey Sterling and John Kiriakou, former FBI translator Shamai Leibowitz, and former National Security Agency executive Thomas Drake. The manner of prosecuting the NSA's Drake was especially surprising. Drake was indicted on April 15, 2010, under the 1917 Espionage Act for presenting documents as part of a complaint to the Inspector General that a $1 billion contract outsourced by the NSA could have been handled in-house for only $3 million—hardly the stuff of espionage. That his prosecution under that law was meant to intimidate other potential whistle-blowers is highly probable. Drake ultimately accepted a misdemeanor plea agreement when the Justice Department's case collapsed.[10]

Rather than recede into memory and history as had other historical cases of mass imprisonment of special populations of prisoners, Guantánamo instead fragmented into several distinct news stories. Although consistent with the increased fragmentation of all political news coverage in the United States in the years since September 11, 2001, it deprived Americans of a single coherent historical narrative that assigned credit and blame for the Guantánamo decision.

American news sources focused on the trials of some of the sixteen "high-value detainees" transferred from CIA custody to Guantánamo in 2006–8 to justify the original Guantánamo decision. In keeping with the practice of the government and press established under the Bush administration, no effort was made by the Obama administration or the press to distinguish this second, smaller group of prisoners from the much more numerous prisoners originally transferred to the camp in 2002. Given that failure, American news consumers could be excused for incorrectly believing that the "high-value" prisoners had been in Guantánamo since 2002 and that the camp had been established for their prosecution.

In the conservative *Wall Street Journal* the military commissions story was framed as one of disruptive behavior by five defendants being prosecuted together—Khalid Sheikh Mohammed, Ramzi bin al-Shibh, Mustafa Ahmad al-Hawsawi, Ali Abd al-Aziz, and Walid bin Attash, and the willingness of their defense counsel to assist them in the exercise during a May 6, 2012, arraignment. Rather than accept the political legitimacy of the trial, the defendants engaged in a "battle of wills" with the beleaguered military judge. Rather than perform their assigned roles representing the guilty in a trial with a foregone conclusion, the defense counsel sought "to put the military commission experiment itself on trial." In what was portrayed as a delaying tactic, they insisted at the arraignment hearing on a full reading of the lengthy charges against the defendants, a formality normally waived in ordinary criminal trials. Of course, this was anything but an ordinary criminal trial. Defense counsel also dared to embarrass the court by raising the issue of the defendants' having been waterboarded at black sites.[11]

An op-ed column in the *Wall Street Journal* by L. Gordon Crovitz deployed a comparison with the Nuremberg trials to express frustration not only about the behavior of the Guantánamo defendants and their defense counsel but also about the deflation of a "cathartic public reckoning" in "at least part of the Muslim world." "After the Nuremberg trials brought detailed information to light," he wrote, "no German could deny the atrocities."[12] By implication, 9/11 is comparable to the war crimes of Nazi Germany, and all Muslims share in responsibility for that attack, just as, in the minds of some, all Germans bore responsibility for the Holocaust. Rarely has a parallel been more over-drawn. Location undermines the comparison. Where the Guantánamo trial was staged on the other side of the planet from an occupied but unpacified Afghanistan, the Nuremberg trials were staged in the heart of occupied and defeated Germany. Unlike the defendants in the dock at Guantánamo, the Nazi leaders tried at Nuremberg had not been tortured or held in secret prisons. Scale too undermines the comparison. All of the deaths from terrorist attacks perpetrated by al-Qaeda are only a tiny fraction of the deaths in atrocities perpetrated by Nazi Germany, in no small part because al-Qaeda could not deploy the military power of an advanced industrial society. Muslims can no more be held collectively responsible for the terrorism of al-Qaeda than Christians can be held collectively responsible for the genocide perpetrated by Nazi Germany. Moreover, the purpose of the Nuremberg trials was different, both more precise and more profound, than compelling Germans to experience a "cathartic public reckoning" with their recent history. Instead, the trial record produced at Nuremberg served as an authoritative narrative that focused responsibility on the Nazi leadership and their ideas rather than on the German population and that identified the perpetrators, victims, and bystanders in the tragedy so that the survivors might move forward in peace with one another. As Crovitz's attribution of collective guilt to all Muslims shows, the Guantánamo trial is unlikely to achieve that purpose.

The *New York Times*, liberal counterpart to the *Wall Street Journal*, complained in an editorial that the trial had been delayed much too long and that the Bush administration, by torturing the defendants and holding them in secret prisons for years, had undermined the legitimacy of the proceedings.[13]

In an article in the *Nation*, Karen J. Greenberg wrote that the weakness of the Guantánamo trial was exposed when the defense counsel interrogated the qualifications of the military judge in a most unusual voir dire:

Challenging a judge beyond his allowable comfort zone is unthinkable in federal court. Each and every attorney has a simple choice: be respectful or be removed—even punished. In the military commissions system, there is no such control. If the silence of the defendants or the vocal protests of their lawyers proclaimed the differences between the two systems, the voir dire illustrated it beyond a reasonable doubt. . . . each and every step of these trials stands to be overwhelmed by the internal contradictions of this system, and the trials themselves will be a platform for vigorous challenges to the commissions' validity.[14]

On May 29, 2012, Guantánamo would once again provide the backdrop for a conservative Republican to posture on national security. Florida's junior senator, Marco Rubio, described as a possible running mate for likely GOP presidential nominee Mitt Romney, toured the prison for several hours.[15] Although the event garnered little coverage, it could be used to bolster his thin foreign policy and national security résumé. The press release issued by his office referred not only to the prison but also to the strategic value of the naval base, a justification for the U.S. presence infrequently heard since September 11, 2001.

Almost lost in the American news coverage was any reference to the original population of prisoners at Guantánamo. The orphaned Uighurs reappeared when two accepted settlement in El Salvador,[16] an unlikely country for them to find a new home but probably better than life on hold in indefinite detention. That left just three Uighurs at Guantánamo who had earlier rejected resettlement in the Maldives and Palau.

The different Guantánamo news stories for national news audiences outside the United States were continuous reminders of the political vexation caused by the Guantánamo decision. In mid-2012, Omar Khadr was once again the leading Guantánamo news story in Canada as Ottawa was criticized by the United Nations Committee Against Torture for moving too slowly to approve his transfer to Canadian custody as well as for participating in the extraordinary rendition of three Arab Canadians, Abdullah Almalki, Ahmad Abou Elmaati, and Muayyed Nureddin, to Egypt and Syria, where they were tortured.[17] The repatriation of Khadr finally took place on September 29, 2012.

By mid-2012 the news story in Britain had long since shifted from the brutal treatment in custody of the released British prisoners to an issue of official secrecy and the constitutional authority of Parliament. The focus of the debate was the Justice and Security Bill, which included a provision allowing judges in civil courts to close proceedings to the press and public at the request of responsible cabinet ministers when secret intelligence material was considered in evidence and a provision creating a Special Immigration Appeals Commission authorized to conduct certain cases in secret.[18] According to the October 2011 *Justice and Security Green Paper* authored by Secretary of State for Justice Kenneth Clarke, the government sought this heightened level of secrecy in judicial proceedings because it had been forced to "reach expensive out-of-court settlements with former Guantanamo detainees because of a lack of an appropriate framework in which civil damages claims involving sensitive material could be heard."[19] That document uses as an example the November 2010 agreement reached with Binyamin Mohammed in which the government paid compensation without admitting liability in his rendition, torture, and imprisonment. The argument for official secrecy is not that the government effectively lost the case because the facts were extremely embarrassing to the intelligence services. How could Mohammed's horrific experience in custody be explained as necessary to protect national security? Instead the green paper cast the need for secret proceedings as necessary to protect the access of the British intelligence services to material given them by "foreign partners." By implication, the Americans will be giving the British less intelligence material unless they can keep it secret.

British civil libertarians joined by opposition members of Parliament countered that the new secrecy would be used to conceal government wrongdoing such as complicity in extraordinary rendition and torture.[20] That point is well taken. London would not have found itself paying Mohammed compensation if it had not been privy to information about his mistreatment.

The fragmentation of the Guantánamo news story into stories about military commission trials of some of the "high-value detainees" for the American news audience and stories about the treatment of individuals who were part of the original population of prisoners for English-language news audiences outside the United States makes the articulation of a single coherent master narrative unlikely. The anti-scandal perpetrated by the Bush administration and abetted by the Obama administration was a success with American public opinion but failed with international public opinion. There is a substantial price to be paid for such incoherence. Guantánamo has become synonymous with gross human rights violations and the hypocrisy of U.S. foreign policy for public opinion even in countries that are America's closest allies. Unless and until a new administration in Washington investigates and reveals the truth about Guantánamo, it will cloud the American title as the champion of liberal democracy. What Briton, Canadian, or Australian, let alone what Pakistani or Yemeni, could now give to any statement made by a U.S. government official about human rights or national security the benefit of the doubt? Without that fundamental trust, the cost of protecting both has become much steeper.

✳   ✳   ✳

What does Guantánamo mean? For Sabin Willett, a Boston attorney who represented several of the Uighur prisoners, it signals not just gross injustice to individuals but also the deterioration of the values that are appropriate to a liberal society, including the U.S. Constitution's limits on the authority of the executive, the basic competence of the military and intelligence services, and respect for fundamental human rights.[21]

Another answer is that Guantánamo signals the collapse of the confidence that once characterized American national spirit. The equanimity with which Americans accepted the presence of the 425,000 Axis prisoners of war in barrack camps strung across the continental United States during the Second World War stands in stark contrast to the hysteria expressed by some Americans about the proposal to transfer 150 prisoners from Guantánamo to a single supermax prison in Illinois. The ratio between those two figures, 28,333 to 1, is a proper gauge of the timidity engendered by eight years of carefully modulated panic since September 11, 2001. One tragic day of terror became a seemingly permanent state of terror. The embarrassing result is collective pusillanimity in the face of nonexistential threats.

Although true, these answers are incomplete. Guantánamo is also an anti-scandal, manifest wrongdoing announced by decision makers in a manner that disarmed critics by aborting the analyis that would have led them to recognize it for what it was. That the official explanation for the decision was a brilliant fraud is evident from the continued articulation of the threat, intelligence, and prosecution rationales without challenge. Logic and evidence betray each of the rationales as either false or wildly exaggerated. There were no terrorist supermen, no intelligence coups, and only a handful of prosecutions. Alternative explanations were also readily available. Comparison with other cases of liberal democracies imprisoning special classes of captives in extraordinarily public geographic isolation points to the spectacle of victory, the punishment of scapegoats, and the announcement of a new international order as a more convincing composite explanation.

Understanding the motivations for the Guantánamo decision is important because it was successful, and political success is usually emulated. The success of the Guantánamo decision is something that neither its apologists nor its critics, captives of the official explanation, seem ever to have grasped. If evaluated against the rationales in the official explanation, then it was an obvious failure. However, if evaluated against the rationales in the alternative explanation, then on balance it was rather fine work.

Success came in the form of an effective spectacle of victory in Afghanistan for the press and public that permitted the Bush administration to launch the war against Iraq that most of its foreign policy decision makers preferred. Success also came in the form of punishment inflicted on symbolic representatives of the leaderships of al-Qaeda and the Taliban. Fear of attack, betrayal, or contamination tempt mass publics to accept or even demand demonstrations of coercive power rather than responses more proportional to the threat. For American audiences in particular, video and photographic images of shackled and blindfolded men in prison-orange behind wire at Guantánamo represented what they had feared. For the foreign policy decision makers in the Bush administration, the same images meant the opportunity to launch a war against Iraq and avoid embarrassing questions about their role in the origins of al-Qaeda.

Only with respect to the hegemony building project of the neocon-servatives was there failure, and even then only partial failure. Neither the U.S. Supreme Court nor the other international powers acquiesced in the Bush administration's effort to carve out a permanent exception for the United States in the international law of war on the treatment of captives. Had the neoconservatives not revealed such obviously grandiose goals, they might have achieved a greater enhancement of the power of the U.S. presidency in conducting foreign policy. Despite overreaching, however, they still managed to make the office more powerful. President Obama has forsworn none of the formal or infor-mal powers acquired by his predecessors in the White House, including his immediate predecessor.

How is the story likely to end? The Obama administration may suc-ceed in closing Guantánamo through a strategy of attrition. At least that is the view of the Departments of Justice, Defense, State, and Homeland Security together with the CIA and Joint Chiefs of Staff in the January 22, 2011, Final Report of the Guantanamo Review Task Force. Old prison camps don't die, they just fade away. What had be-gun so spectacularly would end in anticlimax as the Obama adminis-tration sought to satisfy all parties to the policy dispute by dispers-ing the least offensive prisoners to third countries, prosecuting the handful who had been transferred there in 2006 before both civilian courts and military commissions, and transferring the un-disposable, un-prosecutable remainder to a supermax prison somewhere in the continental United States.

There will be more to the story, however. Guantánamo will still mat-ter because, rather than being an unfortunate exception, it is likely to become a precedent for decisions by future presidential administra-tions. The lesson that they will draw is that, as with the most skillful of magical illusions, the truth may lie hidden in plain sight.

Acknowledgments

Family, friends, colleagues, and students helped make this book possible through their feedback and expressions of impatience. I thank them all for repeating one question: "When will your book be finished?" Special thanks are owed to Delana Hickman and Renee Hickman for their support. Profound thanks are due to my editor, Amy Gorelick, for believing in the project and for her wise advice and kindness.

Appendix 1

Guantánamo in Popular Culture

Direct and indirect references to Guantánamo have appeared in popular fiction and documentary films, television episodes, novels, stage plays, and songs in the years after the Guantánamo decision. Their content ranges from foursquare to muted condemnation.

The 2008 comedy film *Harold & Kumar Escape from Guantanamo Bay*, the sequel to the 2004 *Harold & Kumar Go to White Castle*, involves the misadventures of Harold Lee and Kumar Patel that land them in the Cuban prison camp as a result of their marijuana smoking and the overreactions of a middle-American airline passenger and an ignorant undersecretary of Homeland Security. Although Guantánamo is never mentioned, the opening scene in the third installment of the blockbuster *Pirates of the Caribbean* comedy adventure series, the 2007 *Pirates of the Caribbean: At World's End*, is of a bewigged eighteenth-century British colonial official reading an announcement suspending English common law rights, including the right to counsel and the right to a habeas corpus appeal, to a long line of prisoners being led to the gallows in a tropical prison. Reading it as veiled political commentary is not difficult.

In Michael Moore's 2007 documentary *Sicko*, the attempt by American citizens without medical insurance coverage to gain access to what the film describes as the excellent and free medical facilities for the Guantánamo prisoners is used to illustrate the inequities of U.S. health care provision. In the May 1, 2005, episode of the satiric animated television series *American Dad*, "Threat Levels," Guantánamo is the destination for a real estate agent who is subjected to extraordinary rendition so that her job may be given to one of the central characters, the wife of a CIA agent.

German author Dorothea Dieckmann published *Guantanamo: A Novel* in 2004. Her narrative is written from the immediate perspective of Rashid Bakrani, whose hellish experience includes uncertainty, privation, humiliation, torture during interrogation, and attempted suicide. Dieckmann appears to have drawn upon the experiences of several European celebrity prisoners, including German national Murat Kurnaz, to construct her composite character, a German national in his early twenties from Hamburg with a German Protestant mother and a Muslim Indian father. To drive home the injustice of indefinite imprisonment, the novel ends with the protagonist still confined.

Direct and indirect references to Guantánamo and/or extraordinary rendition appeared in several recent science fiction novels. Two that were published in 2007 by British authors portray Britain in the near future as a police state. Veteran author Brian W. Aldiss's novel *HARM* uses Guantánamo Bay to describe the horrors of torture and indefinite imprisonment. In Ken MacLeod's *The Execution Channel*, both the threat of the prison and of extraordinary rendition are deployed as tactics by an intelligence officer to extract information from a prisoner:

> You see, . . . you do have a choice. . . . You can have a civilized conversation with me and my colleagues. . . . Or, if you say nothing or tell us something that we know isn't true, you can have a series of less civilized conversations with our colleagues in a series of other places. Oh I know you and your friends have joked about Gitmo . . . there are places you can find yourself in where you would wish to God you were in Gitmo.[1]

In the 2008 novel *The Last Theorem*, coauthored by two veteran science fiction writers, Arthur C. Clarke and Frederik Pohl, the innocent protagonist is arrested by security forces because he is in the wrong place at the wrong time, held incommunicado and in solitary confinement for two years, and tortured by being beaten and waterboarded until he confesses to crimes he did not commit.[2] In an interesting postscript, Pohl discloses that he rewrote passages about the protagonist's imprisonment to remove it from the context of the Sri Lankan Civil War to a Guantánamo-like setting to avoid disturbing Sri Lankan authorities. Perhaps. An expatriate Briton, Clarke was a longtime resident of the island nation. But the postscript could be read as intending to avoid disturbing authorities in the United States, where Pohl lives.

In Edward M. Lerner's 2010 science fiction novel *Small Miracles*, the name of the prison has been transformed into a verb in a near-future United States where the Department of Homeland Security appears unrestrained by law. Thus a small population of "supergenius sociopathic terrorist bombers," their intelligence raised far above the norm by medical nanobots, have been "guantanamoed" in an upstate New York psychiatric prison to prevent them from committing further crimes.[3]

Singer Patti Smith wrote the song "Without Chains" about released German prisoner Murat Kurnaz. During a 2002 visit to the naval base, country-and-western entertainer Charlie Daniels improvised an inane new version of his hit song "The Devil Went Down to Georgia" to appeal to the guard force with the lyrics "The Devil went down to Gitmo . . . just looking for a Taliban. . . ."

In 2009 the Guantánamo prison library rejected a donation of Noam Chomsky's book *Interventions*, which had been offered by a military attorney for prisoner Ali Hamza al-Bahlul.[4] Although censorship of prison reading material is the norm not only in the United States but in most countries, the rejection was reported in some news sources as a decision to specifically ban works by Chomsky. Like so much else about the naval base, the prison library is subject to its own peculiar secrecy rules. For example, as of 2010, reporters were free to take photos of available books, including the Arabic translations of the Harry Potter series, but not of the code used to file them.[5] The rules also require review by military censors of all photos taken at the base.

Finally, in May 2007 an employee of a Provo, Utah, company was waterboarded by his supervisor as a motivational exercise.[6] As with Admiral Harry Harris, whose experience with the insertion of nasogastric tubing is mentioned in the introduction, the employee volunteered for the exercise. Unlike Harris, however, the employee did not know precisely what the exercise involved before volunteering. Unsurprisingly, the victimized employee brought suit for damages.

Appendix 2

Island Prisons

Historical examples of prisons established on islands for special categories of prisoners abound. Restoration England used Jersey and the Isle of Man to indefinitely detain antiroyalist political prisoners because the writ of habeas corpus did not run there, a subterfuge that caused Parliament to give the Habeas Corpus Act extraterritorial effect in 1679.[1] Bass Rock in the Firth of Forth, also known as The Bass, was used to imprison Scottish Covenanters in the same period.

A consortium of London merchants took control of Bance Island fifteen miles up the Sierra Leone River from the coast in 1749, reconditioning it as a prison for slaves en route to colonies in the New World.[2] Most of the so-called slave castles, such as the one at Elmina in present-day Ghana, were located on the mainland itself.

Britain used Melville Island in Halifax, Nova Scotia, to intern captured American seamen and privateers during the War of 1812. Today Melville Island is technically a peninsula with a narrow land bridge to the mainland.

First Elba in the Mediterranean and then Saint Helena in the South Atlantic were used to imprison defeated French emperor Napoleon Bonaparte. Britain used Port Blair on South Andaman Island in the Indian Ocean to imprison captured Thuggee in the nineteenth century, rebels from the 1857–58 Indian Mutiny, and Indian nationalist leaders like Vinayak Savarkar in the early twentieth century. Irish Republican Army insurgents were interned on Spike Island in Cork Harbour during the 1919–21 Irish War of Independence. As late as 1956 Britain used the Seychelles in the Indian Ocean to exile Archbishop Makarios III, the rebel leader of the Greek Cypriots.

Deprived of its favorite penal dumping grounds by the American Revolution, Britain pressed into service first Bermuda out in the Atlantic and then Botany Bay in New South Wales, Australia. Botany Bay established its own prison islands for the most incorrigible convicts: Norfolk Island and Pinchgut Island.[3] Later, Saint Helena Island in the mouth of the Brisbane River became the location for a prison operated first by the British colonial government and later by the state government of Queensland, which imprisoned Australian labor leaders there in the late nineteenth century. More recently, Australia has used prison facilities on Nauru, Manus Island off Papua New Guinea, and Christmas Island in the Indian Ocean, to intern Afghan Hazara, Sri Lankan, and Burmese refugees. Canada used Fort Lennox on Île-aux-Noix in the Richelieu River as its first camp for interned enemy aliens and prisoners of war at the beginning of the Second World War.[4]

Historical examples of prison islands are also common across Latin America. The Falkland Islands or Islas Malvinas were the location for an Argentine penal colony whose surviving inhabitants were evacuated by the British navy in 1833 when the islands became a British colony. Argentina also used Isla Martín García in the Río de la Plata as a penal colony for captives taken in campaigns against its indigenous peoples in the late nineteenth century and for a succession of deposed Argentine presidents in the twentieth century. Occupation helped to reinforce Argentina's claim to the island against that of Uruguay. The same motive prompted Argentina to build a prison for repeat criminal offenders in Ushuaia, the capital of the Argentine half of the island of Tierra del Fuego, that was described as the "cemetery of living men."[5] Geographic isolation and the subarctic climate made escape from the island difficult. Using the location as a penal colony had been conceived as far back as the latter sixteenth century, when merchant adventurers from Elizabethan England had designs on controlling the Strait of Magellan.[6]

Chile used Dawson Island to imprison the Selk'nam or Ona, now extinct indigenes from Tierra del Fuego, in the nineteenth century. Minority group deportation, especially of indigenous minority groups, to unfamiliar territory has often resulted in population decline. However, extinction is shocking. Following the 1973 military coup that overthrew the elected democratic government of Salvador Allende, Dawson Island was used to imprison political prisoners. During the period of civil war in the 1950s in Colombia called La Violencia, political prisoners were held on Isla Gorgona. Cuban political prisoners, including Fidel Castro, were imprisoned on Isla de la Juventud before the 1959 Cuban Revolution, and after it as well. Mexico established the Islas Marías Federal Penal Colony in 1905 and continues to use it to imprison convicts associated with the drug cartels. In 1832, Ecuador colonized Charles Island or Isla Santa María in the Galápagos with political prisoners.[7] Panama incarcerated political prisoners on Isla de Coiba.

Continental European states found similar uses for their islands. Solovki, the shortened name for the Solovetski Islands in the White Sea, was originally home to an Orthodox monastery and a Russian naval fortress but later became a feared political prison for both Imperial Russia and the Soviet Union.[8] Imperial Russia also settled Sakhalin Island in the Russian Far East with thousands of convicts judged too incorrigible for exile in Siberia.[9] By 1900 the prisoner colonists outnumbered the indigenes. After the Russian Revolution, Moscow added many more to their number.

Prince Pedro of Portugal held his brother, ousted king Afonso VI, on Terceira in the Azores from 1669 to 1674.[10] Liberal Italy settled the Tuscan Archipelago with ordinary convicts in the nineteenth century, and in the twentieth century the Italian fascist state imprisoned thousands more Italian and colonial political prisoners off the coast of Italy on the Pontine Islands, the Tremiti Islands, and the islands of Favignana, Gaeta, and Ustica. Colonial political prisoners were also imprisoned on Nokra Island in the Red Sea.[11] Among the better known political prisoners of Italian fascism were political theorist Antonio Gramsci, who was imprisoned on Ustica, and Ethiopian leader Ras Imru, who was imprisoned on the Pontine island of Ponza. Mussolini was himself held on Ponza after being overthrown in 1943.

During the White Terror of 1945–46 the Greek dictatorship imprisoned captured communist soldiers on Makronisos Island, captured communist political cadres on Gioura Island, and captured noncombatants who had lived in areas under communist control on Trikeri Island.[12] During the military dictatorship of the 1960s Greece used Yaros Island as a political prison. Postwar Turkey imprisoned political prisoners and criminal convicts on İmrali Island, which is today used to contain a single prisoner, Kurdish Workers Party leader Abdullah Öcelan. Norway confines convicts in the planet's most environmentally friendly prison on Bastoey Island, forty-five miles south of Oslo.

Examples of prison islands can be found across Southeast Asia and the Pacific. The Nationalist Chinese government of Taiwan used Green Island as a political prison during its anticommunist, anti-Formosan-nationalist White Terror of 1947. The military government of Myanmar/Burma established a political prison in the Co Co Islands.[13] Indonesia continues to use Nusakambangan Island to imprison its ordinary convicts and in the 1960s and 1970s used Buru Island to hold its political prisoners, as did the colonial government of the Dutch East Indies before it. Malaysia designated Jerejak Island near Penang Island as a penal colony in 1969. The Maldives uses the South Male Atoll of Maafushi as a prison. The military government of Fiji used Nukulau Island as a political prison from 2000 to 2006. Today, Tonga confines its handful of convicts on Ata Island northeast of Tongatapu.

In Africa, apartheid-era South Africa transformed its naval training base on Robben Island into a prison facility for antiapartheid leaders. Cash strapped before the discovery of offshore oil, tiny independent São Tomé and Príncipe subcontracted as an island prison for small numbers of Spain's Basque ETA prisoners.[14] Ironically, the population of the islands included the descendants of criminals, rebellious slaves, and drought refugees sold by the king of Kongo to the Portuguese in the sixteenth century to work the plantations on the islands.[15]

Successive French regimes have found the use of distant tropical islands as penal colonies for its convicts and political prisoners irresistible. The three Îles du Salut or Safety Islands off the coast of French Guiana were used to imprison dangerous and important prisoners who would otherwise have been held in the penal colony on the mainland at Cayenne. Solitary confinement on Royale and Saint-Joseph was the fate of the most intractable convicts, while political prisoners were held on Île du Diable or Devil's Island. This island was made famous by the imprisonment of Alfred Dreyfus following his wrongful conviction for treason in what became known as the Dreyfus Affair, and later by Henri Charrière's 1970 memoir *Papillon* and its 1973 film adaptation starring Steve McQueen. Less remembered outside France was the use of New Caledonia as a political penal colony. After the defeat of the Paris Commune in 1871, some 35,000 captured Communards who survived the administrative massacre were tried before French military tribunals and 4,500 were ordered deported to New Caledonia, which had become a French possession only in 1853.[16] The island was such a perfect dumping ground that the Communards were later joined by roughly 15,000 convicts and 500 captured Kabyle rebels from Algeria. France exiled Moroccan anticolonial rebel leader Abd el-Krim to Réunion in 1926. France used Con Son Island in the South China Sea, home to the infamous "tiger cages," to imprison its Vietnamese criminal and political prisoners, as did the South Vietnamese government after partition in 1954. Among the most important prisoners of the French on Con Son Island was the future Vietnamese communist leader Le Duc Tho. Islands need not be tropical to make attractive prisons for the French. After the Liberation in 1944, First World War military hero and Second World War fascist collaborator Marshal Philippe Pétain was imprisoned in the fort of Pierre-Levée on Île d'Yeu, eighteen kilometers off the Atlantic coast of France, until his death.[17] The captive Vichy leader had believed that he might be held on the warmer Mediterranean island of Saint-Marguerite.

Notes

Introduction

1. CNN, "Wintry Storm."
2. Lepore, *The Name of War*, x.
3. Blood, *Hitler's Bandit Hunters*, 76–77.
4. Hickman and Bartlett, "Reporting a New Delhi Bias?"
5. Anonymous [Michael Scheuer], *Imperial Hubris*, 135–37.
6. Chehab, *Inside Hamas*, 98.
7. Dalrymple, *The Last Mughal*, 447–48.
8. Clarke, *Against All Enemies*, 30–31; Daalder and Lindsay, *America Unbound*, 104–5; Johnson, *The Sorrows of Empire*, 227–28; Suskind, *The Price of Loyalty*, 72–73; Engelhardt, *The American Way of War*, 23.

Chapter 1. Framing the Decision

1. Angus Reid, "Terrorist Attacks Top Event"; Streatfeild, *History of the World Since 9/11*, 32.
2. Bush, "Address to the Nation"; Bridgman, "Lessons Learned."
3. Freedman, *Evolution of Nuclear Strategy*, 34–36.
4. U.S. Department of Defense, "DoD News Briefing," January 22, 2002.
5. On domestic "superpredator" criminals, see Bennett, DiIulio, and Walters, *Body Count*.
6. Herspring, *Rumsfeld's Wars*, 79–80.
7. U.S. Department of Defense, "DoD News Briefing," February 8, 2002.
8. *Washington Post*, "Guantanamo Bay Timeline."
9. Angus Reid, "There Are Terrorists in U.S."
10. Pew Research Center, "Despite Years of Terror Scares."
11. For an overview, see S. E. Bennett et al., "Citizens' Knowledge."
12. DiMaggio, *Mass Media, Mass Propaganda*, 143–44; Louw, "The 'War Against Terrorism.'"

13. Dadge, *War in Iraq*, 31.

14. White House, "President Welcomes German Chancellor."

15. White House, "Press Conference," June 14, 2004.

16. Ibid.

17. On the distortion of historical memory, see Bothmer, *Framing the Sixties*.

Chapter 2. Strange Consensus

1. Serge, *What Every Radical Should Know*, 102–4.

2. Mayer, *The Dark Side*, 83.

3. Lepore, *The Name of War*, 88–89; Hasian, *In the Name of Necessity*, 63–76; Lieder and Page, *Wild Justice*, 32–33.

4. U.S. Department of Defense, "DoD News Briefing," February 8, 2002.

5. Mayer, *The Dark Side*, 188.

6. Rose, *Guantánamo*, 79–128.

7. Ibid., 137–39.

8. Greenberg, *The Least Worst Place*, 4, 2, 146.

9. Ibid., 47.

10. Ibid., 49.

11. Otterman, *American Torture*, 145.

12. B. Graham, *By His Own Rules*, 318–21.

13. Ibid., 374–75.

14. Grey, *Ghost Plane*, 164–69.

15. Shephard, *Guantanamo's Child*, 89–91.

16. Wittes, *Law and the Long War*, 160–62.

17. Mahler, *The Challenge*, 32.

18. Ibid.

19. Saar and Novak, *Inside the Wire*, 27.

20. Sands, *Lawless World*, 153.

21. Fletcher and Stover, *The Guantánamo Effect*, 119–20.

22. Smith, *Eight O'Clock Ferry*, 28.

23. Rotunda, *Honor Bound*, 87.

24. Ibid., 59.

25. Ibid., 139–40.

26. McEvoy and Shirlow, "Re-Imagining DDR," 33.

27. Fletcher and Stover, *The Guantánamo Effect*, 112–13.

28. L. James, *Fixing Hell*, 5.

29. Ibid., 28.

30. Ibid., 41.

31. Welsh-Huggins, "Ohio Won't Pursue Gitmo Abuse Claim."

32. Cucullu, *Inside Gitmo*, 194.

33. Ibid., 239.

34. Ibid., 214.

35. Kurnaz, *Five Years*, 62.

36. Begg, *Enemy Combatant*, 138–39.

Chapter 3. Three Comparable Historical Cases

1. Lieder and Page, *Wild Justice*, 26–27; Kraft, *Gatewood and Geronimo*, 140.

2. Lieder and Page, *Wild Justice*, 32–33.

3. Adams, *Education for Extinction*, 36–44.

4. Welsh, *Apache Prisoners*, 19.

5. Robertson, *The Tyrannicide Brief*, 349.

6. Halliday, *Habeas Corpus*, 310–12.

7. Panayi, "Prisoners of Britain," 30.

8. Gillman and Gillman, *"Collar the Lot!"* 7–8.

9. Lafitte, *The Internment of Aliens*, 168.

10. Andrew, *Defend the Realm*, 227.

11. Gillman and Gillman, *"Collar the Lot!"* 44.

12. Macklin, "Hail Mosley," 10–12.

13. Renton, *Fascism, Anti-Fascism*, 22–23.

14. Dupuy, *Haiti in the New World Order*, 139–40.

15. Skop, "Race and Place," 450.

16. Goldstein, *Storming the Court*, 56; T. Miller, "Impact," 231–32.

17. Frelick, "Haitian Boat Interdiction," 679.

18. Plummer, *Haiti and the United States*, 201.

19. Stepick, "Haitian Boat People," 172–73.

20. Koh, "America's Offshore Refugee Camps," 146.

21. Reynolds, *Skillful Show of Strength*, 14.

22. Goldstein, *Storming the Court*, 181; Koh, "America's Offshore Refugee Camps," 149.

23. Koh, "Haiti Paradigm," 2397.

24. Gott, *Cuba*, 298–300.

25. Shenon, "U.S. Chooses Guantánamo."

26. Lipman, *Guantánamo*, 220.

Chapter 4. Extraordinary Threat

1. Pressley, "Detainees Arrive."

2. U.S. Department of Defense, "DoD News Briefing," January 11, 2002.

3. Herspring, *Rumsfeld's Wars*, 95–96.

4. U.S. Department of Defense, "DoD News Briefing," January 22, 2002.

5. White House, "Vice President Appears on Fox."

6. WikiLeaks, "Classified Guantanamo Bay Detention Criteria."

7. *Congressional Record,* "Military Commissions Act of 2006."

8. Begg, *Enemy Combatant,* 129.

9. Fox, "Cheap Watches."

10. Simkin, "Chinese Muslims"; Gordon, "Montrealer Sold to U.S. Troops."

11. Associated Press, "Most Gitmo Detainees."

12. Heintz, "Russia."

13. Cody, "China Demands."

14. Rhem, "Detainees Living in Varied Conditions."

15. Glidden, "Internment Camps."

16. Krammer, "German Prisoners," 68, 70.

17. Lewis and Mewha, *Prisoner of War Utilization,* 112.

18. Rhem, "Troops Deal with Stress."

Chapter 5. Intelligence Collection

1. U.S. Department of Defense, "DoD News Briefing," January 22, 2002.

2. Stephen Kenny, e-mail to author, December 22, 2010.

3. U.S. Department of Defense, "DoD News Briefing," January 11, 2002.

4. U.S. Department of Defense, "DoD News Briefing," January 22, 2002.

5. Miles, "Detainees Treated Humanely."

6. Office of the Director of National Intelligence, "High Value Terrorist Detainee Program"; Stolberg, "President Moves 14."

7. McCoy, *A Question of Torture,* 50–54; Watson, *War on the Mind,* 265–87; Wade, "Technology in Ulster," 1103–6; Shallice, "Ulster Depth Interrogation"; Bishop, "Law in Control," 161–62.

8. Walters, *Kinesic Interview and Interrogation,* 291–92.

9. Dodds, "Kuwaiti Detainees."

10. Biderman, "Social-Psychological Needs," 126.

Chapter 6. Prosecution

1. U.S. Department of Defense, "DoD News Briefing," January 22, 2002.

2. Duffy, *War on Terror,* 389.

3. Bravin, "At Guantánamo."

4. Hamdan v. Rumsfeld, 548 U.S. 557 (2006).

5. Sheed, "Guantánamo Abuse 'VideoTaped'"; Rhem, "Military Trials for Two."

6. Melia, "Australian Convicted."

7. Amnesty International, "USA: Letter"; Carrell, "Children of Guantánamo." The presence of juveniles in a prison camp is a source of concern for both U.S. officials and international observers.

8. Associated Press, "Detainee Lawyer."

9. Yates and Whitford, "Presidential Power."

10. Dunne, *Mr. Dooley's Opinions*, 26.

11. Halliday, *Habeas Corpus*, 169–74.

12. Warshauer, *Andrew Jackson*, 197–203.

13. Ex Parte Milligan, 71 U.S. 1 (1866).

14. Irons, *People's History of the Supreme Court*, 188.

15. Hasian, *In the Name of Necessity*, 64–76.

16. Brown, *Bury My Heart at Wounded Knee*, 59–64.

17. Hibbert, *The Great Mutiny*, 132.

18. Solomon, "Saya San," 209–10.

19. Wolfowitz, "Order Establishing Combatant Status Review Tribunal"; Wolfowitz, "Administrative Review Procedures."

20. Donagan, "Atrocity, War Crime, and Treason," 1140–41. The dilemma in recognizing enemies as more than rebels was debated by King Charles I and his advisors with regard to exchanges of prisoners between the Royalists and Parliamentarians during the English Civil War. Fortunately for the prisoners, principle was sacrificed to save lives.

21. [Geneva Convention], Convention . . . 1929.

22. [Geneva Convention], Convention (III) . . . 1949; ICRC, "States Party to the Main Treaties." The Geneva Convention of 1949 has been signed by every recognized state in the international system save Estonia and the Vatican.

23. [Geneva Convention], Convention (III) . . . 1949, Article 3.

24. Ex Parte Quirin, 317 U.S. 1 (1942).

25. Fisher, *Nazi Saboteurs on Trial*, 95–96; Dobbs, *Saboteurs*, 238–39. Three of the nine justices had interests in the case that ought to have disqualified them from hearing it.

26. Johnson v. Eisentrager, 339 U.S. 763 (1950).

27. [Geneva Convention], Protocol Additional . . . (Protocol I).

28. U.S. Department of Defense, "President Determines."

29. Hamdi v. Rumsfeld, 542 U.S. 507 (2004).

30. White House, "President Signs Authorization."

31. Rumsfeld v. Padilla, 542 U.S. 546 (2004).

32. Ibid.

33. Padilla v. Hanft, 547 U.S. 1062 (2006).

34. Rasul v. Bush, 542 U.S. 466 (2004).

35. Allen, "DeLay Takes Fight to Talk Radio."

36. U.S. Department of Defense, "Defense Department Special Briefing."

37. I. James, "Lawyer Unable to Meet Guantanamo Client."

38. Kennedy, *Just Law*, 60.

39. Garwood, "Afghan Insurgency Said Won't Slow."
40. Hamdan v. Rumsfeld, 344 F. Supp. 2d 152 (D.C.C. 2004).
41. Hamdan v. Rumsfeld, 548 U.S. 557 (2006).
42. White House, "Press Conference," July 7, 2006.
43. Miles, "England Memo."
44. Leahy, "Statement."

Chapter 7. Spectacle of Victory

1. Clodfelter, *The Dakota War*, 59.
2. I. James, "Lawyer Unable to Meet Guantanamo Client," 32.
3. Sanders, *While in the Hands of the Enemy*, 56–61.
4. Lewis and Mewha, *Prisoner of War Utilization*, 46; McCoy, *Policing America's Empire*, 70.
5. Capozzola, *Uncle Sam Wants You*, 173, 184.
6. Cannato, *American Passage*, 350–60.
7. Ackerman, *Young J. Edgar*, 190–91.
8. Schrader, "Containing the Spectacle of Punishment."
9. Larson and Savych, *American Public Support*, 108–9; E. Rosenberg, *Date Which Will Live*, 176–79.
10. Authorization for Use of Military Force, Public Law No. 107-40 (2001), Sect. 2(a).
11. Grimmett, *Authorization . . . : Legislative History*.
12. McClellan, *What Happened*, 120–21.
13. Population Census Organization, "Population by Mother Tongue."
14. Roy, *Lessons of the Soviet/Afghan War*, 10–13.
15. Roberts, *Origins of Conflict in Afghanistan*, 14–215.
16. Wright, *The Looming Tower*, 173–75.
17. Mamdani, *Good Muslim, Bad Muslim*, 119–77; Coll, *Ghost Wars*, 168; Johnson, *Blowback*, 10–11, 27–28; Weaver, *Pakistan*, 62–64.
18. National Commission, *The 9/11 Commission Report*, 55–56.
19. Reagan, "Proclamation 4908."
20. White House, "Humanitarian Aid."
21. Jones, *Pakistan*, 15–17. Attempting to deprive his Islamist opponents of issues, Bhutto had already decreed that members of the Ahmedi or Qadiani religious minority were not Muslims and announced a number of laws against gambling and making Friday rather than Saturday the weekly holiday. For General Zia's greater severity, see Richter, "Islamic Resurgence in Pakistan," 548.
22. Abbas, *Pakistan's Drift into Extremism*, 109–10.
23. Filkins, *The Forever War*, 23.

24. McCoy, *Policing America's Empire*, 443–45.

25. Paris, "Air Power."

26. Oshinsky, *Polio*, 54–55, 256–57.

27. Hogan, *Irish Soldiers of Mexico*, 57–81, 160–96. Historical precedent for religious identity motivating U.S. citizens to fight with an enemy against the U.S. military can be found in the Mexican-American War, during which hundreds of Irish Roman Catholics in the U.S. Army deserted and fought with the Mexican Army. Following their capture, some 50 soldiers of the Batallón de San Patricio or St. Patrick's Battalion were hanged, and the remainder were branded on the cheek with the letter *D* for "deserter." Far from replying in kind with the execution of captured Americans, the Mexican Army protected its American prisoners from reprisals by angry civilians. The "San Patricios" were among 9,207 soldiers who deserted from the U.S. Army during that war.

28. The *Tarawa*-class helicopter carrier, tentatively named USS *Da Nang* and then USS *Khe Sanh*, was commissioned in 1980 as the USS *Peleliu*, a name that refers to the Second World War battle for the island of Peleliu in the western Carolines, during which some 10,000 Japanese and 2,000 Americans died between September and November 1944.

29. Smucker, *Al Qaeda's Great Escape*, 116–21; Lambeth, *Air Power against Terror*, 149–54.

30. Gellman and Ricks, "U.S. Concludes Bin Laden Escaped."

31. Musharraf, *In the Line of Fire*, 264–65.

32. Bernstein, "Bin Laden Bribed Afghan Militias."

33. Burns, "Document"; Gellman and Ricks, "U.S. Concludes Bin Laden Escaped."

34. Burns, "Document."

35. Seeley, *Therapy after Terror*, 156–61.

Chapter 8. Punishment

1. Angus Reid, "World Rejects Torture." These figures are consistent with those in a November 2005 public opinion poll in advanced industrial democracies; see Angus Reid, "Eight Countries Reject."

2. Sageman, *Understanding Terror Networks*, 87.

3. B. Jenkins, "There, Where Words Fail," 143.

4. Harbury, *Truth, Torture, and the American Way*, 145–46.

5. Wenk-Ansohn, "The Verge of Pain," 64–65.

6. Ortiz, "The Survivors' Perspective," 30.

7. Gilmore, "Bad Troops, Poor Leaders."

8. S. Graham, "U.S. Admits Afghanistan Vigilante Ties"; Shah, "Bogus Afghan Jailers"; Agence France Presse, "More Vigilantes."

9. Agence France Presse, "American on Trial"; R. Moore, *Hunt for Bin Laden*, 141–44. Idema's actions are discussed at length in Moore's gushing popular history of the early war in Afghanistan.

10. Shah, "U.S. Prisoner Leaves Afghanistan."

11. M. Moore, "Villagers."

12. Dow, *American Gulag*, 143; I. James, "Detainee Says He Was Abused"; Sherman, "Muslim Mistreatment."

13. Agence France Presse, "80 Afghans Released."

14. Shah, "Afghan Protesters."

15. Mackey and Miller, *The Interrogators*, 191, 232, 286, 319.

16. Kurnaz, *Five Years*, 56–78.

17. Jehl, "Army Details Scale of Abuse"; Golden, "In U.S. Report, Brutal Details."

18. Aussaresses, *Battle of the Casbah*, 128–31. Note the conversation between a torturer and a doctor standing over the body of a dead torture victim.

19. Golden, "In Final Trial, G.I. Is Acquitted."

20. Golden, "Years after 2 Afghans Died."

21. Golden, "Army Faltered."

22. Dunham, "U.S. Military Calls 2 Dozen Detainee Deaths Homicide."

23. Jehl and Schmitt, "Inmate Deaths May Be Homicide."

24. Saar and Novak, *Inside the Wire*, 117–18.

25. Verbitsky, *The Flight*, 51; Argentina, Comisión Nacional sobre la Desaparición de Personas, *Nunca Más: The Report*, 221; Roht-Arriaza, *The Pinochet Effect*, 22–24.

26. Vietnam Veterans against the War, *The Winter Soldier Investigation*, 101–5, 106–9. See the statements of Steve Noetzel, Ernie Sachs, and Murphy Lloyd. See also Brinkley, *Tour of Duty*, 350.

27. Kurnaz, *Five Years*, 109–10. Kurnaz reports that some prisoners' war wounds went untreated at Guantánamo.

28. Khan, *My Guantánamo Diary*, 34–35.

29. Lewis, "Guantánamo Inmate Complains."

30. Vischer, *Barbed Wire Disease*, 25–26.

31. Agence France Presse, "Guantanamo Detainee Hicks."

32. Kurnaz, *Five Years*, 183–85.

33. Agence France Presse, "French Guantánamo Inmates"; C. Rosenberg, "Detainee Who Was Forced"; Dodds, "AP: Gitmo Soldier Details Sexual Tactics."

34. Isikoff and Barry, "Gitmo: SouthCom Showdown"; BBC News, "Riots" and "Saudi Ire."

35. Otterman, *American Torture*, 103–4.

36. Carrell, "Coded Letters."

37. Mayer, *The Dark Side*, 190, 226.

38. Buncombe, "Guantanamo Bay Prisoner."

39. Fox, "Guantánamo Detainee Threatens Suicide."

40. Risen and Golden, "3 Prisoners Commit Suicide."

41. Voglis, *Becoming a Subject*, 136.

42. Agence France Presse, "US Medics Implicated."

43. Slavin and Stevens, "Detainee's Medical Files Shared."

44. U.S. Department of Defense, "Medical Program Support."

Chapter 9. Announcement

1. Record, *Dark Victory*, 25–26.

2. P. Jenkins, *Decade of Nightmares*, 89–90.

3. Xenos, *Cloaked in Virtue*, 16–17.

4. Strauss, *Natural Right and History*, 160.

5. *Quod licet Jovi, non licet bovi* is a Roman complaint against double standards that may be translated as "gods may do what cattle may not."

6. Pileggi and Scorsese, *Goodfellas*; Berlinski, *Menace in Europe*, 110–15. So committed to order as a value are some neoconservatives that they endorse organized crime for the same reasons that they endorse organized religion. For example, interethnic peace in Marseille is attributed to the city's mafiosi politics.

7. The geopolitical priorities of the neoconservatives differed only slightly from the amoral Realpolitik of Henry Kissinger, a figure that many of them despised. In a June 1969 meeting with Chilean foreign minister Gabriel Valdés, Kissinger is reported to have said, "Nothing important can come from the South. History has never been produced in the South. The axis of history starts in Moscow, goes to Bonn, crosses over to Washington, and then goes to Tokyo" (Hersh, *The Price of Power*, 263).

8. Immerman, *Empire for Liberty*, 217–19.

9. Boot, "What Next?"

10. Love, *Race over Empire*, 158–200.

11. One of the peculiar consequences of Puerto Rico's peculiar status is that Puerto Ricans and other U.S. citizens living on the island do not vote in U.S. presidential elections. However, they may vote in U.S. presidential elections if they live anywhere else in the United States or abroad.

12. Triay, *Bay of Pigs*, 135–36.

13. Rose, "Guantánamo Bay on Trial," 62. Photo of the Camp Delta cells.

14. Brown and Luce, *Hostages of War*, 33–35; Valentine, *The Phoenix Program*, 347–50.

15. *Life*, "The Tiger Cages of Con Son."

16. Briody, *The Halliburton Agenda*, 219.

17. Koh, "America's Jekyll-and-Hyde Exceptionalism," 116–17.

18. Legro, *Rethinking the World*, 13–16.

19. Ibid., 168.

20. Richardson, *China, Cambodia*, 26, 55–56.

Chapter 10. Closing Guantánamo

1. Obama, "War We Need to Win," 5, 6.

2. *Congressional Quarterly*, "Obama Interviewed."

3. White House, "National Security."

4. Rhem, "Alleged Guantanamo Abuse."

5. Miles, "Detainees Treated Humanely."

6. Sher, "Rep. Gingrey."

7. The full text of Article 1 reads: "The physician shall not countenance, condone or participate in the practice of torture or other forms of cruel, inhuman or degrading procedures, whatever the offense of which the victim of such procedures is suspected, accused or guilty, and whatever the victim's beliefs or motives, and in all situations, including armed conflict and civil strife."

8. Among the research objectives was data collection for use in perfecting waterboarding and sleep deprivation and in determining whether abusive tactics should be used in sequence or simultaneously. See Raymond et al., *Experiments in Torture*, 7.

9. Webber, "Thomson Prison in Illinois."

10. Webber, "Thomson Correctional Center Eyed."

11. Weiser, "Life Sentence."

12. Higham and Finn, "At Least $500 Million."

13. Cloud and Barnes, "U.S. May Expand Use of Its Prison."

14. Finn, "Guantanamo Detainee Naji."

15. Pogatchnik, "Ireland to Take 2"; Reuters, "U.S. Sends Two."

16. Stark, "Germans Moving Closer."

17. Andrea Prasow, e-mail to author, December 21, 2010.

18. Angus Reid, "Public Support."

Chapter 11. After Guantánamo

1. "Petitioner's Motion."

2. Murray and Kane, "Obama Rejects Truth Panel."

3. *National Journal*, "Text: Statements from Holder, Panetta."

4. Ibid.

5. New America Foundation, "Year of the Drone"; Raghaven, "In Yemen."

6. Becker and Shane, "Secret 'Kill List.'"

7. Pilkington, "Bradley Manning's Treatment."

8. WikiLeaks, "Collateral Murder."

9. *Guardian*, "US Embassy Cables."

10. Wheeler, "Government Case."

11. Bravin, "Guantanamo Judge."

12. Crovitz, "From Nuremberg to Guantanamo."

13. *New York Times*, "Road We Need Not Have Traveled."

14. Greenberg, "Military Commissions on Trial."

15. Wong, "Rubio Visits Guantanamo Bay."

16. Savage, "Pair of Guantanamo Detainees Freed."

17. Milewski, "Canada Accused."

18. Doyle, "Time to Stop Paying Out to Terrorists."

19. Secretary of State for Justice, *Justice and Security Green Paper*, 7.

20. Bowcott and Norton-Taylor, "Secret Courts Bill."

21. Sabin Willett, e-mails to author, December 19 and 21, 2010.

Appendix 1. Guantánamo in Popular Culture

1. MacLeod, *The Execution Channel*, 72–73.

2. Clarke and Pohl, *The Last Theorem*, 86–101.

3. Lerner, *Small Miracles*, 361–62.

4. C. Rosenberg, "Noam Chomsky's Works Banned."

5. Peters, "Guantánamo Offers a Look, but Little Else."

6. Vick, "Team-Building or Torture?"

Appendix 2. Island Prisons

1. Robertson, *The Tyrannicide Brief*, 349.

2. Blackburn, *The Making of New World Slavery*, 389–90.

3. Keneally, *A Commonwealth of Thieves*, 114–18.

4. Auger, *Prisoners of the Home Front*, 24–28.

5. Paz, *Durruti*, 81.

6. Andrews, *Trade, Plunder, and Settlement*, 161.

7. Parks and Rippy, "The Galápagos Islands," 38.

8. Malsagoff, *An Island Hell*.

9. Reid, *The Shaman's Coat*, 151.

10. Duncan, *Atlantic Islands*, 115–16.

11. Bosworth, *Mussolini's Italy*, 329–31; Labanca, "Italian Colonial Internment," 29–30; Annussek, *Hitler's Raid to Save Mussolini*, 107.

12. Gerolymatos, *Red Acropolis, Black Terror*, 204–5.

13. Wakeman and Tin, *No Time for Dreams*, 10–11.

14. Ghazvinian, *Untapped*, 213.
15. J. Miller, *Way of Death*, 116.
16. Bullard, "Self-Representation," 183–84; Bullard, *Exile to Paradise*, 204.
17. Williams, *Pétain*, 262–63.

Works Cited

Books, Articles, and Communiqués

Abbas, Hassan. *Pakistan's Drift into Extremism: Allah, the Army, and America's War on Terror*. Armonk, N.Y.: M. E. Sharpe, 2005.

Ackerman, Kenneth D. *Young J. Edgar: Hoover, the Red Scare, and the Assault on Civil Liberties*. New York: Carroll & Graf, 2007.

Adams, David Wallace. *Education for Extinction: American Indians and the Boarding School Experience, 1875–1928*. Lawrence: University Press of Kansas, 1995.

Agence France Presse. "80 Afghans Released from U.S. Custody in Afghanistan." January 17, 2005.

———. "American on Trial for Private 'War on Terror' Claims Rumsfeld Link." July 21, 2004.

———. "French Guantánamo Inmates Placed Under Investigation by Anti-Terror Judges." August 1, 2004.

———. "Guantanamo Detainee Hicks Feared US Interrogators Would Shoot Him." April 3, 2007.

———. "More Vigilantes Could Be Operating in Afghanistan: US Military." July 25, 2004.

———. "US Medics Implicated in Prisoner Abuse at Iraqi Prison: Lancet." August 20, 2004.

Aldiss, Brian W. *HARM*. New York: Ballantine, 2007.

Allen, Mike. "DeLay Takes Fight to Talk Radio." *Washington Post*, April 20, 2005.

Amnesty International. "USA: Letter to President Bush—Children in Guantánamo Bay." April 24, 2003. portland.indymedia.org/en/2003/04/63228.shtml.

Andrew, Christopher. *Defend the Realm: The Authorized History of MI5*. New York: Knopf, 2009.

Andrews, Kenneth R. *Trade, Plunder, and Settlement: Maritime Enterprise and the Genesis of the British Empire, 1480–1630*. Cambridge: Cambridge University Press, 1984.

Angus Reid. "Eight Countries Reject U.S.-Backed Secret Interrogations." December 9, 2005. angus-reid.com/polls/13644/eight_countries_reject_us_backed_secret_interrogations/.

———. "Public Support for Guantanamo Drops in U.S." June 29, 2006. angus-reid.com/polls/9345/public_support_for_guantanamo_drops_in_us/.

———. "Terrorist Attacks Top Event in 75 Years." September 12, 2003. angus-reid.com/polls/26784/terrorist_attacks_top_event_in_75_years/.

———. "There Are Terrorists in U.S., Say Americans." September 1, 2003. angus-reid.com/polls/26878/there_are_terrorists_in_us_say_americans/.

———. "World Rejects Torture in Terrorism Cases." October 24, 2006. angus-reid.com/polls/7013/world_rejects_torture_in_terrorism_cases/.

Annussek, Greg. *Hitler's Raid to Save Mussolini: The Most Infamous Commando Operation of World War II.* Cambridge, Mass.: Da Capo, 2005.

Anonymous [Michael Scheuer]. *Imperial Hubris: Why the West Is Losing the War on Terror.* Washington, D.C.: Brassey's, 2004.

Argentina. Comisión Nacional sobre la Desaparición de Personas. *Nunca Más: The Report of the Argentine National Commission on the Disappeared.* New York: Farrar, Straus & Giroux, 1986.

Associated Press. "Detainee Lawyer Wants Interrogation Halted." July 8, 2005.

———. "Most Gitmo Detainees Freed Elsewhere: Four-Fifths of 'Vicious Killers' Released after Return to Home Countries." December 16, 2006.

Auger, Martin F. *Prisoners of the Home Front: German POWs and "Enemy Aliens" in Southern Quebec, 1940–46.* Vancouver: UBC Press, 2005.

Aussaresses, Paul. *The Battle of the Casbah: Terrorism and Counter-Terrorism in Algeria, 1955–1957.* Translated by Robert L. Miller. New York: Enigma, 2002.

BBC News. "Riots Over US Koran 'Desecration.'" May 11, 2005. news.bbc.co.uk/2/hi/4535491.stm.

———. "Saudi Ire at Koran 'Desecration.'" May 13, 2005. news.bbc.co.uk/2/hi/middle_east/4543373.stm.

Becker, Jo, and Scott Shane. "Secret 'Kill List' Proves a Test of Obama's Principles and Will." *New York Times,* May 29, 2012.

Begg, Moazzam. *Enemy Combatant: My Imprisonment at Guantánamo, Baghram, and Kandahar.* With Victoria Brittain. New York: New Press, 2006.

Bennett, Stephen Earl, et al. "Citizens' Knowledge of Foreign Affairs." *Harvard International Journal of Press/Politics* 1, no. 2 (1996): 10–29.

Bennett, William J., John J. DiIulio Jr., and John P. Walters. *Body Count: Moral Poverty . . . and How to Win America's War against Crime and Drugs.* New York: Simon & Schuster, 1996.

Berlinski, Claire. *Menace in Europe.* New York: Crown Forum, 2006.

Bernstein, Richard. "Bin Laden Bribed Afghan Militias for His Freedom, German Says." *New York Times,* April 13, 2005.

Biderman, Albert D. "Social-Psychological Needs and 'Involuntary' Behavior as Illustrated by Compliance in Interrogation." *Sociometry* 23, no. 2 (1960): 120–47.

Bishop, Joseph W. "Law in Control of Terrorism and Insurrection: The British Laboratory." *Law and Contemporary Problems* 42, no. 2 (Spring 1978): 140–201.

Blackburn, Robin. *The Making of New World Slavery: From the Baroque to the Modern, 1492–1800.* London: Verso, 1997.

Blood, Philip W. *Hitler's Bandit Hunters: The SS and the Nazi Occupation of Europe.* Washington, D.C.: Potomac, 2006.

Boot, Max. "What Next? The Foreign Policy Agenda beyond Iraq." *Weekly Standard,* May 5, 2003. cfr.org/iraq/next-foreign-policy-agenda-beyond-iraq/p5930.

Bosworth, R. J. B. *Mussolini's Italy: Life under the Fascist Dictatorship, 1915–1945.* New York: Penguin, 2006.

Bothmer, Bernard von. *Framing the Sixties: The Use and Abuse of a Decade from Ronald Reagan to George W. Bush.* Amherst: University of Massachusetts Press, 2010.

Bowcott, Owen, and Richard Norton-Taylor. "Secret Courts Bill U-Turn Fails to Silence Critics." *Guardian,* May 29, 2012.

Bravin, Jess. "At Guantánamo, Even 'Easy' Cases Have Lingered." *Wall Street Journal,* December 18, 2006.

———. "Guantanamo Judge Grapples with Disruptive Terror Suspects." *Wall Street Journal,* May 6, 2012.

Bridgman, Jon. "Lessons Learned from Two Days of Infamy." *Seattle Post-Intelligencer,* December 1, 2001.

Brinkley, Douglas. *Tour of Duty: John Kerry and the Vietnam War.* New York: Morrow, 2004.

Briody, Dan. *The Halliburton Agenda: The Politics of Oil and Money.* Hoboken, N.J.: Wiley, 2004.

Brown, Dee. *Bury My Heart at Wounded Knee.* New York: Bantam, 1970.

Brown, Holmes, and Don Luce. *Hostages of War: Saigon's Political Prisoners.* Washington, D.C.: Indochina Mobile Education Unit, 1973.

Bullard, Alice. *Exile to Paradise: Savagery and Civilization in Paris and the South Pacific, 1700–1900.* Stanford, Calif.: Stanford University Press, 2000.

———. "Self-Representation in the Arms of Defeat: Fatal Nostalgia and Surviving Comrades in French New Caledonia, 1871–1880." *Cultural Anthropology* 12, no. 2 (1997): 179–212.

Buncombe, Andrew. "Guantanamo Bay Prisoner 'Tried to Commit Suicide a Dozen Times.'" *Independent* (London), April 27, 2006.

Burns, Robert. "Document: Bin Laden Evaded U.S. Forces." Associated Press, March 23, 2005.

Bush, George W. "Address to the Nation." September 20, 2001. presidentialrheto
ric.com/speeches/09.20.01.html.

Cannato, Vincent J. *American Passage: The History of Ellis Island.* New York:
Harper, 2009.

Capozzola, Christopher. *Uncle Sam Wants You: World War I and the Making of the
Modern American Citizen.* Oxford: Oxford University Press, 2008.

Carrell, Severin. "The Children of Guantánamo Bay." *Independent* (London), May
28, 2006.

———. "Coded Letters from Briton in Guantánamo Reveal 'Regime of Violence.'" *Independent*, August 8, 2004.

CBS News. "Obama: We Are Going to Close Gitmo: But Says No Decision Has
Been Made on Prosecuting Bush Administration Personnel Accused of
Torture." February 11, 2009. cbsnews.com/stories/2009/01/11/national/
main4713038.shtml.

Chehab, Zaki. *Inside Hamas: The Untold Story of the Militant Islamic Movement.*
New York: Nation Books, 2007.

Clarke, Arthur C., and Frederik Pohl. *The Last Theorem.* New York: Ballantine,
2008.

Clarke, Richard A. *Against All Enemies: Inside America's War on Terror.* New York:
Free Press, 2004.

Clodfelter, Michael. *The Dakota War: The United States Army versus the Sioux,
1862–1865.* Jefferson, N.C.: McFarland, 1998.

Cloud, David S., and Julian E. Barnes. "U.S. May Expand Use of Its Prison in
Afghanistan." *Los Angeles Times*, March 21, 2010.

CNN. "Wintry Storm Blasts Country; Missing Boys Found; Hiker Found after
Weeks in Woods; Martin Luther King Remembered; Gitmo Commander
Discusses Policies." *CNN Newsroom*, January 15, 2007. transcripts.cnn.com/
TRANSCRIPTS/2007.01.15.html.

Cody, Edward. "China Demands That Albania Return Ex-U.S. Detainees." *Washington Post*, May 10, 2006.

Coll, Steve. *Ghost Wars: The Secret History of the CIA, Afghanistan, and Bin Laden,
from the Soviet Invasion to September 10, 2001.* New York: Penguin, 2004.

Congressional Quarterly. "CQ Transcript: President-Elect Obama Interviewed on
ABC's 'This Week.'" January 11, 2009.

Congressional Record. "Military Commissions Act of 2006." September 27, 2006,
S10243–S10274. fas.org/irp/congress/2006_cr/s092706.html.

Crovitz, L. Gordon. "From Nuremberg to Guantánamo." *Wall Street Journal*, May
13, 2012.

Cucullu, Gordon. *Inside Gitmo: The True Story behind the Myths of Guantánamo
Bay.* New York: HarperCollins, 2009.

Daalder, Ivo H., and James M. Lindsay. *America Unbound: The Bush Revolution in Foreign Policy*. Washington, D.C.: Brookings Institution Press, 2003.

Dadge, David. *The War in Iraq and Why the Media Failed Us*. Westport, Conn.: Praeger, 2006.

Dalrymple, William. *The Last Mughal: The Fall of a Dynasty: Delhi, 1857*. New York: Knopf, 2007.

Dieckmann, Dorothea. 2007. *Guantanamo: A Novel*. Translated by Tim Mohr. Brooklyn, N.Y.: Soft Skull Press, 2007.

DiMaggio, Anthony R. *Mass Media, Mass Propaganda: Examining American News in the "War on Terror."* Lanham, Md.: Lexington, 2008.

Dobbs, Michael. *Saboteurs: The Nazi Raid on America*. New York: Knopf, 2004.

Dodds, Paisley. "AP: Gitmo Soldier Details Sexual Tactics." Associated Press, January 28, 2005.

————. "Kuwaiti Detainees in Guantánamo Say They Made False Confessions to Stop Abuse and Torture by U.S. Troops." Associated Press, February 7, 2005.

Donagan, Barbara. "Atrocity, War Crime, and Treason in the English Civil War." *American Historical Review* 99, no. 4 (1994): 1137–66.

Dow, Mark. *American Gulag: Inside U.S. Immigration Prisons*. Berkeley: University of California Press, 2004.

Doyle, Jack. "Time to Stop Paying Out to Terrorists, Says Clarke: Bill Will Let Security Services Fight Unfounded Compensation Cases." *Daily Mail*, May 29, 2012.

Duffy, Helen. *The "War on Terror" and the Framework of International Law*. Cambridge: Cambridge University Press, 2005.

Duncan, T. Bentley. *Atlantic Islands: Madeira, the Azores and the Cape Verdes in Seventeenth-Century Commerce and Navigation*. Chicago: University of Chicago Press, 1972.

Dunham, Will. "U.S. Military Calls 2 Dozen Detainee Deaths Homicide." Reuters, March 16, 2005.

Dunne, Finley Peter. *Mr. Dooley's Opinions*. New York: R. H. Russell, 1901.

Dupuy, Alex. *Haiti in the New World Order: The Limits of the Democratic Revolution*. Boulder, Colo.: Westview, 1997.

Engelhardt, Tom. *The American Way of War: How Bush's Wars Became Obama's*. Chicago: Haymarket, 2010.

Filkins, Dexter. *The Forever War*. New York: Knopf, 2008.

Finn, Peter. "Guantanamo Detainee Naji Sent Back to Algeria against His Will." *Washington Post*, July 20, 2010.

Fisher, Louis. *Nazi Saboteurs on Trial: A Military Tribunal and American Law*. Lawrence: University Press of Kansas, 2003.

Fletcher, Laurel E., and Eric Stover. *The Guantánamo Effect: Exposing the Conse-*

quences of U.S. Detention and Interrogation Practices. Berkeley: University of California Press, 2009.

Fox, Ben. "Cheap Watches Trouble for Gitmo Prisoners." Associated Press, March 10, 2006.

———. "Guantánamo Detainee Threatens Suicide." Associated Press, May 20, 2007.

Freedman, Lawrence. The Evolution of Nuclear Strategy. New York: St. Martin's Press, 1981.

Frelick, Bill. "Haitian Boat Interdiction and Return: First Asylum and First Principles of Refugee Protection." Cornell International Law Journal 26 (1993): 675–94.

Garwood, Paul. "Afghan Insurgency Said Won't Slow." Associated Press, April 21, 2006.

Gellman, Barton, and Thomas E. Ricks. "U.S. Concludes Bin Laden Escaped at Tora Bora Fight: Failure to Send Troops in Pursuit Termed Major Error." Washington Post, April 17, 2002.

Gerolymatos, André. Red Acropolis, Black Terror: The Greek Civil War and the Origins of Soviet-American Rivalry, 1943–1949. New York: Basic Books, 2004.

Ghazvinian, John. Untapped: The Scramble for Africa's Oil. Orlando, Fla.: Harcourt, 2007.

Gillman, Peter, and Leni Gillman. "Collar the Lot!": How Britain Interned and Expelled Its Wartime Refugees. London: Quartet, 1980.

Gilmore, Gerry J. "Bad Troops, Poor Leaders Responsible for Detainee Abuse." American Forces Press Service, July 22, 2004. defense.gov/news/newsarticle. aspx?id=25668.

Glidden, William B. "Internment Camps in America, 1917–1920." Military Affairs 37, no. 4 (1973): 137–41.

Golden, Tim. "Army Faltered in Investigating Detainee Abuse." New York Times, May 22, 2005.

———. "In Final Trial, G.I. Is Acquitted of Abusing Jailed Afghans." New York Times, June 2, 2006.

———. "In U.S. Report, Brutal Details of 2 Afghan Inmates' Deaths." New York Times, May 20, 2005.

———. "Years after 2 Afghans Died, Abuse Case Falters." New York Times, February 13, 2006.

Goldstein, Brandt. Storming the Court: How a Band of Yale Law Students Sued the President—and Won. New York: Scribner, 2005.

Gordon, James. "Montrealer Sold to U.S. Troops." Montreal Gazette, July 11, 2005.

Gott, Richard. Cuba: A New History. New Haven, Conn.: Yale University Press, 2004.

Graessner, Sepp, Norbert Gurris, and Christian Pross, eds. *At the Side of Torture Survivors: Treating a Terrible Assault on Human Dignity*. Translated by Jeremiah Michael Riemer. Baltimore: Johns Hopkins University Press, 2001.

Graham, Bradley. *By His Own Rules: The Ambitions, Successes, and Ultimate Failures of Donald Rumsfeld*. New York: Public Affairs, 2009.

Graham, Stephen. "U.S. Admits Afghanistan Vigilante Ties." Associated Press, July 23, 2004.

Greenberg, Karen. *The Least Worst Place: Guantanamo's First 100 Days*. Oxford: Oxford University Press, 2009.

———. "Military Commissions on Trial in Guantanamo." *Nation*, May 11, 2012.

Grey, Stephen. *Ghost Plane: The True Story of the CIA Rendition and Torture Program*. New York: St. Martin's Press, 2006.

Grimmett, Richard F. *Authorization for Use of Military Force in Response to the 9/11 Attacks (P.L. 107-40): Legislative History*. CRS [Congressional Research Service] report for Congress, January 4, 2006.

Guardian. "US Embassy Cables: Terror Suspects, Canada and the Law." December 14, 2010.

Halliday, Paul D. *Habeas Corpus: From England to Empire*. Cambridge, Mass.: Belknap Press of Harvard University Press, 2010.

Harbury, Jennifer K. *Truth, Torture, and the American Way: The History and Consequences of U.S. Involvement in Torture*. Boston: Beacon Press, 2005.

Hasian, Marouf, Jr. *In the Name of Necessity: Military Tribunals and the Loss of American Civil Liberties*. Tuscaloosa: University of Alabama Press, 2005.

Heintz, Jim. "Russia: Ex-Guantanamo Detainee Killed." Associated Press, June 27, 2007.

Hersh, Seymour M. *The Price of Power: Kissinger in the Nixon White House*. New York: Summit, 1983.

Herspring, Dale R. *Rumsfeld's Wars: The Arrogance of Power*. Lawrence: University Press of Kansas, 2008.

Hibbert, Christopher. *The Great Mutiny: India, 1857*. New York: Viking, 1978.

Hickman, John, and Sarah Bartlett. "Reporting a New Delhi Bias? A Content Analysis of AP Wire Service Stories on the Conflicts in Sri Lanka and Kashmir." *Jouvert: A Journal of Post-Colonial Studies* 6, no. 3 (2002). english.chass.ncsu.edu/jouvert/v6i3/con63.htm.

Higham, Scott, and Peter Finn. "At Least $500 Million Has Been Spent Since 9/11 on Renovating Guantanamo Bay." *Washington Post*, June 7, 2010.

Hogan, Michael. *The Irish Soldiers of Mexico*. Guadalajara: Fondo Editorial Universitario, 1997.

ICRC [International Committee of the Red Cross]. "States Party to the Main Treaties." August 20, 2012. icrc.org/eng/resources/documents/misc/party_main_treaties.htm.

Immerman, Richard H. *Empire for Liberty: A History of American Imperialism from Benjamin Franklin to Paul Wolfowitz*. Princeton, N.J.: Princeton University Press, 2010.

Irons, Peter. *A People's History of the Supreme Court*. New York: Viking, 1999.

Isikoff, Michael, and John Barry. "Gitmo: SouthCom Showdown." *Newsweek*, May 9, 2005.

James, Ian. "Detainee Says He Was Abused in Afghanistan." Associated Press, August 8, 2004.

———. "Lawyer Unable to Meet Guantanamo Client." Associated Press, June 23, 2004.

James, Larry C. *Fixing Hell: An Army Psychologist Confronts Abu Ghraib*. With Gregory A. Freeman. New York: Grand Central, 2008.

Jehl, Douglas. "Army Details Scale of Abuse of Prisoners in an Afghan Jail." *New York Times*, March 12, 2005.

Jehl, Douglas, and Eric Schmitt. "U.S. Military Says 26 Inmate Deaths May Be Homicide." *New York Times*, March 16, 2005.

Jenkins, Britta. "There, Where Words Fail, Tears Are the Bridge: Thoughts on Speechlessness in Working with Survivors of Torture." In Graessner, Gurris, and Pross, *At the Side of Torture Survivors*, 142–52.

Jenkins, Philip. *Decade of Nightmares: The End of the Sixties and the Making of Eighties America*. Oxford: Oxford University Press, 2006.

Johnson, Chalmers. *Blowback: The Costs and Consequences of American Empire*. New York: Metropolitan, 2000.

———. *The Sorrows of Empire: Militarism, Secrecy, and the End of the Republic*. New York: Metropolitan, 2004.

Jones, Owen Bennett. *Pakistan: Eye of the Storm*. New Haven, Conn.: Yale University Press, 2002.

Keneally, Thomas. *A Commonwealth of Thieves: The Improbable Birth of Australia*. New York: Nan A. Talese/Doubleday, 2006.

Kennedy, Helena. *Just Law*. London: Chatto & Windus, 2004.

Khan, Mahvish Rukhsana. *My Guantánamo Diary: The Detainees and the Stories They Told Me*. New York: Public Affairs, 2008.

Koh, Harold Hongju. "America's Jekyll-and-Hyde Exceptionalism." In *American Exceptionalism and Human Rights*, edited by Michael Ignatieff, 111–44. Princeton, N.J.: Princeton University Press, 2005.

———. "America's Offshore Refugee Camps." *University of Richmond Law Review* 29 (1994): 139–73.

———. "The 'Haiti Paradigm' in United States Human Rights Policy." *Yale Law Journal* 103 (1994): 2391–2435.

Kraft, Louis. *Gatewood and Geronimo*. Albuquerque: University of New Mexico Press, 2000.

Krammer, Arnold P. "German Prisoners of War in the United States." *Military Affairs* 40, no. 2 (1976): 68–73.

Kurnaz, Murat. *Five Years of My Life: An Innocent Man in Guantanamo*. With Helmut Kuhn. Translated by Jefferson Chase. New York: Palgrave Macmillan, 2008.

Labanca, Nicola. "Italian Colonial Internment." In *Italian Colonialism*, edited by Ruth Ben-Ghiat and Mia Fuller, 27–36. New York: Palgrave Macmillan, 2005.

Lafitte, François. *The Internment of Aliens*. 1940. London: Libris, 1988.

Lambeth, Benjamin S. *Air Power against Terror: America's Conduct of Operation Enduring Freedom*. Santa Monica, Calif.: Rand Corporation, 2005.

Larson, Eric V., and Bogdan Savych. *American Public Support for U.S. Military Operations from Mogadishu to Baghdad*. Santa Monica, Calif.: Rand Corporation, 2005.

Leahy, Patrick J. "Statement of Sen. Patrick J. Leahy, Ranking Member, Judiciary Committee, Hearing on *Hamdan v. Rumsfeld*: Establishing a Constitutional Process." July 11, 2006. votesmart.org/public-statement/189790/statement-of-senator-patrick-leahy-on-hamdan-v-rumsfeld-establishing-a-constitutional-process.

Legro, Jeffrey W. *Rethinking the World: Great Power Strategies and International Order*. Ithaca, N.Y.: Cornell University Press, 2007.

Lepore, Jill. *The Name of War: King Philip's War and the Origins of American Identity*. New York: Knopf, 1998.

Lerner, Edward M. *Small Miracles*. New York: Tor, 2009.

Lewis, George G., and John Mewha. *History of Prisoner of War Utilization by the United States Army, 1776–1945*. Washington, D.C.: Department of the Army, 1955. dtic.mil/cgi-bin/GetTRDoc?AD=ADA438000.

Lewis, Neil A. "Guantánamo Inmate Complains of Threats and Long Isolation." *New York Times*, August 7, 2004.

Lieder, Michael, and Jake Page. *Wild Justice: The People of Geronimo vs. the United States*. New York: Random House, 1997.

Life. "The Tiger Cages of Con Son." July 17, 1970, 24–29.

Lipman, Jana K. *Guantánamo: A Working-Class History between Empire and Revolution*. Berkeley: University of California Press, 2008.

Louw, Eric P. "The 'War against Terrorism': A Public Relations Challenge for the Pentagon." *Gazette: The International Journal for Communication Studies* 63, no. 3 (2003): 211–30.

Love, Eric T. L. *Race over Empire: Racism and U.S. Imperialism, 1865–1900*. Chapel Hill: University of North Carolina Press, 2004.

Mackey, Chris, and Greg Miller. *The Interrogators: Inside the Secret War Against Al Qaeda*. New York: Little, Brown, 2004.

MacLeod, Ken. *The Execution Channel*. New York: Tor, 2007.

Macklin, Graham D. "'Hail Mosley and F' Em All': Martyrdom, Transcendence and the 'Myth' of Internment." *Totalitarian Movements and Political Religions* 7, no. 1 (2006): 1–23.

Mahler, Jonathan. *The Challenge: Hamdan v. Rumsfeld and the Fight over Presidential Power.* New York: Farrar, Straus & Giroux, 2008.

Malsagoff, S. A. *An Island Hell: A Soviet Prison in the Far North.* London: A. M. Philpot, 1926.

Mamdani, Mahmood. *Good Muslim, Bad Muslim: America, the Cold War, and the Roots of Terror.* New York: Pantheon, 2004.

Margulies, Joseph. *Guantánamo and the Abuse of Presidential Power.* New York: Simon & Schuster, 2006.

Mayer, Jane. *The Dark Side: The Inside Story of How the War on Terror Turned into a War on American Ideals.* New York: Doubleday, 2008.

McClellan, Scott. *What Happened: Inside the Bush White House and Washington's Culture of Deception.* New York: Public Affairs, 2008.

McCoy, Alfred W. *Policing America's Empire: The United States, the Philippines, and the Rise of the Surveillance State.* Madison: University of Wisconsin Press, 2009.

———. *A Question of Torture: CIA Interrogation, from the Cold War to the War on Terror.* New York: Henry Holt, 2006.

McEvoy, Kieran, and Peter Shirlow. "Re-Imagining DDR: Ex-Combatants, Leadership and Moral Agency in Conflict Transformation." *Theoretical Criminology* 13, no. 1 (2009): 31–59.

Melia, Michael. "Australian Convicted of Terrorism Charge." Associated Press, March 30, 2007.

Miles, Donna. "Detainees Treated Humanely as Task Force Supports Terror War." American Forces Press Service, June 29, 2005. defense.gov/news/news article.aspx?id=16262.

———. "England Memo Underscores Policy on Humane Treatment of Detainees." American Forces Information Service, July 11, 2006. defense.gov/news/newsarticle.aspx?id=114.

Milewski, Terry. "Canada Accused of 'Complicity' in Torture in UN Report." CBC News, June 1, 2012. cbc.ca/news/politics/story/2012/06/01/pol-un-report-torture-canada-milewski.html.

Miller, Joseph C. *Way of Death: Merchant Capitalism and the Angolan Slave Trade, 1730–1830.* Madison: University of Wisconsin Press, 1988.

Miller, Teresa A. "The Impact of Mass Incarceration on Immigration Policy." In *Invisible Punishment: The Collateral Consequences of Mass Incarceration,* edited by Marc Mauer and Meda Chesney-Lind, 214–38. New York: New Press, 2002.

Moore, Molly. "Villagers Released by American Troops Say They Were Beaten, Kept in 'Cage.'" *Washington Post,* February 11, 2002.

Moore, Robin. *The Hunt for Bin Laden: Task Force Dagger*. New York: Random House, 2003.

Murray, Shailagh, and Paul Kane. "Obama Rejects Truth Panel." *Washington Post*, April 24, 2009.

Musharraf, Pervez. *In the Line of Fire: A Memoir*. New York: Free Press, 2006.

National Commission on Terrorist Attacks upon the United States. *The 9/11 Commission Report*. New York: Norton, 2004.

National Journal. "Text: Statements from Holder, Panetta on Decision Not to Investigate CIA Officials." June 30, 2011. nationaljournal.com/text-statements-from-holder-panetta-on-decision-not-to-investigate-cia-officials-20110630.html.

New America Foundation. "The Year of the Drone: An Analysis of U.S. Drone Strikes in Pakistan, 2004–2012." counterterrorism.newamerica.net//drones.

New York Times. "The Road We Need Not Have Traveled." Editorial. April 8, 2012.

Obama, Barack. "Barack Obama: The War We Need To Win; Obama's Plan to Defeat Terrorism Worldwide." BarackObama.com, 2008. obama.3cdn.net/417b7e6036dd852384_luzxmvlo9.pdf.

Office of the Director of National Intelligence. "Summary of the High Value Terrorist Detainee Program."

Ortiz, Sister Dianna. "The Survivors' Perspective: Voices from the Center." In *The Mental Health Consequences of Torture*, edited by Ellen Gerrity, Terence M. Keane, and Farris Tuma, 13–34. New York: Kluwer Academic, 2001.

Oshinsky, David M. *Polio: An American Story*. New York: Oxford University Press, 2005.

Otterman, Michael. *American Torture: From the Cold War to Abu Ghraib and Beyond*. London: Pluto, 2007.

Panayi, Panikos. "Prisoners of Britain: German Civilian, Military and Naval Internees during the First World War." In *"Totally Un-English"? Britain's Internment of "Enemy Aliens" in Two World Wars*, edited by Richard Dove, 29–43. Amsterdam: Rodopi, 2005.

Paris, Michael. "Air Power and Imperial Defence 1880–1919." *Journal of Contemporary History* 24, no. 2 (1989): 209–25.

Parks, E. Taylor, and J. Fred Rippy. "The Galápagos Islands, a Neglected Phase of American Strategic Diplomacy." *Pacific Historical Review* 9, no. 1 (1940): 37–45.

Paz, Abel. *Durruti in the Spanish Revolution*. Translated by Chuck Morse. Oakland, Calif.: AK Press, 2007.

Peters, Jeremy W. "Tour of Guantánamo Offers a Look, but Little Else." *New York Times*, August 12, 2010.

Pew Research Center. "Despite Years of Terror Scares, Public's Concerns Remain Fairly Steady." December 2, 2010. pewresearch.org/pubs/1815/poll-worried-about-terrorist-attack-america-anti-terror-campaign.

Pileggi, Nicholas, and Martin Scorsese, script. *Goodfellas*. DVD. Directed by Martin Scorsese. Burbank, Calif.: Warner Brothers, 1990.

Pilkington, Ed. "Bradley Manning's Treatment Was Cruel and Inhuman, UN Torture Chief Rules." *Guardian*, March 12, 2012.

Plummer, Brenda Gayle. *Haiti and the United States: The Psychological Moment*. Athens: University of Georgia Press, 1992.

Pogatchnik, Shawn. "Ireland to Take 2 Guantanamo Detainees." *Huffington Post*, July 29, 2010. huffingtonpost.com/2009/07/09/ireland-to-take-2-guantan _n_246785.html.

Population Census Organization, Statistics Division, Ministry of Economic Affairs and Statistics, Government of Pakistan. "Population by Mother Tongue." 1998 Census. census.gov.pk/MotherTongue.htm.

Pressley, Sue Anne. "Detainees Arrive in Cuba Amid Very Tight Security." *Washington Post*, January 12, 2002.

Raghavan, Sudarsan. "In Yemen, U.S. Airstrikes Breed Anger, and Sympathy for al-Qaeda." *Washington Post*, May 29, 2012.

Raymond, Nathaniel, et al. *Experiments in Torture: Evidence of Human Subject Research and Experimentation in the "Enhanced" Interrogation Program*. Physicians for Human Rights, 2010. phrtorturepapers.org.

Reagan, Ronald. "Proclamation 4908—Afghanistan Day." March 10, 1982. www. reagan.utexas.edu/archives/speeches/1982/31082c.htm.

Record, Jeffrey. *Dark Victory: America's Second War against Iraq*. Annapolis, Md.: Naval Institute Press, 2004.

Reid, Anna. *The Shaman's Coat: A Native History of Siberia*. New York: Walker, 2002.

Renton, Dave. *Fascism, Anti-Fascism, and Britain in the 1940s*. New York: St. Martin's Press, 2000.

Reuters. "U.S. Sends Two Guantanamo Detainees to Spain, Latvia." July 22, 2010. reuters.com/article/idUSTRE66L56N20100722.

Reynolds, Nicholas E. *A Skillful Show of Strength: U.S. Marines in the Caribbean, 1991–1996*. Washington, D.C.: History and Museums Division, Headquarters, U.S. Marine Corps, 2003.

Rhem, Kathleen T. "Alleged Guantanamo Abuse Did Not Rise to Level of 'Inhumane.'" American Forces Press Service, July 13, 2005. defense.gov/news/ newsarticle.aspx?id=16651.

———. "Detainees Living in Varied Conditions at Guantanamo." American Forces Information Service, February 16, 2005. defense.gov/news/news article.aspx?id=25882.

———. "Military Trials for Two Guantánamo Detainees to Resume Soon." American Forces Press Service, July 18, 2005. defense.gov/news/newsarticle. aspx?id=16616.

————. "Troops Deal with Stress of Working 'Inside the Wire.'" American Forces Press Service, February 22, 2005. defense.gov/news/newsarticle.aspx?id =25835.

Richardson, Sophie. *China, Cambodia, and the Five Principles of Peaceful Coexistence*. New York: Columbia University Press, 2010.

Richter, William L. "The Political Dynamics of Islamic Resurgence in Pakistan." *Asian Survey* 19, no. 6 (1979): 547–57.

Risen, James, and Tim Golden. "3 Prisoners Commmit Suicide at Guantánamo." *New York Times*, June 11, 2006.

Roberts, Jeffery J. *The Origins of Conflict in Afghanistan*. Westport, Conn.: Praeger, 2003.

Robertson, Geoffrey. *The Tyrannicide Brief: The Story of the Man Who Sent Charles I to the Scaffold*. New York: Pantheon, 2005.

Roht-Arriaza, Naomi. *The Pinochet Effect: Transnational Justice in the Age of Human Rights*. Philadelphia: University of Pennsylvania Press, 2005.

Rose, David. *Guantánamo: America's War on Human Rights*. London: Faber & Faber, 2004.

————. "Guantánamo Bay on Trial." *Vanity Fair*, January 2004. vanityfair.com/ politics/features/2004/01/guantanamo200401.

Rosenberg, Carol. "Detainee Who Was Forced to Bark Like a Dog Sues for His Freedom." *Miami Herald*, October 13, 2005.

————. "Noam Chomsky's Works Banned at Guantánamo Prison Camp." *Boston Herald*, October 12, 2009.

Rosenberg, Emily S. *A Date Which Will Live: Pearl Harbor in American Memory*. Durham, N.C.: Duke University Press, 2003.

Rotunda, Kyndra Miller. *Honor Bound: Inside the Guantanamo Trials*. Durham, N.C.: Carolina Academic Press, 2008.

Roy, Olivier. *The Lessons of the Soviet/Afghan War*. Adelphi Papers 259. Oxford: Brassey's, for the International Institute for Strategic Studies, 1991.

Saar, Erik, and Viveca Novak. *Inside the Wire: A Military Intelligence Soldier's Eyewitness Account of Life at Guantánamo*. New York: Penguin, 2005.

Sageman, Marc. *Understanding Terror Networks*. Philadelphia: University of Pennsylvania Press, 2004.

Sanders, Charles W., Jr. *While in the Hands of the Enemy: Military Prisons of the Civil War*. Baton Rouge: Louisiana State University, 2005.

Sands, Philippe. *Lawless World: America and the Making and Breaking of Global Rules from FDR's Atlantic Charter to George W. Bush's Illegal War*. New York: Viking, 2005.

————. *Torture Team: Rumsfeld's Memo and the Betrayal of American Values*. New York: Palgrave Macmillan, 2008.

Savage, Charlie. "Pair of Guantanamo Detainees Freed, the First in 15 Months." *New York Times*, April 20, 2012.

Scheuer, Michael. *See* Anonymous.

Schrader, Abby M. "Containing the Spectacle of Punishment: The Russian Autocracy and the Abolition of the Knout, 1817–1845." *Slavic Review* 56, no. 4 (1997): 613–44.

Secretary of State for Justice, United Kingdom. *Justice and Security Green Paper.* Command paper Cm 8194, October 2011. www.official-documents.gov.uk/document/cm81/8194/8194.pdf.

Seeley, Karen M. *Therapy after Terror: 9/11, Psychotherapists, and Mental Health.* Cambridge: Cambridge University Press, 2008.

Serge, Victor. *What Every Radical Should Know about State Repression: A Guide for Activists.* Melbourne: Ocean Press, 2005.

Shah, Amir. "Afghan Protesters Take Aim at U.S. Base." Associated Press, July 26, 2005.

———. "Bogus Afghan Jailers May Face Prison Time." Associated Press, July 14, 2004.

———. "U.S. Prisoner Leaves Afghanistan." Associated Press, June 13, 2007.

Shallice, T. "The Ulster Depth Interrogation Techniques and Their Relation to Sensory Deprivation Research." *Cognition* 1, no. 4 (1972): 385–405.

Sheed, John. "Guantánamo Abuse 'VideoTaped.'" *Australian*, March 21, 2005. commondreams.org/headlines05/0321-06.htm.

Shenon, Philip. "U.S. Chooses Guantánamo Bay Base in Cuba for Refugee Site." *New York Times*, April 7, 1999.

Shephard, Michelle. *Guantanamo's Child: The Untold Story of Omar Khadr.* Mississauga, Ont.: John Wiley & Sons Canada, 2008.

Sher, Andy. "Rep. Gingrey Says Guantánamo Detainees Are Treated Fairly." *Chattanooga Times Free Press*, June 10, 2003.

Sherman, Mark. "Muslim Mistreatment Cited at U.S. Prison." Associated Press, March 12, 2005.

Simkin, Mark. "Chinese Muslims Stuck in Guantanamo Limbo." Australian Broadcasting Corporation, January 17, 2006. abc.net.au/7.30/content/2006/s1549632.htm.

Skop, Emily H. "Race and Place in the Adaptation of Mariel Exiles." *International Migration Review* 35, no. 2 (Summer 2001): 449–71.

Slavin, Peter, and Joe Stevens. "Detainee's Medical Files Shared: Guantánamo Interrogator's Access Criticized." *Washington Post*, June 10, 2004.

Smith, Clive Stafford. *Eight O'Clock Ferry to the Windward Side: Seeking Justice in Guantánamo Bay.* New York: Nation Books, 2007.

Smucker, Philip. *Al Qaeda's Great Escape: The Military and the Media on Terror's Trail.* Washington, D.C.: Brassey's, 2004.

Solomon, Robert L. "Saya San and the Burmese Rebellion." *Modern Asian Studies* 3, no. 3 (1969): 209–23.

Stark, Holger. "Germans Moving Closer to Accepting Guantanamo Detainees." *Spiegel Online*, March 29, 2010. spiegel.de/international/world/0,1518, druck-686168,00.html.

Stepick, Alex. "Haitian Boat People: A Study in the Conflicting Forces Shaping U.S. Immigration Policy." *Law and Contemporary Problems* 45, no. 2 (1982): 163–96.

Stolberg, Sheryl Gay. "President Moves 14 Held in Secret to Guantanamo." *New York Times*, September 7, 2006.

Strauss, Leo. *Natural Right and History*. Chicago: University of Chicago Press, 1953.

Streatfeild, Dominic. *A History of the World Since 9/11: Disaster, Deception and Destruction in the War on Terror*. New York: Bloomsbury, 2011.

Suskind, Ron. *The Price of Loyalty: George W. Bush, the White House, and the Education of Paul O'Neill*. New York: Simon & Schuster, 2004.

Triay, Victor Andres. *Bay of Pigs: An Oral History of Brigade 2506*. Gainesville: University Press of Florida, 2001.

U.S. Department of Defense. "Defense Department Special Briefing on Combatant Status Review Tribunals." March 29, 2005. defense.gov/transcripts/transcript.aspx?transcriptid=2504.

———. "DoD News Briefing—Secretary Rumsfeld and Gen. Myers." January 11, 2002. defense.gov/transcripts/transcript.aspx?transcriptid=2031.

———. "DoD News Briefing—Secretary Rumsfeld and Gen. Myers." February 8, 2002. defense.gov/transcripts/transcript.aspx?transcriptid=2624.

———. "DoD News Briefing—Secretary Rumsfeld and Gen. Pace." January 22, 2002. defense.gov/transcripts/transcript.aspx?transcriptid=2254.

———. "Medical Program Support for Detainee Operations." Instruction 2310.08E. June 6, 2006. fas.org/irp/doddir/dod/i2310_08.pdf.

———. "President Determines Enemy Combatants Subject to His Military Order." July 3, 2003. defense.gov/releases/release.aspx?releaseid=5511.

Valentine, Douglas. *The Phoenix Program*. New York: William Morrow, 1990.

Verbitsky, Horacio. *The Flight: Confessions of an Argentine Dirty Warrior*. Translated by Esther Allen. New York: New Press, 2004.

Vick, Karl. "Team-Building or Torture? Court Will Decide." *Washington Post*, April 13, 2008.

Vietnam Veterans against the War. *The Winter Soldier Investigation: An Inquiry into American War Crimes*. Boston: Beacon Press, 1972.

Vischer, Adolf Lukas. *Barbed Wire Disease: A Psychological Study of the Prisoner of War*. Translated by S. A. Kinnier Wilson. London: John Bale, 1919.

Voglis, Polymeris. *Becoming a Subject: Political Prisoners during the Greek Civil War*. New York: Berghahn, 2002.

Wade, Nicholas. "Technology in Ulster: Rubber Bullets Hit Home, Brainwashing Backfires." *Science* 176 (June 9, 1972): 1102–6.

Wakeman, Carolyn, and San San Tin. *No Time for Dreams: Living in Burma Under Military Rule*. Lanham, Md.: Rowman & Littlefield, 2009.

Walters, Stan B. *Principles of Kinesic Interview and Interrogation*. 2nd ed. Boca Raton, Fla.: CRC Press, 2003.

Warshauer, Matthew. *Andrew Jackson and the Politics of Martial Law*. Knoxville: University of Tennessee Press, 2006.

Washington Post. "Guantanamo Bay Timeline." projects.washingtonpost.com/ guantanamo/timeline/.

Watson, Peter. *War on the Mind: The Military Uses and Abuses of Psychology*. London: Hutchinson, 1978.

Weaver, Mary Anne. *Pakistan: In the Shadow of Jihad and Afghanistan*. New York: Farrar, Straus & Giroux, 2002.

Webber, Tammy. "Thomson Correctional Center Eyed for Guantanamo Terror Suspects." *Saukvalley.com*. November 15, 2009. saukvalley.com/articles/ 2009/11/14/43879029/index.xml.

———. "Thomson Prison in Illinois Is Leading Choice in Obama's Search for Stateside Gitmo." *Huffington Post*, November 14, 2009. huffingtonpost. com/2009/11/14/thompson-prison-in-illinoi_n_358069.html.

Weiser, Benjamin. "Life Sentence without Parole for Former Detainee." *New York Times*, January 26, 2011.

Welsh, Herbert. *The Apache Prisoners in Fort Marion, St. Augustine, Florida*. Philadelphia: Office of the Indian Rights Association, 1887.

Welsh-Huggins, Andrew. "Ohio Won't Pursue Gitmo Abuse Claim." Associated Press, February 3, 2011.

Wenk-Ansohn, Mechthild. "The Verge of Pain: Psychosomatic Disorders among Survivors of Torture." In Graessner, Gurris, and Pross, *At the Side of Torture Survivors*, 57–69.

Wheeler, Marcy. "Government Case against Whistleblower Thomas Drake Collapses." *Nation*, June 13, 2011. thenation.com/article/161376/government-case-against-whistleblower-thomas-drake-collapses.

White House. "President Signs Authorization for Use of Military Force Bill." September 18, 2001. georgewbush-whitehouse.archives.gov/news/releases/ 2001/09/20010918-10.html.

———. "President Welcomes German Chancellor Merkel to the White House." January 13, 2006. georgewbush-whitehouse.archives.gov/news/releases/ 2006/01/20060113-1.html.

———. "Press Conference by the President." July 7, 2006. georgewbush-white house.archives.gov/news/releases/2006/07/20060707-1.html.

———. "Press Conference of the President." June 14, 2006. georgewbush-white house.archives.gov/news/releases/2006/06/20060614.html.

———. "Remarks by the President on National Security." May 21, 2009. white house.gov/the-press-office/remarks-president-national-security-5-21-09.

———. "U.S. Humanitarian Aid to Afghanistan." October 11, 2002. 2001-2009. state.gov/p/sca/rls/rm/14330.htm.

———. "The Vice President Appears on Fox News Sunday." January 27, 2002. georgewbush-whitehouse.archives.gov/vicepresident/news-speeches/ speeches/vp20020127-1.html.

Wikileaks. "Classified Guantanamo Bay Detention Criteria (2003)." January 10, 2008. http://wikileaks.org/wiki/Classified_Guantananmo_Bay_deten tion_criteria_(2003).

———. "Collateral Murder." April 5, 2010. http://wikileaks.org/wiki/Collateral_ Murder,_5_Apr_2010.

Williams, Charles. *Pétain: How the Hero of France Became a Convicted Traitor and Changed the Course of History*. New York: Palgrave Macmillan, 2005.

Wittes, Benjamin. *Law and the Long War: The Future of Justice in the Age of Terror*. New York: Penguin, 2008.

Wolfowitz, Paul, Deputy Secretary of Defense. "Administrative Review Procedures for Enemy Combatants in the Control of the Department of Defense at Guantánamo Bay Naval Base, Cuba." Order issued May 11, 2004. defense. gov/news/May2004/d20040518gtmoreview.pdf.

———. "Order Establishing Combatant Status Review Tribunal." Memo to Secretary of the Navy, July 7, 2004. defense.gov/news/Jul2004/d20040707 review.pdf.

Wong, Scott. "Rubio Visits Guantanamo Bay." *Politico*, May 29, 2012. politico. com/blogs/on-congress/2012/05/rubio-visiting-guantanamo-bay-124706. html.

World Medical Association. *Declaration of Tokyo*. 1975. http://www.wma.net/ en/30publications/10policies/c18/index.html.

Wright, Lawrence. *The Looming Tower: Al-Qaeda and the Road to 9/11*. New York: Knopf, 2006.

Xenos, Nicholas. *Cloaked in Virtue: Unveiling Leo Strauss and the Rhetoric of American Foreign Policy*. New York: Routledge, 2008.

Yates, Jeff, and Andrew Whitford. "Presidential Power and the United States Supreme Court." *Political Research Quarterly* 51 (1998): 539–50.

Laws and Legal Actions

Authorization for Use of Military Force, Public Law No. 107-40, 115 Stat. 224 (2001). gpo.gov/fdsys/pkg/PLAW-107publ40/pdf/PLAW-107publ40.pdf.

Ex Parte Milligan, 71 U.S. 2 (1866).

Ex Parte Quirin, 317 U.S. 1 (1942).

[Geneva Convention]. Convention Relative to the Treatment of Prisoners of War. Geneva, 27 July 1929. icrc.org/ihl.nsf/FULL/305?OpenDocument.

———. Convention (III) Relative to the Treatment of Prisoners of War. Geneva, 12 August 1949. icrc.org/ihl.nsf/FULL/375?OpenDocument.

———. Protocol Additional to the Geneva Conventions of 12 August 1949, and Relating to the Protection of Victims of International Armed Conflicts (Protocol I), 8 June 1977. icrc.org/ihl.nsf/FULL/470?OpenDocument.

Hamdan v. Rumsfeld, 548 U.S. 557 (2006).

Hamdan v. Rumsfeld, 344 F. Supp. 2nd 152 (D.C.C. 2004).

Hamdi v. Rumsfeld, 542 U.S. 507 (2004).

Johnson v. Eisentrager, 339 U.S. 763 (1950).

Padilla v. Hanft, 547 U.S. 1062 (2006).

"Petitioner's Motion for Injunctive or Declarative Relief Regarding Respondents' Wikileaks Guidance." Abdullah Omer Mahmoud Faraj v. Barack H. Obama et al., United States District Court for the District of Columbia, civil action 05-1490. fas.org/sgp/jud/faraj/motion279.pdf.

Rasul v. Bush, 542 U.S. 466 (2004).

Rumsfeld v. Padilla, 542 U.S. 426 (2004).

Index

Daniels, Charlie, "The Devil Went Down to Gitmo," 233
Dasch, George, 108
Davis, David, 99–100
Deception, detection and denouncement of, 22–23
DeLay, Tom, 119
Deobandism, 6–7, 146
Department of Defense: CIA and, 25; Combatant Status Review Tribunals, 70; Defense Planning Guidance, 187; military construction contractors for, 195; recidivism rate claimed by, 35–36. *See also* Rumsfeld, Donald H.
Department of Justice, Office of Legal Counsel, 27, 30
Dieckmann, Dorothea, *Guantanamo*, 231–32
Dilawar, 41–42, 173, 174
Dirty bombs, 91
Disraeli, Benjamin, 104
Al-Doussari, Jumah, 179
Drake, Thomas, 220
Drone strikes, 218
Dunant, Henri, 103–4
Dunne, Finley Peter, 95
Durbin, Richard, 210

Elmaati, Ahmad Abou, 223
Enemy combatant, defined, 121. *See also* "Unlawful combatants"
England, Gordon, 123, 129
Ex Parte Milligan, 97–100, 109, 111, 112–13, 118
Ex Parte Quirin, 36, 108–10, 111, 113, 125
Extraordinary renditions: Grey on, 28; of Mohammed, 33–34, 91; Obama and, 217–18; O'Connor on, 115; prisoners taken captive in, 18

False information from interrogation, 81–82
Faraj, Abdullah, 216
Fascist fifth columns, 52
Fear, exploitation of, 44. *See also* Threat rationale
Field, David Dudley, 98

First World War, 49–50, 72
Flanagan, Timothy, 30
Fletcher, Laurel E., *The Guantánamo Effect*, 32–33, 68
Florida: Cuban refugees and, 57–58; internment of Apaches in, 43, 46, 47, 48, 138
Force-feeding of prisoners, 2, 34
Foreign policy: after 9/11, 182–83; Bush administration and, 198–99, 212; neoconservatism and, 183–85; Supreme Court and, 95–96. *See also* Announcement rationale
Foreign powers, irregular forces created by, 153–54
France, island prisons of, 238–39
Freeman, Gregory A., 38
Frist, Bill, 65

Garfield, James A., 98–99
Gates, Robert, 203
Geneva Conventions: Bush on, 128–29; enforcement of, 126–27; Lieber Code and, 24; of 1929, 106–7, 111; of 1949, 107, 111–12; origins of, 103–6; prohibition of torture under, 80; Rumsfeld on, 14; on soldiers in armed forces, 87
German and German-American saboteurs in World War II, 15, 29, 36, 85, 108
German nationals, 50, 72–73, 110, 133, 139. *See also* Kurnaz, Murat
Germany: chancellor of, 17–18; 9/11 hijackers in, 78; Nuremberg trials in, 221–22; prisoners transferred to, 67, 213; in World War I, 49–50; in World War II, 50–52, 185, 186–87
Geronimo, 46, 47
Ghailani, Ahmed Khalfan, 210
Gibbons, John J., 120
Gibney, Alex, 41
Gingrey, Phil, 208, 209
Gonzalez, Alberto, 30
Gordon, Jeffrey, 179
Graham, Bradley, *By His Own Rules*, 28
Grant, Ulysses S., 47
Greenberg, Karen, 222–23; *The Least Worst Place*, 26–27, 28

Grey, Stephen, *Ghost Plane*, 28
Guam, 190, 191
Guantánamo Bay: base at, 138; internment of refugees at, 56–57, 193; as island prison, 139–40; military tribunals at, 215–16; in popular culture, 231–33; population of, 193; "preventive detention" at, 216; prison camps at, 176, 194; repatriations from, 67–69, 212–13; suicides at, 179; as symbol, 225–27. *See also* Closing Guantánamo Bay; Guantánamo decision
Guantánamo decision: analysis of, 22–23; as anti-scandal, 1–2, 225–26; first news of, 11; Mahler on, 30–31; motivation for, 3, 226; public opinion and, 214; rationales for, 12, 17–18; success of, 226; sunk costs argument for, 19–20, 211; survival of, 215–25; Wittes on, 29–30. *See also* Announcement rationale; Intelligence rationale; Official explanations; Prosecution rationale; Punishment rationale; Spectacle rationale; Threat rationale
Guevara, Che, 166–67
Gunning, Christine E., 216
Guzmán, Abimael, 166, 167

Habeas corpus: *Ex Parte Milligan*, 97–100, 109, 111, 112–13, 118; *Ex Parte Quirin*, 36, 108–10, 111, 113, 125; *Hamdan v. Rumsfeld*, 127–30; *Hamdi v. Rumsfeld*, 113–16; *Johnson v. Eisentrager*, 110–11, 127; as Obama campaign promise, 204; *Rasul v. Bush* and *Al Odah v. United States*, 117–21, 127; *Rumsfeld v. Padilla*, 116–17; writs of, 93–94, 96, 97–98, 99
Habib, Mamdouh, 88, 118
Habibullah, Mullah, 173, 174
Hague Regulations of 1899, 106
Haitian refugees, 44, 53–59, 60
Al-Haj, Sami, 34
Halliburton, 194, 195
Hamdan, Salim Ahmed, 30, 31, 87, 88, 126–27, 177
Hamdan v. Rumsfeld, 19, 30, 88, 107, 127–30

Hamdi, Esam Fouad, 113–14
Hamdi, Yaser Esam, 113–14, 115, 159
Hamdi v. Rumsfeld, 113–16, 128
Harkin, Tom, 196
Harold & Kumar Escape from Guantanamo Bay (film), 231
Harris, Harry, Jr., 2–3, 179, 233
Haupt, Herbie, 109–10
Hawaii, 191–92
Hawkins, Augustus F., 195, 196
Al-Hawsawi, Mustafa Ahmad, 221
Haynes, William J., 28, 30
Hefley, Joel, 207
Hicks, David Matthew, 75, 87, 88–89, 90, 118, 177, 212
Historical cases: British fascists, 49–53; Chiricahua Apache, 44–49; Haitian refugees, 53–59; overview, 43–44; parallels between, 59–61
Holder, Eric, 217
Hood, Jay, 79
Hostage rationale, 133–34
Hunger strikes, 2, 34
Hussein, Saddam, 130

Idema, Jack, 170–71
Indian Mutiny, 101
Insurgency, origins of, 147
Intelligence rationale: abandonment of, 18–19; actionable intelligence and, 75–77; background political intelligence and, 77–79; critique of, 13–14; Fletcher, Stover, and, 32–33; James and, 38; Margulies and, 33; Mayer and, 25; overview, 75; public acceptance of, 79–80; Rose and, 25; Saar on, 31; Sands on, 31–32; Smith and, 34; for torture, 27, 28. *See also* Interrogation
International Committee of the Red Cross, 37, 104, 112
International Court of Justice, 197, 198
International law: Japan and, 200; neoconservatism and, 135, 182–83, 186, 197–98, 226–27. *See also* Geneva Conventions
International Military Education and Training funds, 197–98

Pearl Harbor attack, 11, 142, 148
Pelosi, Nancy, 216
Perp walks, 137
Persons employing violence, terminology
  for, 5–8
Philippines, 190, 191
Phillips, Kyra, 2–3
Pirates of the Caribbean: At World's End
  (film), 231
Pohl, Frederik, *The Last Theorem*, 232–33
Police violence, 165–66
Powell, Colin, 203
Prasow, Andrea, 213
President, authority of, 94–95, 96, 135,
  185–86, 227
"Preventive detention," 216
Prisoner-of-war camps, 72–73, 244n7
Prisoners: deaths of, 173, 174–75; defined,
  7; due process rights of, 101–2, 122–23,
  125–26; force-feeding of, 2, 34; images
  of, 136; isolation of, 176–77; memoirs
  of, 39–42; "orphan," 212–13, 223; politi-
  cal-legal identities of, 103; transfers of
  custody of, 66, 130, 175–76, 209–10, 211
Prisoners of war: in civil wars, 104–5;
  defined, 7; denial of status of, 86, 112;
  display of, 136–37; in Japan, 200; U.S.
  constitutional law and, 93–94. *See also*
  Geneva Conventions; Lieber Code
Prisons: Abu Ghraib, 13, 14, 37, 164, 180; in
  Afghanistan, 169–71, 211–12; at Guantánamo, 176–77; on islands, 138–40, 141,
  235–39
Propaganda, 5–6
Prosecution rationale: Combatant Status
  Review Tribunals and, 86–87; critique
  of, 14–17, 84–85; defendants chosen,
  87–91, 92–93, 113, 123–24; public
  opinion on, 83–84; Rotunda and, 36–37;
  Rumsfeld on, 83; war crimes and,
  92–94. *See also* Habeas corpus; Military
  tribunals/commissions
Puerto Rico, 190, 191
Punishment rationale: denial of rights
  and, 176–77; evidence for, 135–36; overview, 4, 134–35; prison memoirs and,
  39–42; psychological regression and,

177–78; Saar on, 31; success of, 226; for
  torture, 27; transfers of custody and,
  175–76. *See also* Torture

Al-Qahtani, Jabran Said bin, 87, 90
Al-Qahtani, Mohammed, 179
Al-Qosi, Ibrahim Ahmed Mahmoud, 87, 91

Rasul, Shafiq, 33, 118
Rasul v. Bush, 33, 102, 117–21, 127
Rationales: hostage, 133–34; overview
  of, 12, 17–18. *See also* Announcement
  rationale; Intelligence rationale; Official
  explanations; Prosecution rationale;
  Punishment rationale; Spectacle ratio-
  nale; Threat rationale
Reagan administration: birth of al-Qaeda
  and, 78, 140–41, 142, 147–48, 156–57;
  Pakistan and, 149–50; refugees and, 55,
  56; Soviet-Afghan War and, 150–51
Realpolitik, 188, 249n7
Refugees: Haitian, 44, 53–59, 60; intern-
  ment of at Guantánamo, 56–57, 193
Rehnquist, William, 112
Reid, Richard, 92
Religious fundamentalism, 26, 152, 159–60
Repatriations from Guantánamo, 67–69,
  212–13
Republicans and Guantánamo Bay, 206–10
Rhem, Kathleen T., 73
Rights of prisoners, denial of, 101–2,
  122–23, 125–26, 176–77
The Road to Guantánamo (documentary
  film), 41
Roosevelt administration, 15, 29, 85, 108
Rose, David, *Guantánamo*, 25–26
Rothermere, Lord, 51
Rotunda, Kyndra Miller, *Honor Bound*,
  35–37
Rubio, Marco, 223
Rudolph, Eric, 159–60
Rumsfeld, Donald H.: Defense Policy
  Board, 13; Graham biography of, 28;
  intelligence rationale and, 75, 76; mili-
  tary reforms of, 171, 195; news briefing
  by, 12, 13–14, 62, 83; on prisoners,
  63–64

John Hickman is associate professor of government at Berry College in Rome, Georgia, where he teaches international relations and comparative politics. An army brat raised in Würzburg, Germany; El Paso, Texas; Oxford, Mississippi; and Springfield, Missouri, he holds a PhD in political science from the University of Iowa and a JD from Washington University in St. Louis. His professional experience includes service as an administrator at Florida A&M University, teaching at Reitaku University in Tokyo, a Fulbright in Romania, and field research in Sri Lanka.

✳   ✳   ✳

The University Press of Florida is the scholarly publishing agency for the State University System of Florida, comprising Florida A&M University, Florida Atlantic University, Florida Gulf Coast University, Florida International University, Florida State University, New College of Florida, University of Central Florida, University of Florida, University of North Florida, University of South Florida, and University of West Florida.